Sacred Havens

Sacred Havens

A Guide to Spiritual Places in Manhattan

TERRI COOK

A Crossroad 8th Avenue Book
The Crossroad Publishing Company
New York

This printing: 2001

Every effort has been made to ensure the accuracy of information throughout this book. However, schedules are changing continually. Readers should verify information before making final plans.

The Crossroad Publishing Company
481 Eighth Avenue, New York, NY 10001

Printed in the United States of America

Library of Congress Cataloging-in-Publication Data

Cook, Terri, 1942-
    Sacred havens: a guide to spiritual places in Manhattan/ Terri Cook.
p. cm.
"A Crossroad 8th Avenue book"
ISBN 0-8245-1960-4 (alk. Paper)
1. New York (N.Y.)—Religion. 2. Sacred space—New York (N.Y.)

I. Title
  BL2527.N7 C66 2001
  291.3'5'097471—dc21

2001003579

TO PEOPLE OF COURAGE AND CONVICTION:

my son
CHRISTOPHER A. COOK

my mother
MARY KATE MCNALLY CONNOLLY (1905–1994)

my father
MICHAEL J. CONNOLLY (1902–1965)

my friend
DAVID J. OESTREICHER (1930–1999)

my favorite patriot
THOMAS DONGAN (1634–1715)

and caretakers of our records
LIBRARIANS AND ARCHIVISTS

THIS BOOK IS LOVINGLY DEDICATED

ACKNOWLEDGEMENTS

I am grateful to all those who care for spiritual places and who generously give their time to help visitors.

I am indebted to my family and friends for their encouragement, and to my editor and knowledgeable New Yorker, Alison Donohue.

Thanks also to the New-York Historical Society, the New York Landmarks Conservancy, the New York Public Library, the New York Municipal Library, the Smithsonian Archives, the Avery Library at Columbia University, and the New York City Parks and Recreation Department.

And, finally, a prayer of thanksgiving for those individuals who contribute financially to the preservation of New York City's sacred sites.

TABLE OF CONTENTS

LOWER MANHATTAN and LOWER EAST SIDE
Battery Park to East 14th Street

EAST SIDE OF MANHATTAN
north of 15th Street to 103rd Street

Features

By The Way

UPPER MANHATTAN and HARLEM
North of 105rd Street

WEST SIDE AND GREENWICH VILLAGE
South of 103rd Street to West Houston Street

Table of Contents

September, 2001

Happy are those who dwell in thy house; they never cease from praising thee. Happy the people whose refuge is in thee, whose hearts are set on the pilgrim's ways! As they pass through the thirsty valley, they find water from a spring; and the Lord provides even men who lose their way with pools to quench their thirst. —Psalm 84

Today, as we go to press, we have even more reason to give thanks for all the churches, temples and spiritual spaces around the city of New York. During the recent days of terror and grief they were indeed Sacred Havens offering shelter and consolation in concrete and tangible ways. They overflowed with people determined to prevail in faith, hope and love.

T.C.

INTRODUCTION

A cabdriver may tell you that the best way to see Manhattan's pulsating streets and skyscrapers is from the top of the Empire State Building. I invite you on a quieter and more enlightening journey: through spiritual places and sacred havens belonging to many ethnic and religious groups. These temples of reverence for the Creator are filled with rich history and inspirational works of art. All are architectural gems.

This revealing tour takes you from America's oldest Methodist church to the world's largest synagogue, and from a Buddhist temple in Chinatown to the church in which Jacqueline Kennedy Onassis prayed. The story is more than stone walls and marble columns. It is a vivid chronicle of New York City's immigrants, who found a land where they could worship freely. They built sacred havens in thanksgiving for this fundamental American right and used them as centers of their social and cultural lives.

This book will guide you through Manhattan's neighborhoods to visit these buildings and sites, which are open to the public at convenient hours. As you make the rounds, take a moment to reflect on the vision of the clergy and congregations who provided courageous leadership in the fight against discrimination and injustice down through the years. Enjoy your visits to these sanctuaries, to the public gardens, and other sites representing our ancestors' faith and hope in their adopted country. These sacred havens are New York City's precious jewels, to be shared by everyone.

To understand why some havens are located in isolated or commercial spots, remember the following events that caused Manhattan's neighborhoods to dramatically change:

1814   Fulton Ferry opens
1837   NY & Harlem Railroad (now Metro North) begin service along Fourth Avenue (now Park Ave.)
1883   Brooklyn Bridge is completed
1868   First elevated line along Ninth Avenue to 30th Street
1880   Thomas Edison invents the electric light
1882   Elevated lines extended to village of Harlem
1898   Cities of Brooklyn & NY merge
1899   Carnegie Hall opens at 57th Street & Seventh Avenue
1901   Macy's Department Store opens
1903   Williamsburg Bridge to Brooklyn opens
1904   IRT Subway opens
1909   Manhattan Bridge opens
1910   Queensboro Bridge on East 59th Street opens
1910   Penn Station on West 34th Street opens
1913   New Grand Central Terminal opens
1913   Woolworth Building opens as world's tallest site
1927   Holland Tunnel on Canal Street opens
1930   Chrysler Building opens
1931   Empire State Building opens as world's tallest site
1939   Rockefeller Center opens
1940   Queens Midtown Tunnel on East 34th Street opens
1952   United Nations moves to new site (East 42nd to 49th Streets)
1962   Lincoln Center opens on West 62nd Street
1973   World Trade Center opens as world's tallest site
2001   World Trade Center is destroyed by terrorist attacks

LOWER MANHATTAN AND THE LOWER EAST SIDE

❖ ❖ ❖ ❖

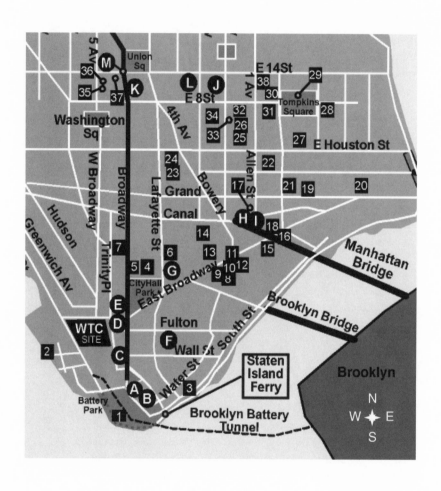

LOWER MANHATTAN AND THE LOWER EAST SIDE

BATTERY PARK TO EAST 14TH STREET

Be sure to get the free NYC Transit Authority Bus and Subway Maps as transportation guides. You can purchase your Metro Card at any subway station.

FEATURES:

A. *National Museum of the American Indian*
B. *Shrine of Elizabeth Ann Seton*
C. *Trinity Church*
D. *St. Paul's Chapel of Trinity Church*
E. *St. Peter's Church*
F. *John Street United Methodist*
G. *Church of St. Andrew*
H. *Eldridge Street Synagogue*
I. *Sung Tak Buddhist Association*
J. *St. Mark's-in-the-Bowery Church*
K. *Grace Church*
L. *St. Ann's Armenian Cathedral*
M. *The Gandhi Garden*

BY THE WAY:

1. East Coast Memorial
2. The Upper Room
3. Vietnam Veterans Memorial
4. African Burial Ground
5. New Ring Shout
6. Triumph of Human Spirit & Still I Rise
7. Civic Center Synagogue
8. St. James Church
9. Shearith Israel Cemetery
10. Mariner's Temple
11. Kimlau War Memorial
12. Lin Ze Yu
13. Church of the Transfiguration
14. Eastern States Buddhist Temple
15. First Chinese Presbyterian Church
16. St. Teresa
17. St. Barbara Greek Orthodox
18. Mahayana Buddhist Temple
19. St. Mary's Church
20. Bialystoker Synagogue
21. Beth Hamedrash Hagodol
22. First Roumanian-American Congregation
23. St. Patrick's Old Cathedral
24. St. Michael's Church
25. Russian Orthodox Cathedral of the Holy Virgin Protection
26. NYC Marble Cemetery
27. The Most Holy Redeemer
28. Saint Brigid's Church
29. Slocum Memorial Fountain
30. St. Nicholas of Myra
31. Saint Stanislaus
32. Max D. Raiskin Center
33. Middle Collegiate Church
34. Saint George's Ukranian Catholic Church
35. Brofman Center at NYU
36. Conservative Synagogue of Fifth Avenue
37. The Village Temple
38. Immaculate Conception Church

❖ ❖ ❖ ❖

NATIONAL MUSEUM OF THE AMERICAN INDIAN

A LEGACY OF NATIVE AMERICAN WISDOM AND SPIRITUALITY

Indians of America, who revered the earth, the sky, the forests, and all God's creatures, had no houses of worship. But their spiritual beliefs and traditions have been beautifully preserved in this museum, a branch of the Smithsonian Institution in Washington, D.C. Exhibition halls echo with the wisdom and spirituality of America's proud tribes: Sioux, Cherokee, Seminole, Apache, Navajo, Choctaw, Shinnecock, Algonquin, Blackhawk, Mescalero, and many others. They call their God by many names: the Creator, the Great Spirit, Mother Earth, the Divinity. All are one in the soul, and all deserve infinite love, respect, and care. Jacki Rand, of Choctaw descent, says, "Native people have much to say. They want the museum to break the silence between the Indian and non-Indian worlds, to serve as a meeting ground where Native people can say, 'You have entered Indian country, and this is who we are.' "

HISTORY

The museum was opened in 1994 in the Alexander Hamilton United States Custom House, a structure built in 1907 to collect tariffs on the huge volume of international trade arriving by ship through nearby New York Harbor. The site once held the Whitehall Street mansion of Governor Peter Stuyvesant, who retired to his farm after British forces seized his Dutch colony (see St. Mark's-in-the-Bowery). With the advent of the computer age and the nearby twin towers of the World Trade Center, the custom house became obsolete and was closed in 1973. The Smithsonian saw the building as a perfect space to display Indian artifacts that had been collected by George Gustav Heye (1874–1957), an engineer born in New York City and a student of Indian culture.

Heye, whose name is pronounced "high," often participated in an Indian social gathering called the *potlatch* — a ritual giveaway in which members of various nations and tribes are lauded for their generosity. He gathered a huge store of artifacts, which might have otherwise been lost to posterity, and donated it to the Smithsonian. The Heye

Collection, shown in an ever-changing series of exhibits, contains nearly one million pieces gleaned from the Arctic Circle to South America. Curators cataloged the priceless items with the help of many Native Americans.

Audio and video presentations explain Native American languages, literature, history, and art. Visitors will grasp the destruction of the Indian way of life by Europeans who, in the name of development, exploited the Native peoples' land and customs. The museum, established by an Act of Congress in 1989, also celebrates contemporary Native American creativity with videos of Indian storytellers, scholars, and tribal descendants interpreting objects and giving new twists to Native American culture. The displays put many myths to rest. For instance, some may be surprised to learn that opinions of women were given special value because it was believed their experience as mothers would help avoid unnecessary conflict. In some tribes a woman could become a chief or sit on a war council.

Don't miss a charming display of moccasins, multicolored and multisized, surrounded by a mysterious spirit all their own. You may feel their movements as they celebrate and symbolize the necessity of living in harmony with the earth.

Computer terminals, a video room, and two bookstores are available for additional information.

ARCHITECTURE

Cass Gilbert (1859–1934), American architect of the Woolworth Building, the George Washington Bridge (along with the engineer Othmar Ammann), and the U.S. Supreme Court Building in Washington, designed the United States Custom House in French Beaux-Arts tradition — an American interpretation, of course, covering 450,000 square feet.

Four massive marble statues by Daniel Chester French line the front plaza. They were completed between 1903 and 1907 and represent the continents of Asia, America, Europe, and Africa. America, to the left of the main entrance, holds a torch of liberty and a bundle of stalks that represents material richness. A human figure, representing labor, turns the wheel of industrial power, while an Indian, looking out from the right, reminds America of her history. Look up to the twelve limestone sculptures that span the cornice. They represent the old and new worlds of commerce—Greece and Rome, Phoenicia, Genoa, Venice, Spain, Holland, Portugal, Denmark, France, and England. Note that Belgium is a name change; it was labeled Germany before World War I.

The interior of the building is as majestic as the exterior. A marble rotunda holds murals by Reginald Marsh of ships entering New York

Harbor, and Labor and Commerce paintings by Carl Paul Jennewein. Desks of customs inspectors ring the main hall.

The museum is a proud testimony to Native Americans, who see the earth as religious ground and themselves as caretakers.

ADDRESS: *1 Bowling Green (near Battery Park), New York, NY 10004*
PHONE: *212-514-3700*
HOURS: *Daily: 10:00 A.M.–5:00 P.M./Closed December 25/Admission Free*
WEB SITE: *www.si.edu/nmai*
LANDMARK DESIGNATION

❖ ❖ ❖ ❖

SHRINE OF ST. ELIZABETH ANN SETON

AND CHURCH OF OUR LADY OF THE ROSARY
HOME TO A SAINT, A TRADER, AND IMMIGRANT GIRLS

Skyscrapers of steel, glass and concrete seem to huddle protectively over this historic Roman Catholic Church that sits upon a unique spot—poised as a beacon at the southern tip of Manhattan with a commanding view of New York Harbor and the Statue of Liberty.

HISTORY

The eighteenth and nineteenth century red brick complex has three separate buildings blending as one, with each section having its own history: a home to the Seton family; a house built for James Watson, a prosperous trader; and a shelter for young girls. Elizabeth Bayley Seton (1774-1821) gave birth in this house to Rebecca, the last of her five children, and lived there from 1801 to 1803, until her husband, William Magee Seton, died. She was widowed at the age of 29 with limited means to support her family. Consoled by the spirituality of the Filicchis family, who were business associates of William, and inspired by their faith, Elizabeth converted to Roman Catholicism (see Grace Church). She joined St. Peter's Catholic Church, on nearby Barclay Street.

In June 1808 Elizabeth moved her family to Baltimore, Maryland to open a school that became the basis of the American parochial school system. Elizabeth also founded in the same year the first American religious order, the Sisters of Charity, to educate children and help needy immigrants.

Shrine of St. Elizabeth Ann Seton

In 1885 the property was purchased by the Catholic Church to fulfill a promise made to Charlotte O'Brien, daughter of the Irish patriot William Smith O'Brien. Charlotte had traveled from Ireland to America and was horrified by the lack of housing and support for young girls immigrating to New York in quest of a new life. Miss O'Brien pioneered the idea of a shelter with Archbishop John Ireland. The prelate promised to help, but Charlotte sailed back to Ireland, never knowing that her indignation would turn into the mission of Our Lady of the Rosary. The shelter would welcome more than 150,000 women to its haven.

Today the Shrine of Elizabeth Ann Seton holds daily services and is visited by tens of thousands of people every year. The shrine is a testimony to Elizabeth, a woman of remarkable faith and charity, who was canonized in Rome on September 14, 1975 as the first American-born saint.

ARCHITECTURE

As the visitor faces the red-brick exterior of 7 State Street, the oldest section of the Georgian house is to the far right and measures only two windows wide. Built in 1793, it has a traditional white marble plaque over two second-floor windows. The Seton family resided in this old three-story section.

In 1806 a Federal-style wing was added, with a curved porch holding stately Ionic columns made from ships' masts. It is attributed to an architect of City Hall, John McComb Jr. The addition was built for James Watson, a wealthy trader who could watch from the porch as his cargo ships sailed into New York harbor. The wing has been restored to its original appearance with the addition of white cornices and a distinctive balustrade on the roof.

Our Lady of the Rosary Church was added in 1885 at the left side of the site, and built in the same Federal style. A life size image of Elizabeth Seton is tucked into an alcove over entryway facing Battery Park where the Seton family often strolled. The interior of the building retains the gracefulness of early 19th century architecture. The cream-colored sanctuary had once served as the ballroom in James Watson's time, and has a traditional Federal balcony. Three pale yellow stained-glass panels, set in Federal-style frame, fill the front wall and depict scenes from Elizabeth's life. In one frame, Elizabeth is portrayed in the robes of the religious order she founded; in another, she is shown lovingly with her children. It is interesting to note that before Elizabeth converted to Catholicism she was a member of nearby Trinity Church where she and her five children were baptized.

Sit for a moment in the soft lighting provided by elegant brass chandeliers, and feel the spirituality and serenity that fills this gracious sanctuary, dedicated to a guiding light for all who are overcome by life's routine.

ADDRESS: *7-8 State Street (at South Ferry) New York, NY* 10004
PHONE: *212-269-6865*
HOURS: *Mon.-Fri.: 6:30 A.M.-5:00 P.M. Sat.-Sun.: 8:00A.M-6:00P.M.*
LANDMARK DESIGNATION

TRINITY CHURCH

WITNESS TO THE BIRTH OF AMERICA

This Episcopal church witnessed the formation of both New York City and the United States of America. It has lived through the colonial period, the American Revolution, the birth of the nation, the Civil War, and the technological advances of the twentieth century. Fierce debates over religious ritual, the church charter, and political party affiliations dominated much of its history, but Trinity survived it all.

HISTORY

In 1696 British colonists in New York started a branch of the Church of England. This property outside the fortified wall built by the Dutch (Wall Street takes its name from the barricade) was purchased from Lutherans for twenty pounds sterling. A charter granted by King William III stated that Trinity was to be the colony's central church and was required to send the Crown an annual token of one peppercorn.

In 1705 Queen Anne gave the church 250 acres of farmland that ran from Fulton to Christopher Streets, and from Broadway to the Hudson River. Today, five percent of the Queen's farm is still owned by Trinity, with 28 commercial buildings on the property. King's College, now Columbia University, started in a room at the church and opened its first school in 1760 on Murray Street after receiving an endowment of land from the trustees.

In 1776, at the beginning of the American Revolution, a fire destroyed most of New York City, including Trinity. Flames stopped

Graveyard at Trinity Church

just short of St. Paul's, Chapel where scorched gravestones can still be seen. All during the war Trinity's congregation was fiercely divided between loyalists to England and patriots. The clergy remained loyal to the Crown and continued to include a prayer for King George in all services. In 1789 George Washington was inaugurated president of the new nation, and Trinity Church was granted a charter from New York State. Allegiance to the throne was omitted from services.

The congregation met in St. Paul's Chapel until the new Trinity was completed in 1790. Because of structural problems that church had to be torn down in 1839; the present building was consecrated in 1846. Along the way many disagreements arose. A proposal to install a cross atop the steeple stirred objections from puritanical parishioners who favored a weather vane, the device that capped most Protestant churches. Legend has it that a cross mysteriously appeared one night and so settled the debate.

Symbolism in the stained-glass windows was also questioned. Note the chancel's window, which caused a commotion among traditional church members: YH, the Jehovah symbol for Yahweh; a bishop's miter; a chalice; the eye of Providence, which is on the back of the U.S. dollar bill; and Hebrew lettering. High versus low church rituals were further emotional issues (see Church of St. Mary the Virgin). Thomas Cole, a painter who worked on the interior, wrote to a friend in 1844, "We are too much fettered by puritanical opinion."

In 1913 All Saints' Chapel was added to Trinity solely for prayer and meditation. It was dedicated to the Reverend Morgan Dix, rector from 1862 to 1908, who led a divided city and congregation through the Civil War, when Northern families were often torn over their loyalty to Southern friends and relatives.

ARCHITECTURE

Richard Upjohn designed the Gothic Revival brownstone structure, whose nave soars to 80 feet and whose 25-story steeple is topped with a gilded cross.

Bronze doors, illustrated with scenes and personalities from the Bible, fill the entranceways. They were designed in 1896 by Richard Morris Hunt as a memorial to John Jacob Astor from his son, William Waldorf Astor, who renounced his American citizenship, moved to England, and became a baron.

Trinity's stained-glass windows are among the oldest in the nation. Upjohn designed the chancel window above the high altar, but his clerestory windows were replaced by the Rohlf Glass Company in New York in the 1960s, when it was discovered that the tinted windows lost all color after being washed. Upjohn used richly dyed German glass to focus on the chancel image of Jesus and his Apostles, Peter, Matthew, Mark, Luke, John, and Paul, and had all the windows made in Abner Stephenson's workshop on the church grounds.

Frederick Clarke Withers built the elaborate reredos (the sanctuary wall behind the high altar), which stretches 20 feet across the chancel. Gray stone from France, Italian white marble, and pink stone from Portugal are used on panels that portray the passion of Jesus. Atop the reredos, angels playing musical instruments welcome the risen

Jesus. The handsome English oak pulpit, holding Trinity's original red-velvet pennant, has been the platform for many well-known people. Bishop Desmond Tutu of South Africa, former President Jimmy Carter, and Queen Elizabeth II have spoken at Trinity. When the queen visited in 1976, she was paid all back rent as outlined in the original charter. The 279 peppercorns were presented in a crystal bowl.

For a more intimate spot, visit All Saints' Chapel, created in 1911 by the architect Thomas Nash. It can be reached through an archway on the north aisle.

Stop by the museum on the premises and read the original charter or watch an informative video. Before you leave glance up at the plaster ceiling, which is faux Gothic; the appearance of flying buttresses is only a cosmetic touch.

Once outside, stroll through the churchyard and look for memorials of prominent families and historic figures, including Alexander Hamilton, Robert Fulton, and Francis Lewis, the only signer of the Declaration of Independence buried in Manhattan. Be sure to see the intricately carved Astor Cross, over 15 feet high, which memorializes Caroline Webster Astor, the hostess known for gathering The 400, the elite of New York City society. Nearby is one of the best stones in the yard. Adam Allyn, "Comedian," is remembered with a unique inscription dated February 15, 1768: "this stone was erected by a American company as a testimony of their unfeignd regard. he possessed many good qualities. But he was a man. He had the Frailties Common to man's Nature."

Adam, obviously a well-loved rascal, is forgiven publicly for whatever his transgressions were. A fine thought for all visitors to carry away.

ADDRESS: 74 Trinity Place (on Broadway at Wall St.) New York, NY 10006
PHONE: 212-602-0800
HOURS: Daily: 8:00 A.M.–4:00 P.M. Call for service schedule and
museum hours. Mon.–Fri.: free guided tour at 2:00 P.M.
WEB SITE: www.trinitywallstreet.org
LANDMARK DESIGNATION

ST. PAUL'S CHAPEL

OF TRINITY CHURCH
WHERE GEORGE WASHINGTON PRAYED

A fter General George Washington took the oath of office as the first president of the United States on the balcony of Federal Hall, he walked to nearby St. Paul's Chapel for a service of thanksgiving. He was accompanied on that day, April 30, 1789, by his Congress, to whom he would later say, "The establishment of our new Government seemed to be the last great experiment for promoting human happiness."

HISTORY

St. Paul's Chapel opened in 1766 under the auspices of Trinity Church and stood in a field outside the city wall. It is the oldest public building and only remaining colonial church in Manhattan. Shortly

before the British occupation of New York in 1776, St. Paul's services were suspended as war threats increased between colonists and the Crown. The chapel, several city blocks away from Trinity, escaped the Great Fire of 1776, which burned down most of the city. St. Paul's became the religious center of the Episcopal community until Trinity Church was rebuilt in 1790.

Among those who worshiped in the chapel were General Charles William Cornwallis, the British field commander who surrendered to Washington's forces in 1781, Lord William Howe, who led the British forces in New York, and a young visitor from England, Prince William (later King William IV). You will see General Richard Montgomery, hero of the Battle of Quebec, immortalized in a white marble bust below the east window. The colorful royal arms hanging on the interior gallery are from George III, the last king to rule the American colonies. Many prominent New York families attended services in the chapel and are buried in its graveyard. Enjoy a walk along the paths while reading the memorial stones.

ARCHITECTURE

Archivists say that Thomas McBean probably designed the chapel, but there is no written document to prove it. Built in true Georgian style, St. Paul's resembles the London masterpiece St. Martin-in-the-Fields Church, designed by James Gibbs. McBean was thought to have paid tribute to Gibbs, his teacher, by using the same architectural elements.

The exterior is Manhattan schist, a coarse-grained metamorphic rock. Note that the chapel's main entrance, with its large porch, faces Broadway and the churchyard. The portico, with Ionic columns and Palladian window, was completed in 1767. Stop to look up at brownstone tower and steeple, also inspired by St. Martin's Church, which were added in 1794 by James Crommelin Lawrence. The clock still works.

The French architect Pierre Charles L'Enfant is said to have designed much of the interior before becoming city planner of Washington, D.C., and after serving Washington's Continental Army as a major in the Corps of Engineers. L'Enfant's white-and-gold reredos, entitled "Glory," is poised above the high altar. The work represents Mount Sinai, with clouds, lightning, and two Tablets of the Law inscribed with the Ten Commandments. At the top is the Hebrew symbol for God. Outside the altar rail, the hand-carved wooden pulpit with a graceful winding staircase is surmounted by a coronet and six feathers—thought to be the only emblem of British nobility surviving in its original spot in New York City.

True to colonial tradition, the chapel walls are painted in a pastel aqua, and the woodwork is white with gilded touches. Rich mahogany trims the pews and altar railing. Clear-glass windows, more than 10 feet high, flood the chapel with light. Fourteen original Irish Waterford chandeliers add a touch of splendor to the nave and gallery. In the north aisle is the pew that George Washington used. On the wall above is a painting, the first rendition in oil, of the Great Seal of the United States, which was adopted in 1782. George Clinton, first governor of New York, is commemorated in the south aisle. His pew is used today by elected representatives of New York State, whose coat of arms hangs on the wall above.

ADDRESS: *Broadway and Fulton Street, New York, NY 10006*
PHONE: 212-602-0800
HOURS: Daily: 9:00 A.M.–3:00 P.M.
LANDMARK DESIGNATION

ST. PETER'S CHURCH

FIRST ROMAN CATHOLIC PARISH IN NEW YORK STATE

This parish is a survivor. Once all but given up as a victim of the changing city, the church lives on, persevering on the site where it was established. Today it is surrounded by skyscrapers and bustling commerce and has become a church away from home for thousands of people who work at local businesses.

After the Revolutionary War, New York City, as capital of the new nation, welcomed many foreign diplomats and businessmen. Those who were Roman Catholic attended services in the home of the Spanish ambassador Don Diego de Gardoqui. Governor Peter Stuyvesant hated Roman Catholic Spain, victor of many battles with the Dutch, so Catholicism was never tolerated. Under England's rule Catholic colonists would fare no better. No charter was issued to build a Roman Catholic church until well after other religions were established.

Five lots at the corner of Barclay and Church Streets were leased from Trinity Church, and the cornerstone for New York's first Roman Catholic church was laid on October 5, 1785. Don Diego led the ceremony. A thousand silver dollars from King Charles III of Spain provided initial financial help. In 1792 Trinity Church canceled all back debt and sold the land to St. Peter's for a thousand pounds. But the church would survive its growing pains only through subsidies sent by Catholics in Mexico and Spain.

During the yellow fever epidemics that swept the city in 1795, 1798, and 1805, Pastor William O'Brien and his fellow priests worked selflessly. Church records show that they earned the gratitude of the Board of Health for their care of the afflicted. In 1800 St. Peter's established the first free Catholic school in New York State. A lay staff taught both secular subjects and religious doctrine. In 1831 three Sisters of Charity arrived from Emmitsburg, Maryland, sent by the founder of the order, Elizabeth Bayley Seton, who was received into Catholicism at St. Peter's altar in 1805.

Pierre Toussaint (1766–1853), a Haitian-born slave freed upon the death of his owner, was also a member of the parish. Toussaint became so successful in the hairdressing business that he was able to purchase the freedom of his sister and his future wife, Juliette Noel. He raised and educated many orphans, who lived at St. Patrick's Old Cathedral School, and nursed the sick during yellow fever epidemics. In December 1996 Toussaint was declared Venerable, a step toward sainthood, by Pope John Paul II. He is interred at St. Patrick's Cathedral but is remembered at St. Peter's with an exterior memorial plaque.

In 1837 the old church was razed and replaced by the present building. Some members of the congregation, noting the neighborhood's change from residential to business, wanted St. Peter's to be sold and the money used to build a new church elsewhere in the city. But John Cardinal McCloskey intervened, saying, "St. Peter's will never be alienated."

ARCHITECTURE

The architects John R. Haggerty and Thomas Thomas designed this Greek Revival building in the classical tradition of many churches in Rome. The six-column portico complements smooth granite walls and the low-angled pediment. A small entryway leads into a pale green nave with three crystal chandeliers and white marble columns. Checkered marble flooring extends to the spacious high altar. The walls of the side aisles are lined with brass lamps reminiscent of nineteenth-century lighting.

Over the main altar hangs the church's focus, *The Crucifixion*, a dramatic oil painting by the Mexican artist José Vallejo, a gift from Archbishop Nuñez de Haro of Mexico City in 1789. A life-size marble statue of Elizabeth Bayley Seton reminds visitors that it was on this site that the young widow was consoled by her faith and went on to become a formidable role model for American women (see Shrine of St. Elizabeth Ann Seton).

Before you walk down the exterior staircase, take a moment to read the plaques attached to the church's facade. Thomas Dongan (1634-1715) is lauded for the contribution he made serving as colonial governor of New York from 1682 to 1688. Dongan founded the first representative assembly and passed the Charter of Rights and Privileges, which granted religious toleration, trial by jury, immunity from martial law, and freedom from arbitrary arrest for all colonists. James, Duke of York, was furious with Dongan's policies and removed him. Dongan, born in Castletown, Ireland, returned to England in 1691 and became the second Earl of Limerick, but he will always be remembered at St. Peter's for planting the seeds of American liberty.

ADDRESS: *16 Barclay Street (at Church St.), New York, NY 10007*

PHONE: 212-233-8355
HOURS: Mon.–Fri.: 7:00 A.M.–6:00 P.M. Sat.: 8:00 A.M.–5:00 P.M.
Sun.: 8:00 A.M.–1:00 P.M.
LANDMARK DESIGNATION

JOHN STREET
UNITED METHODIST CHURCH

OLDEST METHODIST CHURCH IN THE UNITED STATES

The story is told of Barbara Heck, a German Irish immigrant in colonial New York who called on friends one evening and found them playing cards. To Miss Heck, this was a symbol of moral decay stemming from a lack of spiritual guidance. In righteous anger she contacted her cousin, Philip Embury, who had been a lay preacher in his native Ireland and a follower of the Anglican reformers John and Charles Wesley. Tradition has it that she said: "Philip, you must preach to us, or we shall all go to hell!" Embury took up the challenge, held a meeting in his home on October 12, 1766, and subsequently organized the first Methodist society as a division of the Church of England and a forerunner to John Street United Methodist Church.

HISTORY

A deed dated March 29, 1768, shows the purchase of this site on John Street from the estate of the Reverend Henry Barclay, a Trinity Church rector whose name graces a nearby street. The society dedicated its first church, named for the Wesleys, on October 30, 1768. One of the craftsmen was said to be the founder, Philip Embury. Look in the church museum for an oak pulpit that the skilled carpenter built.

As colonial New York began to flex its muscle against British tyranny, the John Street congregation remained loyal to England, ensuring the church's survival through the years of British occupation. The church had attracted large numbers of black Africans, who made up about 20 percent of the congregation. Peter Williams, a slave who converted to Methodism and had his freedom purchased by the congregation for forty pounds, became sexton in 1778. After paying his debt and starting a tobacco business, Williams, with his fellow member James Varick, participated in establishing the first African Methodist Episcopal Church in 1796 (see Mother AME Zion Church). He never left the John Street congregation and would see his son ordained the first black Episcopal priest (see St. Philip's Church).

In 1817, when city planners widened John Street, the old church was leveled, and the current building was dedicated on April 27, 1841. As development engulfed Lower Manhattan and residents moved north, the New York State Legislature issued a special charter in 1866 stating that John Street Methodist Church must be forever maintained as a place of public worship on its present site.

ARCHITECTURE

William Hurry designed the simple brownstone building in Greek Revival style with an Italianate touch. The center of the facade holds a white-framed Palladian window, a northern Italian detail popular in England.

The warm, cream-colored interior has remain unchanged since its opening in 1841, with many of the furnishings coming from the 1768 church. Graceful brass candelabra, attached to the gallery, were originally gaslights.

Stop for a moment by an old stained-glass window mounted on the back wall. It is an image of Bishop Francis Asbury, who came to America in 1771 as a volunteer minister and was appointed cogeneral of the Methodist Society along with Thomas Coke. In keeping with the spirit that followed the American Revolution, Asbury was democratically elected in 1784 as the first bishop of the new American Methodist Church. (It is interesting to note that the Wesley brothers, advocates of reform who inspired many followers, would never leave the Church of England.) By the way, the city of Asbury Park on the New Jersey shoreline was named after the bishop.

Visit the museum, located under the sanctuary, and discover how the people of John Street lived and worshiped when New York City was home to sailors and artisans, slaves and soldiers, carpenters and candlemakers. An eighteenth-century English wall clock, a gift from John Wesley, hangs there, still watching the ever-changing parade of immigrants.

ADDRESS: *44 John Street (between Nassau & William Sts.)*
  New York, NY 10038
PHONE: *212-269-0014*
HOURS: *Mon., Wed., Fri.: 12:00–4:00 P.M. Sun.: 11:00 A.M.–1:00 P.M.*
LANDMARK DESIGNATION

❖ ❖ ❖ ❖

CHURCH OF ST. ANDREW

"BLESSED ARE THEY WHO WALK IN THE LAW OF THE LORD"

Tucked away in the courthouse complex of Foley Square, this Roman Catholic church offers respite and solace in an area humming with public servants, university students, and citizens carrying out their responsibilities as jurors. The area is known as Civic Center—the governmental heart of the city. The church is within easy reach of City Hall, the Municipal Building, Police Headquarters, Pace University, and a federal jail. Its Latin motto, prominently written in the stone portal above the church doors, fittingly describes St. Andrew's civic ministry: Beati Qui Ambulant in Lege Domini; Blessed Are They Who Walk in the Law of the Lord.

HISTORY

Founded by Bishop John Hughes in 1842, St. Andrew's reflects the human experience of immigrants who streamed into New York City in the nineteenth century. The church, originally at Duane and Augustus Streets, was surrounded by the city's worst slums. Beginning in 1845, a thousand Irish immigrants arrived daily, ignored by city government but cared for by St. Andrew's compassionate priests.

As Lower Manhattan developed, tenements were replaced by printing plants and the area became known as Newspaper Row. In 1901, to accommodate night staffs of morning newspapers, St. Andrew's initiated the Printer's Mass, celebrated at 2:30 A.M. In 1906 the clergy met the needs of civic and judicial workers and started noon-day Mass. The Catholic Lawyers' Guild sponsored the first Red Mass in 1928, a tradition still widely attended that marks the beginning of the judicial calendar in September. It is a time for lawyers and judges to contemplate the gravity of their work.

In 1929 St. Andrew's became the owner of its present site through a swap of Duane Street property with the city. The present parcel once held the birthplace of Patrick Cardinal Hayes, the fifth archbishop of New York, and Carroll Hall, a meeting place for Catholic discussion groups. On November 30, 1939, Francis Cardinal Spellman dedicated St. Andrew's final home. Priests and brothers who care for the congregation are members of the Congregation of the Most Blessed Sacrament, founded in 1856 by St. Peter Julian Eymard, a French priest who was canonized in 1962. A statue honoring Eymard stands to the left of the altar.

ARCHITECTURE

The federal-style building was designed by Maginnis & Walsh in collaboration with Robert J. Reiley. Its exterior of limestone and red brick, with a belfry holding the Duane Street bell, recalls colonial New York.

The warmth of the sanctuary is accented by walnut panels and oil paintings in gilded frames. Small circular stained-glass windows under the gallery tell the story of St. Andrew's life—his work as a disciple of John the Baptist, leading his brother Simon Peter to Jesus, and his crucifixion on an X-shaped cross. Look up in the gallery for stained-glass windows honoring saintly women who have played an important role in American society. Elizabeth Seton started the American parochial school system (see Shrine of St. Elizabeth Ann Seton), and Mother Frances Xavier Cabrini, who arrived in New York City in 1883, helped educate Italian immigrants. Blessed Kateri Tekakwitha, a Mohawk Indian from New York State who was rejected by her tribe for becoming a Catholic, is venerated as the Lily of the Mohawks.

Stop by Sinners' Corner on the left as you enter the sanctuary. Featured in stained-glass are Matt Talbot, a reformed alcoholic whose virtue in overcoming the disease was much admired; Mary Magdalene, a prostitute who anointed the feet of Jesus and received his pardon; Margaret of Cortona, like Magdalene a public sinner; and Dismas, the good thief who was crucified with Jesus. Many candles are lit in this spot. Don't miss the restored painting of the Crucifixion on the side wall of the nave. It is reminiscent of an old master's work in style and color, but its artist and age are unknown.

The metal baptismal font from the Duane Street church was used to christen Patrick Cardinal Hayes (1867–1938), who grew up in the area and served St. Andrew's as an altar boy. The hood of the font bears sculptured symbols of the seven sacraments and is crowned with three-dimensional images of John the Baptist baptizing Jesus. When you leave the church, look for the bust of Cardinal Hayes above the side entrance.

A much admired ecclesiastical leader in New York, he did very well for a neighborhood kid.

ADDRESS: *20 Cardinal Hayes Place (in Federal Plaza), New York, NY 10007*
PHONE: *212-962-3972*
HOURS: *Daily: 6:00 A.M.–6:00 P.M.*
Exposition of the Blessed Sacrament daily 1:30–5:00 P.M.

ELDRIDGE STREET SYNAGOGUE

SPIRITUAL HAVEN WHERE TIME STOOD STILL

This landmark Orthodox synagogue stands as testimony to the waves of Jewish immigrants who poured into New York City's Lower East Side in the late nineteenth century. With only their faith and hope for a new life in America, these Eastern Europeans built this haven as spiritual relief from the pressures of daily life and in thanksgiving for the religious freedom they had sought and won. As years passed the increasingly prosperous congregation moved away from this working-class neighborhood until there were simply not enough members to sustain the cost of daily use. The upper sanctuary was closed in the mid-1950s, and services were held on the basement level. Gerard Wolfe, a writer of popular architectural guidebooks, discovered the sealed sanctuary and stirred interest to finance a master plan for restoration in 1986 under the auspices of the nonprofit Eldridge Street Project. The architect Giorgio Cavaglieri is returning the landmark to its original grandeur.

HISTORY

Eldridge was built in 1887 for a group of Eastern European Jews who had lived in New York for almost thirty years. The synagogue is officially known as K'hal Adath Jeshurun with Anshe Lubz, meaning People of the Congregation of the Righteous and People of Lubz, Poland—two congregations that merged. At least half of the founding members were new arrivals from Poland and Russia seeking freedom from anti-Jewish laws that had relegated them to ghettos. They were Orthodox Ashkenazi, the sect from which springs 80 percent of American Jewry. Ashkenaz is the old Hebrew word for Germany.

By 1900 membership at Eldridge had risen to a thousand. The congregation included the actors Edward G. Robinson and Sam Jaffe, the chemist Linus Pauling, and the renowned physician Jonas Salk. But by the 1920s members were leaving the Lower East Side in huge numbers.

Today a small but loyal congregation still pray and fondly recall the history of a group that has never missed holding Sabbath service since 1887.

ARCHITECTURE

Peter and Francis William Herter, New York City architects specializing in tenement housing and private homes, built this Moorish-style haven in homage to thirteenth-century Spanish synagogues influenced by Islamic design. A central gable dominates the beige brick and gray terra-cotta facade, with a Star of David roundel placed in the rose window. Lined up beneath the window are keyhole-shaped openings filled with stained glass. The exterior's typical Moorish touches include rounded arches, bell-shaped pinnacles, and intricately carved columns.

But nothing quite prepares you for the sanctuary, a 4,000-square-foot area illuminated by sun pouring in through skylights and stained-glass windows on all four sides. A dark sculptured-wood gallery surrounds the sanctuary and is supported by amber-colored marble columns. Attached to each scagliola (artificial marble) column are three gas jets holding brass fixtures, a charming reminder of an era before electricity.

The bimah, a reading table holding the Torah scroll, is in the center of the sanctuary, a sign of European tradition. At each of the bimah corners a Victorian brass candelabrum (originally a gaslight from the 1920s) holds four colorful glass shades. An enormous brass chandelier hangs from the barrel-vaulted ceiling.

The east wall focuses on the Holy Ark, an Italian walnut cabinet that once held twenty-four Torah scrolls. Carved doors open with the touch of a finger and are still lined with the original red velvet. On either side of the Ark, a trompe l'oeil mural represents white-curtained windows looking toward Jerusalem. Notice the music stand below the lectern on the east wall and a telltale sign that it was well-used by cantors — two footprints are worn through the carpet.

One area of the main sanctuary, still set apart by a red-velvet curtain, was for older women who could not climb to the gallery. In all traditional Orthodox congregations, men and women worship separately. Be sure to go upstairs and see the 70-foot-high sanctuary from a more lofty position. Perhaps you will feel the joy of the Eldridge congregation when they entered for the first time.

ADDRESS: *12 Eldridge Street (between Canal & Division Sts.)*
   New York, NY 10002
PHONE: *212-978-8800*
HOURS: *Tues. & Thurs. 11:30 A.M. & 2:30 P.M. tours*
WEB SITE: *www.eldridgestreet.org*
Group tours and reservations available. Call for worship information.
LANDMARK DESIGNATION

SUNG TAK BUDDHIST ASSOCIATION

TO REALIZE TRUTH

Saffron-robed monks place their hands together and bow their heads in greeting to all who visit this house of worship dedicated to the principles and teachings of Buddha. In the serene Meditation Hall, gifts of fruit, incense, and flowers are left on small altars to thank the deity who helps Buddhists eliminate illusion about life and realize truth. Buddha (Sanskrit for "the enlightened one") is said to have been born of nobility in Nepal and to have lived from about 563 to 483 B.C. His life story, written two hundred years after his death, is shrouded in legend, but his basic philosophy is well recorded. Buddha was concerned with suffering in the lives of ordinary people. He felt that these emotions could be overcome by giving up personal ambition and selfishness, and practicing moderate detachment. The goal was a state of complete bliss, known as Nirvana, which brought the end of rebirths. Buddhists believe that to be reborn in another body is to suffer, repeatedly, the problems of humanity. Buddhism originated in India and spread rapidly as Indian traders introduced its principles to China and Southeast Asia. Three branches — Theravada, Mahayana, and Vajrayana — developed and all have many sects. A different emphasis on Buddha's original philosophy is practiced by each.

Sung Tak Buddhist Temple was dedicated on December 23, 1996. Established by a successful New York City businessman who emigrat-ed from China's southern province of Fujian, the temple was a gift to the monks who had taught him the Buddhist way.

The present group occupies this landmark building built as a syna-gogue in 1903 for the Congregation of the Sons of Israel from Kalwarie, a small town on the Polish-Lithuanian border. Since there was seating for 1,500 people, it was often used for community meetings. In 1913 a dispute flared up between adherents of Orthodox and Reform philosophies. A mob of five thou-sand young Jews forced their way in to hear Rabbi Judah Magnes, from Temple Emanu-El, who had broken with Reform leadership and become an Orthodox follower. The friction led to the birth of the Young Israel Movement, an Orthodox branch of Judaism that adheres to strict rules of conduct and follows Kosher laws. In 1977 the synagogue was aban-doned and fell into disrepair.

The limestone temple rises four stories, with a smooth facade pierced by rounded arches that once held over fifteen stained-glass win-dows. Alfred E. Badt, an architect who also designed row houses, was clearly influenced by the German *Rundbogenstil*, the round-arch style used in Romanesque Revival architecture. Twin lateral stairways lead to a portico guarded by two large terra-cotta fu dogs. A decorative ebony incense pot with an interesting pagoda roof sits in the center of the porch.

Bright red doors are paired at three entranceways leading into the sparse plaster interior. All traces of Judaism have been removed, but Hebrew lettering might be under panels placed over the entrance arches. The street-level entrance, which once held meeting rooms, is now a retail store. The monks live and study on the upper floors.

The Meditation Hall, the main public room, is small and compact. Its focal point is three dramatically decorated altars. The room is a duplication of Buddhist temples in China. Round red cushions dot the marble floor for those who wish to sit and reflect. Gilded statues of three giant Buddhas sit in individual pagodas while a huge bronze bell, encased in a red wooden structure, calls the monks to prayer. Be sure to visit the wall of tiny white Buddhas, as well as the deity that sits in the entrance, guarded by fierce-looking warriors. All Buddhas, be they jolly or austere, teach the way to virtue.

ADDRESS: **15 Pike Street (near the Manhattan Bridge), New York, NY 10002**
PHONE: 212-587-5936
HOURS: Daily: 9:00 A.M.–7:00 P.M.
LANDMARK DESIGNATION

ST. MARK'S CHURCH-IN-THE-BOWERY

THE SPIRIT OF THE DUTCH, THE LURE OF THE ARTS

This Episcopal site stands as a living memorial to the hardy Dutch settlers who pioneered a great mercantile experiment that would become New York City. Today St. Mark's continues not only as a historic sacred haven but as an experimental center for performing arts featuring dance presentations, poetry readings, and innovative works at the Ontological Theater.

Peter Stuyvesant (1610–1672) ruled New Amsterdam, the capital of the Dutch colonial New Netherland, with a stern hand. As the sixth director-general, from 1647 to 1664, he banned the sale of alcohol and ordered all colonists, regardless of their beliefs, to attend St. Nicholas Dutch Reformed Church near his official residence at Whitehall and State Streets (see National Museum of the American Indian). When he surrendered the colony to British forces in 1664, Stuyvesant retired to his 30-acre bouwerie (Dutch for "land"). A chapel stood for almost 150 years where St. Mark's stands today, making the site one of the oldest used continuously for religious services in New York City.

In 1799 St. Mark's Episcopal Church — part of Trinity Church — was consecrated with the financial assistance of Peter Stuyvesant's great-grandson, Petrus Stuyvesant. Under the terms of a charter granted by England, Trinity was to have been the only Episcopal parish in colonial New York. But Alexander Hamilton, soon to become the first United States secretary of the Treasury, found a loophole in the charter and established St. Mark's as the second independent Episcopal church. Hamilton's move set the stage for new Episcopal churches as the city's population increased and its boundaries expanded. Clement Clarke Moore, who served on the vestry of St. Mark's in 1813, donated land to establish General Theological Seminary, St. Luke-in-the-Fields, and St. Peter's Church (see entries).

The spirit of Peter Stuyvesant continues to echo from every nook and cranny of St. Mark's, since his remains, and those of his heirs, are interred in a vault beneath the church. Reflecting the democratic spirit of the New World, Colonel Henry Sloughter, who served as English governor for four months in 1691, is also buried there. Be sure to see the bronze statue of the director-general in nearby Stuyvesant Square, a public park between 15th and 16th Streets on Second Avenue that was once part of his enormous farm. The life-size sculpture by Gertrude Vanderbilt Whitney is realistic — right down to Stuyvesant's stern visage and peg leg, a memento of a battle with Spanish forces on the Caribbean island of Curaçao.

In 1978 fire seriously damaged the interior of the church during restoration. The local architect Harold Edelman (1923–1998), in cooperation with Preservation Youth Project, a church work-training program, restored the fieldstone building as it stands today. The sanctuary reopened on Easter Sunday 1982.

ARCHITECTURE

Construction of St. Mark's took place over long periods of time; its architect is unknown. The fieldstone exterior and round arched windows, belonging to the later Georgian tradition, were completed between 1795 and 1799. The artisan Ithiel Town designed the Greek Revival tower in 1828; the cast-iron porch, made in Italianate tradition, was added in 1854. An exceptional cast-iron fence that still encircles the site is from 1836. Look for street names on the fence, used before there were official posts, and a charming public water fountain attached to the fence's corner pillar.

When you enter the sanctuary, you won't find traditional pews or dark woodwork. Instead, a soaring open space reflects St. Mark's long-standing support for the arts — note the spotlights fixed to wooden columns. Most of the lower windows are filled with stained glass installed in 1885. See images of St. Augustine, St. Mark and, of course, Peter Stuyvesant. The Christmas Tree window is directly over the Stuyvesant vault. To witness the art of stained glass brought into the twentieth century, look up to the clerestory level for Harold Edelman's modern interpretations of life on the Lower East Side. These brilliant jewel-toned windows were installed after the 1978 fire.

Be sure to spend some time walking through the churchyard and find the bust of Peter Stuyvesant that was given to the people of New York by Wilhelmina, queen of the Netherlands. Created by the sculptor Toon Dupuis, the statue was dedicated in 1915 and placed in trust of St. Mark's. Its long inscription details the meeting at The Hague on July 16, 1646, when Stuyvesant was named to head the Dutch colony of New Netherland.

Many families that played roles in the development of New York

City are also interred at St. Mark's, including the Fish family — Hamilton Fish was a powerful twentieth-century member of U.S. House of Representatives. The Fish residence from 1803 stands down

the block at 21 Stuyvesant Street. Nicholas Fish, American Revolutionary War veteran and a founding member of the church, has a marble plaque in the entrance hall stating, "The faithful soldier of Christ and of his country." Daniel Tompkins (1774–1825), who was governor of New York State and vice president of the United States under James Monroe, also rests in the yard. His name graces Tompkins Square Park on Avenue A and 9th Street.

Churchyard plaques honor other church members and artists: W. H. Auden (1907–1973), British-born American poet and parishioner who lived nearby on East 8th Street; and Frank O'Hara (1926–1966), one of the originators of the New York School of poetry and a curator at the Museum of Modern Art. Downtown on Battery Park's fence out-side the Winter Garden, you'll see O'Hara's words emblazoned: "One need never leave the confines of New York."

ADDRESS: *131 East 10th Street (at Second Ave.), New York, NY* 10003
PHONE: 212-674-6377
HOURS: 10:00 A.M.–6:00 P.M.; *Sunday services at* 10:30 A.M.;
Wednesday vespers at 6:15 P.M.
Enter through side entrance in the churchyard
THE ONTOLOGICAL THEATER: 212-533-4650
LANDMARK DESIGNATION

GRACE CHURCH

A COUNTRY CHURCHYARD IN THE BIG CITY

As you walk along lower Broadway, this Episcopal church greets you with a romantic tableau of greenery, wrought-iron gates, carefully tended gardens, and a Gothic Revival complex of mul-tishaped buildings. The setting, reminiscent of an English country vil-lage, owes its mystique to the original owner of the property, Henry Brevoort, an uncle of the architect James Renwick, Jr. Legend has it that Henry insisted his apple orchard be preserved and forced city plan-ners to work around his trees — that's why Broadway leans to the west, and 11th Street dead-ends from Broadway to Fourth Avenue.

HISTORY

Grace Church was established in 1809 as an independent ministry for immigrants at Broadway and Rector Street, directly across from Trinity Church. It was proof that the city was expanding and the Episcopal diocese growing larger. The present church, only two miles uptown from the original building, was dedicated in 1846 by a con-gregation that now included some of the city's wealthiest citizens. A

few walnut prayer stalls are still marked with original brass plaques inscribed with old names.

Look in the Honor Room for two 4-foot-high oak angels that remember the women and children of the nearby German community who perished in 1904, when the ferryboat *Slocum* caught fire and capsized in the East River (see Slocum Memorial Fountain). More than six hundred families in the parish lost loved ones.

The church archivist, Edyth McKitrick, tells the story of Dr. Wright Post, a senior warden at Grace Church and brother-in-law of Elizabeth Seton (see Shrine of St. Elizabeth Ann Seton). Post supported the impoverished Seton family even though the community saw them as outcasts for converting to Roman Catholicism. Look for a white marble plaque with elegant black lettering that was placed by the Post family in 1828; it recalls the physician as "modest, dignified and mild in deportment."

ARCHITECTURE

James Renwick, Jr.(1818–1895), a Grace parishioner and later a vestryman like his father, designed this Gothic Revival landmark in sparkling white marble. Although Renwick trained as an engineer, he was profoundly influenced by the 1836 writings of Augustus Pugin in praise of Gothic architecture. Indeed, the proportions and rich details used by Renwick make Grace Church a monument to the revival of Gothic design in New York City.

Trademark of the Revival, a glorious stained-glass rose window by Clayton & Bell is placed high above the main entrance. Flying buttresses, pointed arches, and forty-six windows fill the nave which holds unique designs in stained glass from many artisans. Above the high altar, a 33-foot-high Te Deum (Praise to God) window by Clayton & Bell dominates. Each of the four vertical sections represents a line from the Te Deum canticle. Jesus is seated in the center, with figures of the Apostles, prophets, and martyrs lifting their faces toward him. Look for Mary Magdalene, with flowing blond hair, holding a canister of healing oils.

The Hugh and Sarah Marsh Auchincloss window of the Heavenly Host from 1886 has an interpretation of adoring angels by the English artisan Charles Booth that captures an exuberant spirit of celebration. It is topped with the good omen of a hexagram. Mary Elizabeth Tillinghast, a pupil of John La Farge, created the Jacob's Dream window using opalescent glass. It was the first window she made, and oral historians note that Grace's vestrymen were not full of praise. The memorial window to Benjamin J. Hutton is now one of the church's most admired pieces.

A charming series of smaller windows showing the seven parables of Matthew is in the Honor Room, on the left side of the nave. Don't miss the choirboys' window — you can almost hear angelic voices chanting prayers. The Honor Room pays tribute to the Boys' Choir, founded in 1894 with sixteen singers. It evolved into the highly rated Grace School.

Detour into the Chantry, an intimate chapel added in 1879 for Sunday school. Construction was made possible by the parishioner Catherine Lorillard Wolfe, a socially prominent patron whose portrait by Alexandre Cabanel hangs in the European gallery of the Metropolitan Museum of Art. She was the first woman to sit on the Met's Board of Trustees.

Be sure to find the bust of a bearded James Renwick, Jr. (sometimes mistaken for St. Peter) high in the left corner of the north transept. In the right corner is an image of the Reverend Henry Codman Potter, a rector of Grace Church who is fondly remembered for his outreach programs as the seventh Episcopal bishop of New York. He began the construction of the Cathedral Church of St. John the Divine following the plan laid out by Horatio Potter, his uncle and former bishop.

As you leave the church, look up at the decorative 25-foot marble steeple from 1883, which replaced the original wooden spire. It can be seen lighting up the evening sky for miles around — a reminder that Grace continues to illuminate all those seeking rest within its Gothic haven.

ADDRESS: *802 Broadway (at 10th St.), New York, NY 10003*
PHONE: *212-254-2000*
HOURS: *Daily: 7:30 A.M.–7:00 P.M. Enter through rectory if door is locked*
WEB SITE: *www.gracenyc.org*
LANDMARK DESIGNATION

ST. ANN'S ARMENIAN CATHEDRAL

ARMENIAN CATHOLIC CATHEDRAL AND
AMERICAN NATIONAL SHRINE

If the site of this cathedral could sing, it would resound with voices of past congregations in four languages: hymns of Baptists in English, Torah readings in Hebrew, prayers of Catholics in Latin, and the solemn liturgies of Eastern Rite Catholics in Armenian. At its beginnings St. Ann was closely tied to Union Square, two blocks north of the church, once the site of elegant mansions, fine shops, and the Academy of Music. Unfortunately, the square also attracted militant advocates staging raucous demonstrations for a variety of causes. Today the busy hum of a weekend green market fills Union Square, and the quiet shelter of St. Ann's still reflects the ethnic diversity of the city.

The congregation first met in 1852 in an old Presbyterian church on Astor Place. The need for a church school prompted their pastor, the Reverend Thomas Preston, to purchase property from Temple Emanu-El and move to the present site on January 1, 1871. A red-brick school was soon built in the rear, facing 11th Street (it is now an apartment building that still has the school logo on its facade).

St. Ann's, which was equipped with a Henry Irben organ, gained worldwide fame when the American premiere of Verdi's Requiem was sung in its sanctuary on October 25, 1874.

Many early parishioners were working-class immigrants from Ireland; others were successful owners of local businesses. Governor Al Smith was a member of the congregation and a lay trustee from 1929 to 1933. In 1929 Pope Pius XI designated the church as the American National Shrine of St. Ann. Annual novenas (nine days of prayer) had traditionally been held in honor of the church's patron, but the papal proclamation added to the church's prestige. After World War II the neighborhood changed dramatically as commercial lofts replaced family housing. The parish census rapidly declined, and the school closed in 1943.

The church entered a new phase in 1984, when Pope John Paul II designated St. Ann an Eastern Rite cathedral. The first Apostolic Exarch of Armenian Catholics in the United States and Canada, the Reverend Nerses Mikael Setian, was installed here. Today St. Ann's is a multicultural parish. Eastern Rite services in Armenian and Roman Rite services in English and Spanish are celebrated every Sunday. On Saturday afternoons a traditional Tricene Latin Mass is celebrated.

The church's gray limestone facade, leaded windows, and single tower are remnants of two antecedents: the 12th Street Baptist Church, which was built in 1847, and Temple Emanu-El, which held services here from 1857 to 1871. The architect Napoleon LeBrun (1821–1901) designed the remainder of the building in thirteenth-century French Gothic style. St. Ann's is not listed among LeBrun's accomplishments, probably because he incorporated the existing facade into his Gothic plans. Little restoration has been done to the design from LeBrun, who was also a parishioner.

The spacious church is 166 feet long and more than 63 feet wide. Majestic Ionic columns and Gothic arches line the nave. The ambula-tory, surrounding the nave, has tributes to the Virgin of Quinche from Ecuador and to St. Ann's founding pastor, Father Thomas Preston. A white marble pietà — sculpture of the dead Christ lying in the arms of his mother, Mary — is a memorial to Preston. This stat-ue also pays homage to Michelangelo, whose original work from 1500 is displayed in St. Peter's Basilica at the Vatican.

The clerestory holds sixteen nonfigurative stained-glass win-dows, probably left by the Baptist congregation. The nave is filled with twenty-eight windows re-calling scenes and saints beloved by the Irish congregation. "Patrick Preaching at Tara" was a gift of Patrick Cardinal Hayes. St. Ann's pink-and-white apse holds the original 1871 marble altar and reredos. A gilded inscription, Ara Privilegiata (Privilege Indulgen-ces), is placed high on the walls to indicate special blessings given there. On both sides life-size marble angels hold original Victorian candelabra.

Be sure to see the tender image of Ann, patron of the cathedral, reading to her young daughter, Mary. Life-size white marble figures, placed on a pedestal in front of a rose-colored drape, are a reminder of the family unity so admirably represented by this cathedral.

ADDRESS: *110 East 12th Street (between Third & Fourth Aves.)*
  New York, NY 10003
PHONE: *212-477-2030*
HOURS: *Mon.–Fri.: 11:30A.M.–2:30 P.M.*
  Sat: 1:00 P.M.–6:00 P.M. 2:00 P.M. Traditional Latin Mass
  Sun: 9:00 A.M.–2:00 P.M. 10:00 A.M. Spanish Mass;
  11:15 A.M. English Mass; 12:30 P.M. Armenian Mass

❖ ❖ ❖ ❖

THE GANDHI GARDEN

"IN A GENTLE WAY, YOU CAN SHAKE THE WORLD."

Union Square has always been buzzing with heavy traffic from public transportation and a popular green market that is held four days a week. In contrast, the Gandhi Garden provides a small space for meditation, perhaps evoking memories of a quiet man whose pacifist preaching shook the British Empire to its very foundation.

HISTORY

The statue, dedicated on Gandhi's birthday in 1986, was made possible by a gift from the Gandhi Memorial International Foundation and the patron Mohan B. Murjani, a successful marketer of Gloria Vanderbilt jeans and Tommy Hilfiger sportswear. Since its unveiling, the site has become a rallying spot for Gandhi's admirers who hold an annual birthday celebration featuring music, speeches, and floral tributes.

Mohandas Karamchand Gandhi, born October 2, 1869, spent his lifetime inspiring his Hindu followers, who called him "Mahatma", meaning teacher or great soul. Gandhi developed the practice of "satyagraha"—nonviolent civil disobedience—to resist the British overlords who ruled India. This fierce nationalist strode across India covered only in white homespun as he preached his message.

Mohandas Karamchand Gandhi: 1869-1948

After India won its liberation from British rule in 1947, the country was divided into Hindu India and Moslem Pakistan. Gandhi unsuccessfully fought the partition. In 1948 he was assassinated by a Hindu extremist who blamed Gandhi for the division.

In his early years, Gandhi was not always the humble man who led India out of subjugation. His autobiography tells stories of his days as an accomplished attorney who personally felt the sting of prejudice and fought for his oppressed countrymen in South Africa's judicial system.

ARCHITECTURE

The Gandhi Garden is a triangular-shaped plot of land on the southern side of Union Square Park. A black wrought iron railing surrounds the well-tended garden and holds the monument. The life-sized bronze statue rests on a granite base which together measures 14 feet in height. Kantilal B. Patel, the sculptor, shows Gandhi wrapped in a dhoti, a garment of homespun cotton. Carrying a walking stick, wearing sandals and wire-rimmed eyeglasses, Gandhi is captured in full stride to show his determination for India's independence.

The pure simplicity of the statue brilliantly recalls this extraordinary leader who believed that "in a gentle way, you can shake the world." Perhaps as you meditate on Gandhi's words, you'll smile back at the Mahatma's kindly gaze.

ADDRESS: *14th Street at Broadway and Union Square*
PHONE: *Maintained by NYC Parks Department*
HOURS: *Public Space*

BY THE WAY

As you make your rounds in LOWER MANHATTAN, you may wish to visit other spiritual places. Some are public, others are open at special times. Be sure to call ahead.

EAST COAST MEMORIAL: 1963. Albino Manca designed this epic-sized bronze eagle clutching a funeral wreath on an pedestal inscribed, "1941–1945, Erected by the United States of America in proud and grateful remembrance of her sons who gave their lives in her service and who sleep in the American coastal waters of the Atlantic Ocean — Into Thy Hands, O Lord." The names of 4,596 heroes have been chiseled into eight granite slabs, 19 feet high, that face the Statue of Liberty and the sea beyond. One sinking claimed the troopship Dorchester and its entire contingent of GI's, including the Reverend Clark Poling, a chaplain from New York City (see Marble Collegiate Church). The memorial was dedicated by President John F. Kennedy, himself a Navy veteran and survivor of an attack in the Pacific campaign. Look for the fingertip ritual, as visitors trace a hero's name in silent tribute.

Battery Park (near South Ferry subway station) Public Space

THE UPPER ROOM: 1987. Ned Smyth created this pink sculptured courtyard, 40 feet high and 75 feet long. It holds an altarlike structure as well as a rectangular table surrounded by twelve seats. The room is a spiritual oasis along the waterfront.

Battery Park City on the Esplanade at Albany St. Public Space

VIETNAM VETERANS MEMORIAL: 1984. This engraved glass-block-and-granite monument by Peter Wormser and William Fellows is powerfully simple. Writings on the 14-foot-high wall from soldiers, newspapers, and the artisan John

The Upper Room

Ferrandino commemorate the men and women who gave their lives in a controversial war. A touching tribute to reconciliation.

55 Water Street (between Coenties Slip & Broad St.) Public Space

AFRICAN BURIAL GROUND: A small visible segment uncovered in 1991 by a construction crew working on the neighboring federal office building holds over four hundred bodies. The cemetery, which was designated a National Historic Landmark and part of a New York Historic District, is believed to have been part of five acres that spread from Chambers to Duane Streets. It was originally outside the city limits and was used from 1712 to 1794; it is estimated that over ten thousand people of African heritage were placed in graves. As the city developed the grounds started to be covered over until the cemetery was forgotten. When it was rediscovered, the bodies were removed and sent to be studied at Howard University in Washington, D.C. Controversy continues over this action, but all remains will be reinterred and a monument erected. Be sure to visit the federal building next door, which has a window overlooking the site, but be prepared to go through a security check because of government offices upstairs.

290 Broadway (between Broadway, Duane & Reade Sts.) Public Space

NEW RING SHOUT: 1994. Artwork embedded in the lobby floor is named after the ring shout dance of celebration that is performed in North America and the Caribbean. The terrazzo and brass circle with a 40-foot diameter was created by the sculptor Houston Conwill, the graphic designer Joseph De Pace, and the poet Estella Conwill Majozo. The "dance floor" is filled with historical references and symbols to honor the African Burial Ground (see entry). Take time to read the words from fourteen black heroes, especially the former slave Sojourner Truth, "I want to see women have their rights, and then there will be no more war." Clara McBride Hale, who cared for thousands of Harlem's children, says, "I'm not an American hero. I'm just a person who loves children." The journalist Ida B. Wells states, "There must always be a remedy for wrong and injustice." A free pamphlet has more details.

Federal Office Building, 290 Broadway (between Broadway, Duane & Reade Sts.)

TRIUMPH OF THE HUMAN SPIRIT: 2000. This sculpture by Lorenzo Pace is set within the historic Foley Square District which includes the African Burial Ground (see entry). The 300-ton black granite monument rising over four stories is an abstract representation of a West African Chi Wara headdress placed in a canoe. The sailing vessel is a tribute to Native Americans as well as slaves and immigrants who traveled by sea to America. Be sure to visit **Still I Rise**, a nearby six-foot-wide bronze medallion by the artist Rebecca Darr, which is set into the sidewalk. Words from Maya Angelou's powerful poem of the same name surround an engraving of an entombed mother cradling her child.

North of City Hall in Foley Square Park Public Space

CIVIC CENTER SYNAGOGUE: 1967. William Breger and Paul Gugliotta created an unusual modern design on a street filled with cast-iron buildings and old tenements. This Orthodox haven has a curved white marble facade that seems to dance with the wind. The congregation was founded in 1938 on Lafayette Street by Jacob Rosenblum, a lawyer and assistant to District Attorney Thomas E. Dewey. New York City razed the group's first building on Duane Street (1961–1964) to build Federal Plaza but traded land for the present site. An influx of residents to Soho and Tribeca has revitalized this spiritual haven whose name remembers its origin.

49 White Street (between Broadway & Church Sts.) 212-966-7141

ST. JAMES CHURCH: 1835. This fieldstone **landmark** is attributed to Minard Lafever. The Greek Revival design with recessed portico and Doric columns has a low-angled gable topping off its brownstone facade. This Roman Catholic parish was established in 1827 just south of the Brooklyn Bridge on Ann Street and was known as Christ Church. The Reverend Felix Varela, a professor of philosophy from Cuba, was appointed pastor. After Christ Church was condemned, land was purchased on James Street. Dedication of the new church to the Apostle James, patron of Spain, is said to have been influenced by Father Varela, who once served there. See an exterior plaque dedicated to the first pastor along with one from the Ancient Order of Hiberians, founded in 1836 to fight bigotry and provide "friendship, unity, and Christian charity." Varela welcomed all newcomers and was among the first to celebrate St. Patrick's Day for Irish immigrants. Some of the original congregation did not want to travel uptown to the new church and formed the Church of the Transfiguration (see entry) with Father Varela as pastor. From 1882 until the Depression of 1929, the parish provided a much needed orphanage for girls. Governor Alfred E. Smith (1873–1944), Democratic presidential candidate in 1928, served St. James as an altar boy and attended its parish school. Hispanic and Chinese immigrants moved in as the old congregation moved on to suburban areas. When entering the church, notice the old opalescent glass in the narthex doors. Look up to the stenciled ceiling filled with murals and note the Arts and Crafts border on the sanctuary walls. The focus of the square interior is a wide chancel with white marble reredos. Above the altar three paintings tucked into round marble arches detail the life of Jesus. An intricately carved marble altar rail was donated from a private home and installed in the 1940s. Since the gallery was removed, the nave glows with color from double tiers of stained-glass windows.

23 Oliver Street (at James & Madison Sts.) 212-233-0161

SHEARITH ISRAEL CEMETERY: Headstones date from 1683 to 1831 in this **landmark** graveyard for Spanish Portuguese Jews who arrived from Brazil in 1654. An annual ceremony with honor guard is held around Memorial Day.

55 St. James Place (near Chatham Sq.)

MARINERS' TEMPLE: 1842. The Greek Revival smooth brownstone is attributed to Isaac Lucas or Minard Lafever who designed this small rectangular building with a recessed Ionic portico and a low-angled pediment. The **landmark** displays a ship's bell outside the portico as a reminder that it was founded for transient seamen who roamed the Port of New York. The church distributed Bibles from the American Bible Society, had a free reading room, and was listed as "unisectarian." The present Baptist congregation features the Voices of Praise Choir, with gospel music resounding every Sunday through the classically designed interior.

3 Henry Street 212-233-0423

LIN ZE YU: 1997. This life-size bronze statue was designed by T. A. Ho of the United States and T. C. Ho and Li Wei Si of China. Lin Ze Yu (1785–1850), a scholar and politician of China's Qing dynasty, banned opium and led troops against British invaders in the Opium

Wars. "Say no to drugs" appears on the base of the statue along with his biography. Next to it is the **Kimlau War Memorial**, 1962, by Poy G. Lee. This simple arch-shaped monument with Asian motifs is inscribed, "In memory of the Americans of Chinese ancestry who lost their lives in defense of freedom and democracy."

Chatham Square and Oliver Street Public Space

CHURCH OF THE TRANSFIGURATION: 1801. This Georgian Gothic **landmark** was built as Zion English Lutheran Church. Henry Engelbert designed the addition with tower in 1868. It became a Roman Catholic church in 1853 under the leadership of Father Felix Varela, a Cuban exile. The congregation dates from 1827 as part of Christ Church that split from the new St. James Church (see entry). The world-famous opera singer Enrico Caruso was a frequent visitor here. Be sure to see the plaque dedicated to Father Varela on the facade.

29 Mott Street (west of Park Row) 212-962-5157

EASTERN STATES BUDDHIST TEMPLE: A storefront on a street celebrated so often in song holds a large collection of golden Buddhas in its heavily incensed atmosphere. Small red cushions are provided to kneel in worship. Chinese and Vietnamese leaflets are available, none in English.

64 Mott Street 212-966-6229

FIRST CHINESE PRESBYTERIAN CHURCH: 1817. This Manhattan schist **landmark** was built as the Northern Dutch Reformed Church. The Federal design has clear-glass Gothic windows placed in stone walls. In 1864 the building was purchased by Hanson K. Corning and donated to the Presbyterian Church. It was designated the Sea and Land Church because of the area's large seafaring population. Services were held in Italian, Greek, Russian, and Spanish. In 1951 a Chinese congregation founded in 1885 by the Reverend Huie Kim began to share the facilities, and they were given the building in 1971. The simple blue nave has one central aisle, mahogany pews with white doors, and a gallery. Marble plaques in the chancel memorialize Colonel Henry Rutgers, who donated the land, and the Reverend William McMurray, first pastor of the original Dutch Reformed

Church, who served until his death in 1835. White Doric columns crowned with a Federal pediment highlight the raised chancel, which holds a white wood pulpit, lectern, and altar. The focus of the sanctuary, a stark white cross, hangs like a bas-relief against a red-draped reredos.

61 Henry Street (Market St.) 212-964-5488

ST. TERESA: 1841. A Gothic Revival gray stone church was built for the First Presbyterian Church by an unknown architect who adorned the bell tower with a public clock (the oldest in the city). A Roman Catholic congregation purchased the site in 1863, and the parish sold its parking lot and air rights to finance reconstruction of the interior after the ceiling collapsed in 1995. Services continued in the auditorium until the restored sanctuary opened in December 2000. The church's patron is Teresa of Ávila (1515–1582), a Spanish Carmelite nun and mystic whose writings are celebrated as masterpieces.

141 Henry Street (Rudgers St.) 212-233-0233

ST. BARBARA GREEK ORTHODOX CHURCH: 1895.

Religious space was built by Ernest W. Schneider and Henry Herter as a Romanesque synagogue for Congregation Mishkan Israel Suwalki, whose immigrant members were tailors from Suwalki and Great Poland, near the German border. In the 1920s the building became a Christian church. In 1932 a Greek congregation organized and purchased the building, naming it for Barbara, who was beheaded by her father for converting to Christianity. Be sure to visit the Shrine of St. Barbara and see the Greek custom of leaving small tin icons with symbols of favors requested. In 1998 fire devastated the interior, forcing the congregation to remove the traditional dome, install wood flooring, and restore paintings. The iconostatis (altar screen) holds European-style murals and is lit by seven hanging lamps. As you leave, look up to the choir loft at the gilded oil painting of a regal Christ, crowned and robed in traditional Byzantine style. This icon was once the focus of the altar screen.

27 Forsyth Street (along the Manhattan Bridge south of Canal St.)
212-226-0499

MAHAYANA TEMPLE BUDDHIST ASSOCIATION: At the

foot of the Manhattan Bridge, this huge temple with its red-and-yellow facade holds an enormous gold Buddha in the main sanctuary. The story of Siddhartha, who became the Buddha Gautama, is told in text and pictures framed on the temple's interior walls. Buddhism aims to free humans from suffering in a constantly shifting world. Noise from the bridge is muffled but the atmosphere of peace prevails.

133 Canal Street (and Grand St.) 212-925-8787

ST. MARY'S CHURCH: 1832. Congregation was founded in 1826 near Broome Street in a Presbyterian church purchased by the Augustinian Fathers. In 1831 that church was destroyed in a fire set by anti-Catholic, anti-Irish, and anti-immigrant groups. The congregation and many non-Catholic friends united to build St. Mary's on Grand Street. It is now the oldest Roman Catholic building in Manhattan and the first to have a bell and steeple, which were forbidden in Ireland by British law. Note the exterior is in two sections: the original is gray stone while the red-brick facade with tall twin towers was added in 1871 by Patrick C. Keely. Frescoes around the main altar were also created at this time. Be sure to see the interior's skylights and vivid stained-glass windows from 1887 by the Mayer Company of Munich and London. A small gift shop tucked into the back of the nave holds a wonderful surprise: a huge stained-glass window of St. Patrick holding a sprig of shamrocks. Irish immigrants who originated the parish placed another favorite, St. Bridget, directly across the aisle, but that window is now located in the reconciliation room. By the 1930s the parish school was closed, but new arrivals from Puerto Rico were moving into the neighborhood's public and cooperative housing. Today the church is thriving with Hispanic and Chinese members.

440 Grand Street 212-674-3266

BIALYSTOKER SYNAGOGUE: 1826. The **landmark** Federal-style stone building, originally Willett Street Methodist Church, was taken over in 1905 by immigrants from Bialystok, (once part of Russia, now Poland). Round arches frame the tripartite entry, with stained-glass windows placed above the doors. The beautiful interior with murals, Victorian lighting fixtures, and original gallery is obviously well cared for by an Orthodox congregation that dates back to 1878.

7 Willett Street (between Grand & Broome Sts.) 212-475-0165

CONGREGATION BETH HAMEDRASH HAGODOL (Great House of Study): 1850. Built as Norfolk Street Baptist Church (forerunner of Riverside Church). This landmark is home to New York City's oldest Russian Orthodox group, founded in 1852 as the first synagogue in America to train rabbis. The congregation moved into the building in 1885. The cream stucco facade with brown Gothic woodwork is a historic highlight of the neighborhood, where squat tenements were replaced by huge housing projects. The synagogue now stands alone, surrounded by its original black wrought-iron fence. In 1997 the sanctuary's five-story Gothic window was destroyed in a windstorm, but it has been repaired with help from neighbors and friends.

60 *Norfolk Street (between Grand & Broome Sts.)* 212-674-3330

FIRST ROUMANIAN-AMERICAN CONGREGATION: 1888. This Romanesque Revival Orthodox synagogue was built as a Methodist church. It became known as the Cantors' Carnegie Hall because many famous cantors, including Jan Peerce and Richard Tucker (stars of the Metropolitan Opera) were members. The congregation moved to this building in 1900 after merging with the German group Shaari Shomoyim (Gates of Heaven) in 1885.

89 *Rivington Street (between Orchard & Ludlow Sts.)* 212-673-2835

ST. PATRICK'S OLD CATHEDRAL: 1815. The first Roman Catholic cathedral in New York City, built by a multinational congregation from 1808, was designed by the architect Joseph-François Mangin, a designer of City Hall. The interior was rebuilt by Henry Engelbert in 1868 after a fire. A wooden reredos, softly-colored murals, and old windows are a treat in the interior, which rises 85 feet and is over 120 feet long. Be sure to visit the historic graveyard, whose high brick walls are seen in Martin Scorsese's film *Mean Streets*. St. Pat's was the Scorsese family church. A labyrinth of restored vaults beneath the **landmark** church holds old New York families and can be visited by appointment. Bishop John Dubois (1764-1842), the cathedral's third bishop, is buried under the sidewalk near the Mott Street entrance. The church historian, the Reverend Thomas J. Shelley, tells a Dubois yarn in which the bishop said, "Bury me where the people will walk over me in death as they wished to do in life." A legend stenciled on the wall of the narthex states that in the 1830s and 1840s the building was often the scene of violent demonstrations by religious bigots. A new cathedral was planned by Old St. Pat's daring leader Bishop John Hughes (1797–1864), who, after dedicating a cornerstone in 1858 on Fifth Avenue and 50th Street, was loudly criticized for building in the wilderness. In 1879, when the presiding bishop, John Cardinal McCloskey, moved uptown to Fifth Avenue, the old cathedral became a parish church. Look for the Federal-style red-brick grammar school from 1825 on Prince Street. It was originally the church's orphanage, supported by Pierre Toussaint, a prosperous Haitian hairdresser and freed slave who is a candidate for sainthood (see St. Peter's Church on Barclay Street). Toussaint, once buried in the cemetery, now rests uptown in the cathedral vault.

262 *Mulberry Street (at Prince St.)* 212-226-8075

ST. MICHAEL'S RUSSIAN CATHOLIC CHAPEL: 1858. This Gothic Revival **landmark** was designed by James Renwick, Jr., and William Rodrigue as the chancery office for St. Patrick's Old Cathedral (see entry). The small red-brick building is three stories high and surrounded by the old cemetery. In 1936 Russian immigrants who were given the first floor for worship, set up a traditional Russian chapel with a decorative iconostatis as the entrance to the altar and a single crystal chandelier. The parish is named for St. Michael, an archangel usually seen defeating the fallen angel Lucifer. This intimate space holds more than fifty worshipers.

266 *Mulberry Street (at Prince St.)* 212-226-2644

RUSSIAN ORTHODOX CATHEDRAL OF THE HOLY VIRGIN PROTECTION: 1860. Church was built as Mount Olivet Memorial Church for a German Reformed group. The Russian congregation who organized in 1926 at St. Augustine Episcopal Chapel on Houston Street dedicated this space in 1943 as the spiritual and administrative center for its church in America while awaiting a legal decision on property rights (see St. Nicholas Russian Orthodox Cathedral). In 1985 the group merged with St. Innocent's Chapel from Westchester, who renovated and renewed the parish, and saved the church from real estate developers. Be sure to study the Byzantine icons

by Daniel Breno and the decorated oak iconostasis (altar screen), which holds a handcrafted Holy Gate (entry only by clergy). Directly across the street is the **New York City Marble Cemetery**, which opened in 1832; it is the resting place for many famous citizens, including Stephen Allen and Isaac Varian, both city mayors; James Lenox, who started a private library that became part of the city system; Preserved Fish, a prominent merchant; and the Kip family, who owned a midtown farm around 34th Street that is known as Kips Bay. The first nonsectarian cemetery of the same name was opened in 1830 with only underground marble vaults; entrance is through an alley off Second Avenue bound by 2nd and 3rd Streets. (In 1847 New York State passed a law forbidding any new burial grounds in Manhattan.)

59 East 2nd Street (between Second & Third Aves.) 212-677-4664

CHURCH OF THE MOST HOLY REDEEMER: 1851. This Romanesque Byzantine design with exterior dome towers over its Lower East Side neighborhood. In 1912 a major renovation added the limestone and granite facade, lowered the tower to 232 feet, and topped the cupola with copper. The present site had held a smaller church built in 1844 for Roman Catholic immigrants from Germany who had been worshiping in the crowded sanctuary of St. Nicholas on 2nd Street. Led by its founder, the Reverend Gabriel Rumpler, Holy Redeemer became the largest German-speaking parish in the city and introduced singing and solemn processions to American services. The ornate interior, which has many altars and artifacts in grand Byzantine motifs, seats more than 2,000. The crypt holds eighty-five Redemptorist priests and brothers who helped immigrants through the city's many smallpox epidemics. In 1860 the church opened St. Joseph's Orphanage on 89th Street (see St. Joseph's Church of Yorkville) to care for children left alone after the epidemics. The Zundel Company of Long Island created stained-glass windows filled with glorious figurative designs. Be sure to see two polychrome wood carvings at the entrance to the nave: the Pietà from 1893 and the Crucifixion from 1896. Also look for the baptismal font, which was fashioned from the carved communion rail when the church was renovated in 1992. Entrance to the church is through the rectory next door.

173 East 3rd Street 212-673-4224

Musical prayer in stained glass at Church of The Most Holy Redeemer

ST. BRIGID'S CHURCH: 1848. Patrick Charles Keely built this church, whose stucco facade and early Gothic interior reflect the structure's age. Its Roman Catholic immigrants from Ireland, the only English-speaking parish in "Kleine Deutschland" (Little Germany), were led by the Reverend Richard Klein who had opened a small chapel on East 4th Street. The original gallery is still on three sides. Note the original Bavarian stained glass and fourteen oil paintings of the Stations of the Cross by L. Chovet of Paris and the unusual carved wood reredos, designed by Keely to reflect the early Gothic spirit. Look up to the music loft to see organ pipes encased in carved wood topped by Gothic spires and angels. A nearby street is named for the jazz innovator Charlie Parker, who lived at 151 Avenue B and is remembered every August in Tompkins Square Park with a spirited jazz festival. The present Hispanic congregation hopes to continue the Brigidines mission of the founders: to live in harmony and glorify God.

119 Avenue B (at East 8th St. facing the park) 212-228-5400

SLOCUM MEMORIAL FOUNTAIN: 1906. This sculpture by Bruno L. Zimm commemorates the worst maritime disaster in American history. "They were earth's purest children loving and fair" is inscribed on the stone facade. More than a thousand lives were lost on June 15, 1904, when the ferryboat *General Slocum*, named after the Civil War's Major General Henry Wagner Slocum, capsized in the East River. Most of the victims were neighborhood women and children from St. Mark's Lutheran Church (see Community Synagogue) who were sailing to a picnic on Long Island Sound. The Reverend George Hass, pastor of St. Mark's, lost his entire family. Nearly every resident in the German immigrant enclave between 14th and Houston Streets was affected by tragedy. A memorial service is held annually at Trinity Lutheran Church in Middle Village, Queens.

Tompkins Square Park, East 10th Street (between Avenues A & B) Public Space

ST. NICHOLAS OF MYRA CARPATHO-RUSSIAN ORTHO-DOX CHURCH: 1871. James Renwick, Jr., and William H. Russell designed this church for St. Mark's Mission Chapel near St. Mark's-in-the-Bowery (see entry) to "church the unchurched" immigrants who were flooding the area. The red-brick Gothic Revival complex, which was financed by the Rutherford Stuyvesant family, is asymmetrically placed on its corner site. It includes a rectory with a Sunday school and an individual bell tower. Original decorative plaques, spires, finials, and stained glass remain intact. High on the facade a red terra-cotta bas-relief holds the symbol of St. Mark, a lion with long, curly mane, standing above the original chapel name. St. Nicholas was founded by immigrants from Czechoslovakia who rented space in 1925 and purchased the site in 1937. The intimate cruciform interior holds three hundred worshipers. Five crystal chandeliers add glorious light to the renovated sanctuary with iconostatis (altar screen), which was dedicated in April 2000. The white marble baldachin in the chancel is engraved with a phrase that translates "Our Father." Be sure to look up to the mural-faced choir loft, shaped like a triptych with Gothic arch openings. The patron, Nicholas, was bishop of Myra (now called Dembre, in Turkey) and is one of the most popular saints in Eastern and Western Christianity. He is fondly remembered as Santa Claus and the patron saint of children.

288 East 10th Street (at Avenue A) 212-254-6685

ST. STANISLAUS ROMAN CATHOLIC CHURCH: 1900.
This Neo-Gothic structure is filled with old world charm for a Polish Roman Catholic congregation that was established in 1872 on Henry Street. Its patron was a bishop of Cracow who spoke out against the king's adultery and was murdered in 1079. A mural above the main altar tells the saga. Don't miss the single stained-glass window of the Black Madonna tucked into the mural. The exterior bronze bust of Pope John Paul II by the sculptor Andrzej Pitynski commemorates the Pope's visit to the church when he was Karol Cardinal Wojtyla of Cracow. Every September a service is held to remember the 1939 assault on Poland by Adolf Hitler that triggered World War II. Liturgies are conducted in Polish and English, because the area is still a strong Polish American neighborhood with great restaurants.

101 East 7th Street (between First Ave. & Avenue A) 212-475-4576

COMMUNITY SYNAGOGUE/ MAX D. RAISKIN CENTER:
1848. This Greek Revival brick temple was built as St. Matthew's

Lutheran Church and purchased by a German congregation in 1857 for St. Mark's Lutheran Church because of an overcrowded sanctuary on Lower Broadway. But the congregation never fully recovered from the Slocum disaster (see Slocum Memorial Fountain) and voted to merge with Zion Lutheran Church (see Zion-St. Mark's Lutheran Church). In 1940 the present Orthodox Jewish congregation, established by local businessmen, moved into the space, adding symbolic roundels to old stained-glass windows and opening a chapel on the lower level. The main sanctuary floor plan with oak pews and a decorative arch that surrounds the Ark were left, but a metal railing was installed to separate the sanctuary, since women and men do not sit together when worshiping. A richly embroidered red-velvet curtain draws all eyes to the Ark, the focus of the sanctuary. The center honors Rabbi Max D. Raiskin, who was the guiding spirit of the East Side Hebrew Institute on Tompkins Square Park, which educated thousands of Lower East Side immigrant children.

325 East 6th Street (between First & Second Aves.) 212-473-3665

MIDDLE COLLEGIATE CHURCH: 1892. Neo-Romanesque granite church by S. B. Reed is a descendant of the first Collegiate Reformed Church from 1628, whose members were the original Dutch settlers in New Amsterdam (see Marble Collegiate Church). Before moving to present site, the Middle Collegiate group worshiped in a Nassau Street church from 1729, and at Lafayette Place and Fourth Street from 1839. A historic bell made in Amsterdam and used by the congregation since 1731 hangs in the corner tower and is known to have rung when the Declaration of Independence was signed. Twelve Tiffany stained-glass windows are the highlight of the intimate interior, which holds an austere white marble altar and interesting memorials. The congregation is filled with visual and performing artists who have made the church a vital community center.

112 Second Avenue (between 6th & 7th Sts.) 212-477-0666

ST. GEORGE'S UKRAINIAN CATHOLIC CHURCH: 1977. This Byzantine Rite traditional design by Apollinaire Osadca replaced a smaller building. An interior dome, rich mosaics, and stained-glass windows are special delights. The congregation, founded in 1905, moved from East 20th Street down to the area known as Little Ukraine. Nearby Taras Shevchenko Place (connecting 6th & 7th Streets) is named for the artist (1814-1861) whose writings called for an independent Ukrainian state at a time when local culture was being crushed by Russia. A three-day outdoor festival is held every May to celebrate the congregation's heritage.

30 East 7th Street (between 2nd and 3rd Aves.) 212-674-1615

Byzantine exterior of St. George's

EDGAR M. BRONFMAN CENTER FOR JEWISH STUDENT LIFE AT NYU: 1887. A Jewish student center, built by Van Campen Taylor as a private town house for the artist Lockwood de Forest, who attempted to revive the art of wood carving. Unique teak carvings adorn the facade as well as the face of the apartment house next door (by Renwick, Aspinwall & Russell). In 1997 New York University completed interior renovations and named the center for its donor, former chairman of Seagram's Corporation. Sabbath services are held for the Egalitarian, Conservative, and Orthodox.

7 East 10th Street (between Fifth Ave. & University Pl.) 212-998-4114

CONSERVATIVE SYNAGOGUE OF FIFTH AVENUE: Tucked between towering apartment buildings, this synagogue is a reminder of old Greenwich Village. A high wrought-iron fence protects the garden and the path that leads into a small white stucco building. The congregation was founded in 1959 in a former two-story private home. An intimate sanctuary, with two bronze menorahs flanking the Ark, holds seventy worshipers. When weather permits, services and social gatherings are held in the garden.

11 East 11th St. (between Fifth Ave. & University Pl.) 212-929-6954

THE VILLAGE TEMPLE: (Congregation B'Nai Israel): A Jewish Reform group founded in 1948 moved into this renovated metal shop in 1957. One founder, Morton Minsky, was the producer of Minsky's

Burlesque. A single window of golden stained glass forms a modern Star of David that is best seen when illuminated in the evening.

33 East 12th Street (between Broadway & University Pl.) 212-674-2340

IMMACULATE CONCEPTION CHURCH: 1894. Built as Grace Chapel and Hospital (which is the present-day rectory) for the Grace Episcopal Church by Barney & Chapman in the late French Gothic style designated Francis I, this beige-brick and terra-cotta complex ministered to a growing population of European immigrants in the Gas House District. Two huge gas tanks were located east of this **landmark** church in the area that is now Con Edison territory. A Roman Catholic group, founded in 1855, moved to the church in 1943, when their building was razed to build Stuyvesant Town. A beautiful collection of stained-glass windows remain from the Episcopal congregation. Most are by Henry Holiday, who created all the windows for the Church of the Holy Trinity (see entry). Look for Ezekiel, a major Old Testament prophet, who holds an impressive ivory yad (torah pointer shaped like a hand). The ornate tower holds the original ten bells, which still peal. Be sure to see the exterior water fountain, topped with the ecumenical inscription "Ho, everyone that thirsteth."

414 East 14th Street (between First Ave. & Avenue A) 212-254-0200

EAST SIDE
OF MANHATTAN

❖ ❖ ❖ ❖

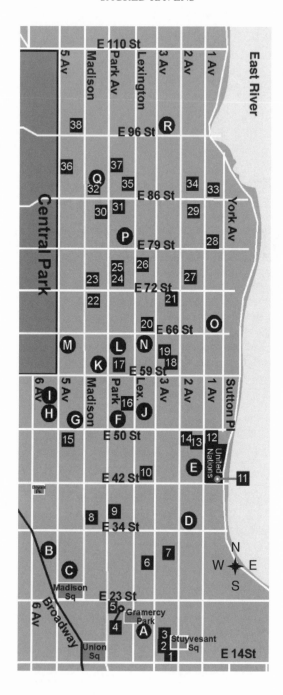

EAST SIDE OF MANHATTAN

Fifth Avenue divides the east and west sides while Central Park borders the Avenue from 59th to 110th Street. NYC's bus system runs north on First, Third and Madison Avenues; and south on Fifth, Lexington and Second Avenues. Major crosstown streets have bus stops going west. An unlimited metro card by the day, week or month lets you take as many trips as you like.

FEATURES:

A. *The Brotherhood Synagogue*
B. *Marble Collegiate Church*
C. *The Church of the Transfiguration*
D. *St. Vartan Armenian Cathedral*
E. *Tillman Chapel*
F. *St. Bartholomew's Church*
G. *The Lady Chapel of St. Patrick's Cathedral*
H. *St. Thomas Church*
I. *Fifth Avenue Presbyterian Church*
J. *Erol Becker Chapel of The Good Shepherd at St. Peter's Church*
K. *Christ Church*
L. *Central Presbyterian Church*
M. *Temple Emanu-El*
N. *Church of St. Vincent Ferrer*
O. *St. John Nepomucene*
P. *The Unitarian Church of All Souls*
Q. *Church of St. Thomas More*
R. *The Islamic Cultural Center*

BY THE WAY:

1. St. Mary's Byzantine
2. Friends Meeting House
3. Saint George's Episcopal Church
4. Calvary Episcopal Church
5. Lutheran Church of Gustavus Adolphus
6. Saint Stephen
7. Church of the Good Shepherd
8. Church of the Incarnation
9. Church of Our Saviour
10. Church of St. Agnes
11. UN Meditation Room
12. UN Gardens
13. Raoul Wallenberg Memorial
14. Church of the Holy Family
15. Church of Sweden
16. Central Synagogue
17. L'Eglise Francaise du Saint Esprit
18. Trinity Baptist Church
19. Our Lady of Peace Church
20. Park East Synagogue
21. St. John the Martyr
22. St James' Church
23. Madison Ave. Presbyterian Church
24. Church of The Resurrection
25. Temple Israel
26. St Jean Baptiste Church
27. Holy Trinity Cathedral
28. St. Monica's Church
29. Zion-St. Mark Lutheran Church
30. St. Ignatius Loyola Church
31. Park Ave. United Methodist Church
32. Park Ave. Synagogue
33. St. Joseph's Church of Yorkville
34. Church of the Holy Trinity
35. Immanuel Lutheran Church
36. Church of the Heavenly Rest
37. Brick Presbyterian Church
38. St. Nicholas Cathedral

THE BROTHERHOOD SYNAGOGUE

MEETING MODERN SOCIETY IN A HISTORIC SETTING

This Conservative synagogue building shares a patina of history with its setting, Gramercy Park. The landmark sits on the southeast corner of this privately owned park, not far from the site where President Theodore Roosevelt was born and grew up, and a few doors west of two private clubs that have been havens of artists and writers for over a century. The Players Club was established in 1885 by the Shakespearan actor Edwin Booth. Sculptured images of Shakespeare, Dante, Goethe, Milton, and Michelangelo appear on the facade of the National Arts Club. Perhaps these portraits will be a reminder of the congregation's message that brotherhood is the hope of the world.

HISTORY

Congregation Beth Achim (House of Brothers), traces its roots to May 14, 1954 when thirty-one people attended services in the Village Presbyterian Church on West 13th Street. Rabbi Irving Block launched the congregation on the basis of a program of social service that would meet the day's needs and avoid uncompromising extremes of Jewish belief. He established an open-door policy for all who wished to participate in Judaism. Several months after the inaugural service, Rabbi Block started a religious instruction school with six children.

The synagogue grew rapidly in the shared facility until the death of Block's good friend, the Presbyterian minister Reverend Dr. Jesse Stitt, and in 1973 a search was launched for another space. The Society of Friends, a Quaker group, owned the present property but had moved in 1958 to join a nearby meetinghouse in Stuyvesant Square. During the Civil War the Gramercy Park house had been a station on the Underground Railroad, which sheltered escaped slaves from the South

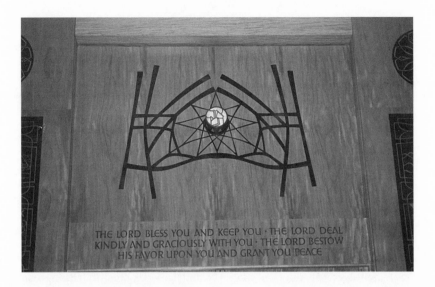

THE LORD BLESS YOU AND KEEP YOU · THE LORD DEAL
KINDLY AND GRACIOUSLY WITH YOU · THE LORD BESTOW
HIS FAVOR UPON YOU AND GRANT YOU PEACE

and assured them safe passage to freedom in North. Time had taken a heavy toll on the building, but the location made the property extremely valuable, and developers, with wrecking balls in hand, were eyeing the site. The neighborhood fought valiantly to save the meetinghouse.

In 1975 the Brotherhood Synagogue purchased the site and joined the community in the campaign for its preservation. Rabbi Block and his congregation drafted a sensitive plan for restoration, and developed the interior space to suit the religious and educational needs of their members.

ARCHITECTURE

The New York architects Gamaliel King and John W. Kellum designed the Italianate-style Quaker meetinghouse in 1859. The austere three-story building has round-arch windows that dominate the facade. Look closely at the windowpanes for a wavering pattern, a sign that the original glass has survived. The exterior sandstone walls are smoothly plastered, and on the right-hand wall the congregation has placed a stylized menorah relief. A triangular pediment crowns the rooftop. James Stewart Polshek, the architect responsible for the restoration work, added to the left side of the building the Garden of Remembrance, a memorial to Holocaust victims.

The classically elegant interior has pastel blue walls, ivory trim, and walnut railings. Be sure to see the red-velvet curtain in the sanctuary's foyer. It dates back to the synagogue's first Ark and is embroidered with golden letters: "Behold how good and how pleasant it is for brethren to dwell together." The sanctuary, encircled by a traditional ivory-colored gallery, is filled with plain wooden pews of deep walnut. The benches date from 1840 and were used in the Friends Meeting House on Orchard Street on Manhattan's Lower East Side.

Spend some time studying the Holy Ark, made from rare honey-colored imbuya and primavera woods. It is by the designer Ismar David. The Ark doors are inscribed with a shortened form of the Ten Commandments, a symbol for the contents of the Torah. Flanking the doors are two panels that depict the symbols of the twelve tribes of Israel, the descendants of the twelve sons of Jacob. Read Isaiah's words inscribed over the doors of the Ark and feel the comfort this serene oasis embodies: "The Lord bless you and keep you. The Lord deal kindly and graciously with you. The Lord bestow His favor upon you and grant you peace."

ADDRESS: *28 Gramercy Park South (on 20th St. between Park & Third Aves.) New York, N.Y. 10003*
PHONE: *212-674-5750*
HOURS: *Admittance through the office during office hours*
LANDMARK DESIGNATION

MARBLE COLLEGIATE CHURCH

AND THE POLING CHAPEL
DUTCH COLONY'S HAVEN AND HERO'S MEMORIAL

This is the home of Norman Vincent Peale (1898–1993), charismatic preacher of "the power of positive thinking," whose sermons were broadcast for more than fifty years. Dr. Peale was a pioneer in merging religion and psychology. Marble Collegiate, whose origins are firmly rooted in the Reformed Church of Holland, is the oldest Protestant church in America. It is governed by elders and deacons; the creed, which relies on the Scriptures, is Calvinist. The main sanctuary is open to visitors, but you will need to check in at the 29th Street desk for an escort. **The Poling Chapel**, however, is available to the public every day.

HISTORY

Marble Collegiate is one of four collegiate churches left in Manhattan whose history is traced to the arrival of New Amsterdam's first minister from the Church of Holland, the Reverend Jonas Michaelius. In 1628 Mr. Michaelius, sponsored by the Dutch West India Company, financier of expeditions to the New World, arrived to conduct services in a grain mill on what is now William Street in Lower Manhattan. Peter Minuit, who was serving as third director-general of New Netherland, was the first elder of church. History remembers Minuit as the resourceful Dutchman who bought this island from the Manhatoe Indians for legendary trinkets valued at twenty-four dollars.

In 1647 the colony's sixth and last Dutch director-general, Peter Stuyvesant, took command (see St. Mark's-in-the-Bowery), decreeing that everyone must observe the Sabbath at St. Nicholas Church, the first sanctuary built in 1642 within the fort of New Amsterdam. When the population increased, two ministers from Holland tended church members, and so began the first collegiate or colleague system of a shared ministry in the New World. While the system is no longer used, the word *collegiate* remains as part of the church name.

Dutch governance of the island ended in 1664, when Stuyvesant surrendered to British forces. King William III of England, who was of Dutch ancestry, granted a full charter to the Dutch Reformed Church in 1696, firmly establishing its right in the British colony of New York. A plaque mounted on the facade commemorates this milestone in the history of religious freedom. The church may have won its independence, but as the colony fought for its freedom, British officials seized all Dutch churches and destroyed them. When independence was won, the hardy Dutch rebuilt on their large land holdings and played a vital role in the new nation. As the city moved northward, so did the collegiate congregation. In 1854 a group moved to the present site, designated the Fifth Avenue Collegiate Church, a name to indicate its location on a dusty country road. In 1906 the designation changed to Marble Collegiate.

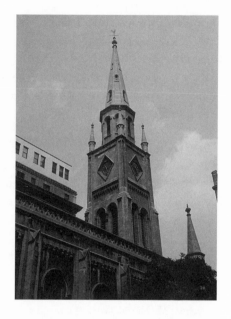

The Poling Chapel was opened in 1965. It is named in memory of the Reverend Clark Poling, one of four military chaplains who with hundreds of American servicemen perished in February 1943, when a German U-boat sank the U.S. troopship *Dorchester* in the North Atlantic. Dr. Daniel Poling, Clark's father, had served as pastor of Marble Collegiate.

ARCHITECTURE

Samuel A. Warner designed this Romanesque Revival building in 1854 using white marble blocks — hence its name. He topped the central tower with a belfry, a clock, and an octagonal spire. The congregation added their old six and one-half foot gilded weathercock — a feature of Dutch churches used as a reminder of the Apostle Peter's denial of Jesus.

The interior, which seats over a thousand, was the first to be designed with free-hanging balconies and no columns. Gold-stenciled fleurs-de-lis (lilies) subtly cover taupe walls in the sanctuary, which has two Tiffany windows, of King David and Moses.

The 29th Street lobby leading into Poling Chapel and the New York Theological Seminary is enhanced by a mosaic entitled *The Lily Among the Thorns*. This flower had been adopted by the sixteenth-century Reformed Church in Holland as a symbol of its struggle for religious freedom. Dutch settlers brought the motif to the New World. In the small chapel, imposing windows made in Chartres, France, by Gabriel Loire fill the southern wall. They tell of the Creation, the Flood, the Nativity, and the Ascension. A serene portrait of Dr. Poling hangs directly opposite these windows.

When you leave the building, don't forget to look inside the cast-iron fence for the lifelike bronze sculpture of the eternal optimist, Dr. Peale, dedicated on his one-hundredth birthday in 1998. The spirit of this eloquent preacher has been skillfully captured by John Soderberg. Incidentally, the fence surrounding the church is very old; it was put up to keep out stray cattle on Marble's dirt road, which became fashionable Fifth Avenue.

ADDRESS: *1 West 29th Street (at Fifth Ave.) Enter through 29th Street
New York, NY 10001*
PHONE: *212-686-2770*
HOURS: *Daily: 10:00 A.M.–5:00 P.M. Sun.: 10:00 A.M.
Prayer Circle in Poling Chapel; 11:15 A.M. Service in Main Sanctuary*
WEB SITE: *www.marblechurch.org*
RADIO BROADCAST: *WOR (710) Cable TV: Odyssey Channel in Manhattan*
LANDMARK DESIGNATION

CHURCH OF
THE TRANSFIGURATION

THE LITTLE CHURCH AROUND THE CORNER
ROMANTIC HOME OF ACTORS, WRITERS, BRIDES,
AND BRIDEGROOMS

For countless numbers of Broadway's guys and dolls, the Episcopal Church of the Transfiguration has served as opening night for married life. Stand at the altar of the Chapel of the Holy Family, usually referred to as the Bridal Chapel, and it is easy to imagine

Damon Runyon's anxious Miss Adelaide finally getting the reluctant Nathan Detroit to say "I do." During World War II as many as 2,900 weddings a year took place here.

HISTORY

There was a time in the United States when actors were treated as second-class citizens, good enough for entertainment but not good enough to be members of a church. They were barred from the sacrament of marriage, even burial. All that changed in December 1870, when Joseph Jefferson, a comic actor, went to a church on Madison Avenue to arrange a funeral for his actor friend George Holland. "No funeral in this church for an actor!" proclaimed the rector. Asked to name a church that would bury Mr. Holland, the rector sniffed, "I believe there's a little church around the corner that does that sort of thing." Jefferson's wish was granted by the Reverend George Hendric Houghton (1820–1897), rector and founder of the Church of the Transfiguration, and the name the Little Church Around the Corner became a permanent symbol of tolerance, love, and understanding.

A stained-glass window commemorating this event is in the south aisle of the nave. On the left, Joseph Jefferson, as Rip Van Winkle, a role he played on the stage for forty years, escorts the shroud-wrapped body of George Holland to the church. Written across the panels is Jefferson's acclamation, "God bless the Little Church Around the Corner." Note that the story of Rip Van Winkle by local author Washington Irving is shown above and below the main panels. The English window was made by the White Friar Studios and includes an icon of a white-robed monk at the bottom.

In 1849 Dr. Houghton, who served as pastor for forty-nine years, opened his one-story church on the present site with twenty-four people. His vision was to minister to poor immigrants, for he believed that faith must always be accompanied by charitable works. Dr. Houghton established Sunday school for black children and sheltered escaped slaves arriving on the Underground Railroad in the 1860s. One black couple, George and Elizabeth Wilson, who helped Dr. Houghton during that time, are immortalized in stained glass in the south transept as "sometime doorkeepers in this House of the Lord."

GOD BLESS ONE LIGGLE CHURCH   AROUND ONE CORNER

ARCHITECTURE

This romantic church, with a mansard slate roof, is Gothic Revival in the style of the early fourteenth century. The architectural team included many artisans who anonymously contributed to the rambling but charming appearance of these brick-and-brownstone buildings. When space was needed, sections were added without any master plan. The first structure, a five-story red-brick rectory built in 1854, is to the far left and carries the painted crest "Fides Opera" (Faith and Works) atop its portal. The Chapel of the Holy Family was part of the original 1849 building and stands next to the rectory; its second story, added in 1852, holds the gabled windows of the Episcopal Actors' Guild, a group established in 1923 to exchange tips of the trade.

The main bell tower, added in 1854, is the third structure. Visitors enter through the tower's wooden doors, which lead to the main sanctuary and chapels. Next in line is an octagonal tower, built in 1906, which holds the Chapel of St. Joseph of Arimathea. It is topped with an eight-sided gray slate roof and crowned with a Gothic cross. Completing the church's exterior is the southern transept, built in 1854 and extended in the 1860s. It holds the shrine "Madonna and Child," designed in 1920 by Ralph Adams Cram, prolific architect of the Gothic Revival (see St. James' on Madison Avenue).

An original black wrought-iron fence separates the serene garden from the street and directs visitors to a unique stone entryway, a lych-gate topped with a shell-shaped copper roof and weather vane (in England, this is the spot where pallbearers wait with a coffin — *lych* meaning "body"). The rector intended this square-shaped lych-gate to be a resting spot for travelers. It was built in 1896 by Frederick Clarke Withers and donated by Mrs. Franklin Delano, the former Laura Astor, who was a grandaunt of President Franklin Delano Roosevelt. In 1920 the lych-gate, along with church, was immortalized on Broadway as a stage set in the grand finale of Florenz Ziegfeld's musical comedy hit *Sally*.

As you walk up the garden path and enter the main sanctuary, be sure to study the high altar with its polychrome reredos designed and rebuilt by Withers in 1880. Standing on either side of the decorative chancel is the unique brass pulpit by Richard Upjohn and an eagle-topped brass lectern. The Bible gracing the lectern was a gift from Edwin Booth (1833-1893), America's first great actor, who as a parish member was buried from church.

Throughout the cozy sanctuary stained-glass windows, largely the work of John La Farge, are remarkable. They depict saintly subjects as well as memorable events in the history of the Little Church. Don't miss the copy of Raffaello's Transfiguration Window from St. Peter's Basilica in Rome. This painted window is in the St. Joseph of Arimathea Chapel, which is enhanced with intricate grillwork at its entrance.

On the west wall of the transept, Edwin Booth, in his world-famous role as Hamlet, appears in a memorial window donated in 1898 by the Players Club, which Booth founded. A commemorative window to Joseph Drexel (1831–1888) glorifies the importance of music with King David playing the harp. Look for the bronze plaque created by Paul Manship in honor of Otis Skinner, one of Broadway's most famous actors. Manship, incidentally, was sculptor of the golden Prometheus in Rockefeller Center's lower plaza. All these tributes and many others make sure that artisans will always be cared for in this haven of faith and good works.

ADDRESS: 1 *East 29th Street (between Fifth & Madison Aves.)*
New York, NY 10016
PHONE: *212-684-6770*
HOURS: *Mon.–Fri.: 8:00 A.M.–6:00 P.M. Sat.: 9:00 A.M.–6:00 P.M.*
Sun.: 8:00 A.M.–6:00 P.M. A guided tour is led each Sunday after the
11:00 A.M. service.
WEB SITE: *www.littlechurch.org*
LANDMARK DESIGNATION

ST. VARTAN ARMENIAN CATHEDRAL

FIRST ARMENIAN CATHEDRAL IN THE NEW WORLD

War, conquest, religious persecution, and incredible suffering make up the history of Armenia — a land of Christians in Asia Minor. Today, halfway around the world from their homeland, Armenian immigrants and their children worship in the splendor of their own cathedral, a gleaming monument to their determination. Armenia became the first country in the world to recognize Christianity as its national religion. While the Armenian Church has no connection with either the Roman Catholic Church or the Eastern Orthodox Church, its rites, sacraments, and beliefs are similar. Liturgy is celebrated here in a medieval poetic dialect of the Armenian language called k'rapar (KUH-rah-parr). The Catholicos, the spiritual leader of the faithful, sits in the Armenian city of Etchmiadzin.

HISTORY

Thousands of Armenians streamed into the United States in the late nineteenth century to escape the brutalities of the Ottoman Empire. Flight to America peaked in 1915, when Turkish Moslems launched a campaign of genocide that killed, by Armenian estimates, 1.5 million Armenian Christians. Many victims died of starvation when Turkish troops evicted them from their homes and banished them to the barren countryside. To this day, the Turkish government denies responsibility. Armenians living in the Middle East came to America in the 1950s to escape political unrest. Another wave of immigration came after an earthquake in 1988 and the fall of Soviet communism.

The Cathedral Project began to take shape in April 1949, when four plots of land were purchased. The site was chosen because a universal symbol of peace and tolerance — the United Nations — stands close by. The cornerstone was dedicated in 1966 and St. Vartan's Cathedral consecrated in April 1968. It is named for Vartan Mamigonian, a fifth-century Armenian prince who opposed Persian forces threatening to supplant Christianity with the cult of Zoroastrianism (in which there is no deity; the source of truth is symbolized by the light of the sun or fire in a universal struggle over darkness).

The building complex serves as the seat of the Armenian Church of North America, which established its first church in 1891 in Worcester, Massachusetts.

ARCHITECTURE

Walker Cain, an American architect, modeled the 12,000-square-foot church on a seventh-century sanctuary near the Armenian city of Yerevan. He captured the majestic simplicity of an ancient house of worship, including two features shared by many Armenian churches — a dome and double-intersecting arches that create a wide-open sanctuary. The beige exterior of smooth Kentucky limestone reflects its

ancient prototype and rises 140 feet. A gilded dome tops off the structure. In a stunning departure from the old, St. Vartan's is placed on a platform 5 feet above street level and features a spacious plaza. Over the entrance is a bas-relief of the patron receiving a blessing from Catholicos Hovsep.

Before going inside, stop by the north wall to see a provocative 14-foot sculpture, *Christ*, by the American artisan Koren Der Harootian.

As you enter the sanctuary, reflections of golden chandeliers, each 14 feet in diameter, shine through the glass partition that encloses the narthex. A dramatic altar holding a Byzantine icon of Mary with the Infant Jesus is crowned with a conical-shaped canopy supported by four columns of red marble. A marble roundel in the center of the nave floor is inscribed with these words of the Apostle Matthew: "Ye are the salt of the earth, but if the salt hath lost His savor, wherewith shall it be salted?" A challenge to all who read it.

Take time to study the symbols and stained-glass windows around the dome depicting the Creation. The Armenian letter in the center translates, "He is."

Throughout the church the New Jersey artisan Bogdan Grom has created a visual history of the Armenian people. He designed all the artistic fixtures in the sanctuary, including the stained-glass windows and bas-relief work, to recall Armenia's past. Particularly touching are two stained-glass windows placed opposite the main altar. The first, dedicated to the victims of the 1915 holocaust, shows Ezekiel commanding skeletons scattered around him to return to life. The revitalized people are shown greeted by an angel. The other window portrays the patron Vartan in his martyrdom and includes the invention of the thirty-six-letter Armenian alphabet in A.D. 404 by St. Mesrob, specifically to translate the Bible. At its pinnacle images of anonymous craftsmen celebrate the construction of the cathedral.

Look also in stained glass for the Apostles Thaddeus and Bartholomew, who introduced Christianity in Armenia, and for Noah's Ark, which, according, to the Book of Genesis, landed with its cargo of animals on Mount Ararat, the highest point in Armenia.

Be sure to the visit two side altars as well. One commemorates St. Gregory the Illuminator, who converted King Tiridates III in A.D. 301 and evangelized the country. The other honors St. Nersess, an eleventh-century Catholicos who drew together a divided church with the motto "Unity in important issues; Freedom in secondary issues; Love among all."

ADDRESS: *630 Second Avenue (between 34th & 35th Sts.)*
    New York, NY 10016
HOURS: *212-686-0710*
HOURS: *Mon.-Fri.: 9:00 A.M.–5:00 P.M. Sun.: 10:00 A.M.–1:00 P.M.*
    Closed Sat.
Enter through Diocesan Center if door is locked
WEB SITE: *www.armenianchurch.org*

TILLMAN CHAPEL

AT THE CHURCH CENTER FOR THE UNITED NATIONS
INTERDENOMINATIONAL FOCUS ON PEACE AND MATRIMONY

If the United Nations is the most visible symbol of humankind's quest for world peace, then the Tillman Chapel is a glorious symbol of unity, mutual respect, and love embodied in the sacred rite of marriage. This chapel has been the scene of thousands of weddings, with sacred vows recited by couples of differing faiths. An illustration of its interdenominational focus is seen on the chapel's walls in cream-colored banners emblazoned with symbols of the world's major religions: Christianity, Judaism, Shinto, Hinduism, Buddhism, and Islam. The inclusive atmosphere is further underscored by a white sculptured exterior window covering the lower facade. The window is a dazzling mural that sheds new light on the human struggle to achieve peace.

HISTORY

In 1952 the United Nations moved to its present site bordering the East River. Many related buildings sprang up on First Avenue, now known as United Nations Plaza, to complement the mission and the modern architecture of the UN. The Church Center, dedicated in

1962, was conceived as an office building with a religious function. It is the national headquarters of several denominations and has a street floor designed to hold an ecumenical chapel. The Tillman Chapel was donated in 1963 by the Women's Division of the Board of Missions of the Methodist Church in honor of Mrs. J. Fount Tillman, a past president.

Since the chapel is small, all ceremonies are intimate. Weddings are customized for each couple, and pictures can be taken in the United Nations Gardens (see entry) across First Avenue. Many celebrities shunning publicity have made their vows here, since no media coverage is allowed.

ARCHITECTURE

William Lescaze, a pioneer of modern architecture, designed the white sandstone Church Center and, with Harold Wagoner, the interior of the chapel, which holds 160 people. Integrated into Lescaze's plan is a wall of glass that, as a major innovation in the art of stained glass, was conceived by the Willet Studios of Philadelphia, and engineered by a team of artisans led by William Stewart. On the exterior a bold sculptured effect is accomplished by using metal and epoxy for a contemporary design by the Belgian artisan and sculptor Benoit Gilsoul (1914–2000). In the interior faceted chunks of glass combine with the strong exterior silhouette to produce a pure jewel-like effect. Wooden pews parallel the window and continue around the sides of the chapel. A raised pedestal, enclosed with a carved wooden rail, sits in the center for the officiating minister.

On the north side, a white marble baptismal font is accompanied by two red-cushioned marble seats. The southern wall holds an electronic organ, and dominating the east wall is the majestic stained-glass window.

Henry Lee Willet, whose studio manufactured this work of art, captured its purpose: "In the universal language of art, I wanted to challenge mankind to seek the truth, to seek peace and preserve it, using traditional symbols transposed to contemporary forms. I assumed only two premises—one, that man almost universally believes in a supreme being, and two, that the only salvation of mankind is in finding the truth that makes man free."

Truth is symbolized by a crystal in the center of the window. Two seekers of truth are shown as groping shapes who pass under the wings of the dove of peace. They change into human-shaped forms joined in love for God and their neighbors. An all-seeing eye, in the form of an ellipse, extends over the entire window. It is the symbol of God. Part of the window on the left is in darkness—a symbol of humankind sinking into the depths, destroying itself in a futile attempt to surpass God's power.

But bright white light symbolizes the human soul. Light rises from a human form for God to use as He wishes, as a symbol of the belief that the soul can never be destroyed. Through sacrificial love, humankind comes into the light, borne on the wings of the spirit to achieve brotherhood and peace.

ADDRESS: 777 United Nations Plaza (44th St. & First Ave.)
   New York, NY 10017
PHONE: 212-661-1762
HOURS: Mon.-Fri.: 9:00 A.M.–6:00 P.M. Sat .& Sun.: 9:00 A.M.–4:00 P.M.
   Enter through office building on 44th Street if door is locked

ST. BARTHOLOMEW'S CHURCH

KNOWN BY ITS DOME

St. Bart's, as it is affectionately known, sits like an island in a sea of gleaming corporate headquarters and high-rise apartment houses on Park Avenue. The church's colorful exterior of pink-colored brick, gray limestone, various shades of marble, and ceramic tiles highlights its juxtaposition among skyscrapers of glass and steel. The majestic dome that crowns this Episcopal church can be easily spotted, despite the city's many distractions.

HISTORY

The congregation of St. Bart's held its inaugural service in 1835, downtown at 193 Bowery Road at a time when the population of New York City was about 250,000. This affluent group was thought to have been founded as a negative response to the Oxford Movement that was stirring up the Anglican Church (see Church of St. Mary the Virgin). A sinking foundation at St. Bart's second home (1872 to 1918 on Madison Avenue at 44th Street) forced the congregation to move uptown to its present location, which was welcomed as an escape from a busy commercial area to a more residential part of town.

On October 20, 1918, this far-from-finished St. Bart's was opened. In 1930 the congregation would finally celebrate its completion when the marble facings on the walls, gold-leafed mosaics and a mammoth pipe organ had added the finishing touches to the interior. More important, the Byzantine dome that crowns the shallow transept crossing was also completed.

St. Bart's remains an architectural jewel among the city's landmark churches, just as it was planned by the original congregation. But the church is not without controversy. Remember the air rights question? St. Bart's and its Community House were declared landmarks in 1989 — a designation that meant the exterior of the buildings could not be

altered without approval from the city's Landmarks Preservation Commission. When the church vestry found itself in a budget crunch, it proposed selling air rights over the Community House, paving the way for yet another midtown skyscraper. Proponents had not reckoned with the likes of the architecture critic Brendan Gill and former First Lady Jacqueline Kennedy Onassis, who opposed such a scheme. After long and heated debates the case wound up in the U. S. Supreme Court, which ruled that the city's Landmark Law was constitutional as it pertains to churches and that St. Bart's must stand as is.

To pave the way into the twenty-first century and answer the challenge for religious education, the church opened its Center for Religious Inquiry, offering a multitude of seminars on Bible history, the world's major religions, and even Gregorian chant.

ARCHITECTURE

Bertram Goodhue (1869–1924), the recognized master builder of ecclesiastical works, used the Romanesque and Byzantine feeling of early Christian churches when he designed St. Bart's, but he died before his work was finished. His associates at Mayers, Murray & Phillip completed the master's plan.

The building's style of architecture harmonizes with the Romanesque portal from the previous church. Designed by Stanford White and donated by Mrs. Cornelius Vanderbilt, the portal was modeled on the Church of St. Gilles-du-Gard at Arles, France. Limestone arches and marble columns frame three sets of bronze doors filled with Old and New Testament illustrations. The majestic center portal features Christ in Glory on a tympanum by Daniel Chester French and Andrew O'Connor.

The recycled portal, which projects from the church entrance, leads into the narthex, a vestibule 73 feet long and 15 feet wide.

Marble pillars support the five-domed mosaic ceiling, filled with the story of the Creation. Like all mosaic work in the church, this dazzling ceiling is the work of the artist Hildreth Meiere.

The vastness of the cruciform nave is spectacular. It is filled with masterful architectural details: sculptured limestone panels above doorway lintels and arches; carved scenes from the life of Jesus on surrounding pillars; a quatrefoil pulpit of yellow Siena marble designed by Lee Lawrie; and clerestory windows filled with rich iconography by Hildreth Meiere.

What a surprise to discover that the baptistry's font is a life-size angel holding a shell. This Neoclassical white marble sculpture is by the Danish artisan Bertel Thorwaldsen. Read the inscriptions on the bronze gates and find the image of St. Patrick surrounded by his icons:

the hull of a boat, a Celtic cross, a staff, and his miter decorated with two shamrocks.

The apse glistens with spectacular gold-leaf mosaics portraying the Transfiguration, and is filled with small windows holding onyx screens and a black marble altar. The space also contains an Aeolian-Skinner pipe organ, the largest in New York City. St. Bart's popular series of concerts features many new works played by world-class musicians.

While regal beauty defines St. Bart's, stop by the charming memorial chapel for a more intimate spot to reflect. As you leave, don't forget the terrace café, a good place to nourish your body after you have renewed your spirit.

ADDRESS: *109 East 50th Street (and Park Ave.)*
    New York, NY 10022
PHONE: *212-378-0200 Center for Religious Inquiry: 212-378-0290*
HOURS: *Daily: 8:00 A.M.–6:00 P.M.*
WEB SITE: *www.stbarts.org*
LANDMARK DESIGNATION

THE LADY CHAPEL

OF ST. PATRICK'S CATHEDRAL
A HIDDEN JEWEL

The immensity of St. Patrick's Roman Catholic Cathedral overshadows one of its most beautiful jewels — the Lady Chapel, a quiet oasis that visitors may miss because it is hidden behind the towering high altar. Edward Cardinal Egan has been known to hold meetings in its intimate space.

HISTORY

St. Patrick's Cathedral, first proposed by Archbishop John Hughes in 1850, would not be opened for worship until 1879 (see St. Patrick's

Old Cathedral). Although the architect James Renwick, Jr., had included the Lady Chapel in his master plan of 1858, it would not be built because of financial constraints. The Civil War would also severely delay all construction. John Cardinal McCloskey officially opened St. Patrick's Cathedral with an area for the Lady Chapel sealed behind a wall. At the same time Thomas Edison was busy demonstrating his electric lightbulb.

In 1901 a gift from the family of Eugene Kelly and a new design by the architect Charles T. Mathews cleared the way for construction. William Renwick, nephew of James and partner in his firm, submitted a design that was rejected. The chapel was built in the space originally planned by Renwick, between the rectory and the archbishop's residence on Madison Avenue. Archbishop Michael Augustine Corrigan celebrated the first Mass in the Lady Chapel on Christmas Day 1906. Today the chapel is a favorite place for marriage proposals, and wedding ceremonies.

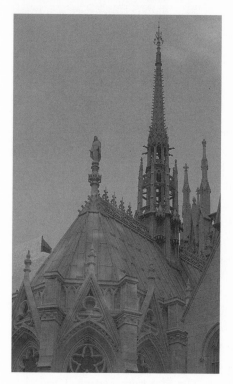

The Lady Chapel

ARCHITECTURE

The chapel is patterned on thirteenth-century French Gothic models. In churches of the Middle Ages, a chapel dedicated to Mary was always placed close to the sanctuary to hold the Blessed Sacrament, which is believed by Catholics to be the consecrated body of Christ. Given the enormity of the cathedral, the chapel is relatively small — 28 feet wide, 56 feet long, and rising 56 feet. The exterior is

Vermont marble and the interior stone. A bank of ivory candles at the entrance lights the way in.

The English artisan Paul Woodroffe added tranquillity to the shrine with royal blue figurative windows. The stained glass chronicles the life of Jesus in relation to his mother, Mary. Five windows surrounding altar illustrate the Glorious Mysteries of the Rosary: the Resurrection, the Ascension, the Descent of the Holy Spirit, the Assumption, and the Coronation of Mary. Look at the round medallions that top each window for easy identification. Also find the small image of Monsignor Michael J. Lavelle at his writing desk with quill in hand; he served as St. Patrick's rector for fifty-two years.

Monsignor Michael J. Lavelle

The focal point of the chapel, a 7foot statue of Mary, was designed by Oronzio Maldarelli and made by the Piccirilli Brothers, prolific local sculptors whose works include the lions outside the New York Public Library. The altar table holds a mosaic front panel with a tribute to the Annunciation showing Mary and the Archangel Gabriel surrounded by a vine of roses, symbols of love. Look down at the Siena marble floor laid out in a Gothic pattern and note the coat of arms of Pope Leo XIII near the entrance. This pontiff was the leader of the Roman Catholic Church when St. Patrick's opened.

In 1978 the final element of Mathews's design was completed with the installation of an 8-foot copper statue of Mary on the ridge of the roof overlooking Madison Avenue. The sculpture, designed and constructed by Anthony Minervini, bestows serenity on all who glance up from the hectic city pace.

James Renwick's original plan for the chapel is in the New York Public Library on 42nd Street. A glimpse of Renwick himself can be found in stained glass installed 1879 in the west wall of the cathedral's

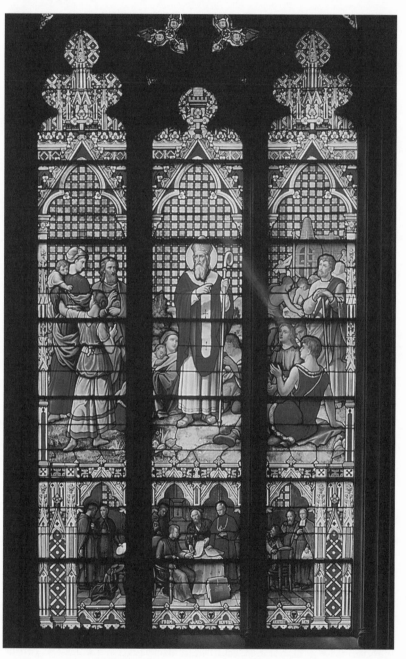

The Gift of James Renwick Jr. to St. Patrick's Cathedral

south transept. This window was his gift to the cathedral and is a fine visual representation of the building's history. In the upper section the patron Patrick, as archbishop of Ireland, appears with a crowd while a church is under construction in the distance. In the lower panels Renwick is seen submitting his plans to the seated Archbishop John Hughes while Hughes's successor, John Cardinal McCloskey, stands with the building plan in his hand. This plan represents alterations the cardinal made to Renwick's original design. Look for a blue portfolio labeled, "James Renwick, Esq., New York." Standing with the group are Nicholas Lorin of France, the window's designer, several priests and monks, an apprentice architect who folds a drawing, and the Reverend John M. Farley, who would succeed McCloskey and officially dedicate the cathedral in 1910.

ADDRESS: *460 Madison Avenue (Fifth Ave. & 50th St.)*
New York, NY 10022
PHONE: *212-753-2261*
HOURS: *Daily: 7:00 A.M.–7:00 P.M. (visit the gift shop for a history of the*
 cathedral)
WEB SITE: *www.stpatrickscathedral.com*
LANDMARK DESIGNATION

ST. THOMAS CHURCH

"BEAUTY . . . TO THE GLORY OF GOD"

While the beauty that fills this traditional Anglican Episcopal sanctuary is a testament to an inspirational clergy, a generous congregation, and a glorious choir, the architect Ralph Adams Cram said, "Beauty of whatever kind in any church is put there to the glory of God and not to the admiration of the passerby." But beauty is what pulls you into this haven. The 80-foot-high reredos, an elaborately sculptured stone wall at the far end of the sanctuary, glows like an amber-colored magnet through the opened doors of the sanctuary and entices travelers to experience quiet time with their spiritual selves.

St. Thomas Church moved to its present site in 1870, only to see its new home destroyed by fire in 1905. The congregation, founded in 1823, had worshiped in two other havens downtown on Broadway and Houston Street. A wooden chapel built on the site served as a temporary place of worship until October 4, 1913, when the church as it is today held its first service.

An important part of the liturgy was always music, and it was raised to new heights in 1902, when the world-famous boys' choir was established. In 1916 the organist and choirmaster Tertius Noble appealed for a school, and Charles Steele, an industrialist, made Noble's dream a reality. The St. Thomas Choir, which includes adult men, is renowned for liturgical recordings and its Tuesday evening concert series.

ARCHITECTURE

This church, which seats about 1,700, is built in Kentucky limestone. It was designed in Classic Gothic, the style used throughout Europe in the Middle Ages, by Ralph Adams Cram and Bertram Grosvenor Goodhue, of the firm of Cram, Goodhue & Ferguson. Cram dealt with the floor plan, which is 214 feet long and 100 feet wide, while Goodhue produced all the details. Many would say that the real beauty of the church is in the details, for no fixture was too insignificant for Goodhue. Two small brass locks in the vestry are sculpted with cameos of six Apostles.

The exterior facade holds forty-eight sculptured figures and a classic rose window, 25 feet wide. The entrance carving was begun only in 1962, thanks to the generosity of the parishioner George S. Scott. Be sure to look at the carvings related to marriage over the bridal door, which is found to the left of the main stairway. An elaborate reredos, reminiscent of that of Winchester Cathedral in England, makes the simple altar table the most prominent feature of the church. Look just above the altar for an image of St. Thomas kneeling before Jesus, no longer doubting His resurrection. Three abstract stained-glass English windows colorfully enhance the multitiered reredos. More than eighty

figures stand on the facade in an array of saints, historic figures, Episcopal bishops, and coats of arms. George Washington is among them. Be sure to get a copy of the church walking tour, which identifies all the images.

While Goodhue conceived the grand design of the reredos, Lee Lawrie carved the sculptures. He was a prolific artist who is well represented throughout the city — for instance, by the bronze sculpture of Atlas directly across from St. Patrick's Cathedral and ten limestone panels in the Rockefeller Center complex.

Visit the Chantry Chapel, which is used for daily services and baptisms. An octagonal font has an elaborate oak cover and a pedestal that holds pieces of the old church. Over the chantry's altar, a polychrome triptych shows Jesus performing his first miracle at the wedding feast in Cana. All the figures are richly colored with gilded accents. Noteworthy are stained-glass windows in this vaulted chapel that honor historic women of the church. Be sure to see Helena, mother of the Emperor Constantine, St. Elizabeth, Queen of Hungary, and the charitable Dorcas and Phoebe.

Nine other huge windows surround the 95-foot-high nave. The Spirit Bay, in the fourth bay from the back of the nave, was the last clerestory window to be installed. It was dedicated in 1974 by Terence Cardinal Cooke of St. Patrick's Cathedral. Remembered are Mohandas K. Gandhi, Eleanor Roosevelt, Adlai Stevenson, Ralph Bunche, who won the 1950 Nobel Peace Prize, John Muir, Albert Einstein, with lots of hair, Oliver Wendell Holmes, and a cherubic Pope John XXIII. St. Paul, the son of a Jew who became Apostle to the Gentiles, is the central figure in the window.

Study the face of the parapet that encloses the high altar. It holds eight mosaics — four represent the church while four others pay tribute to American history: The first settlement at Jamestown, Virginia, in 1607; Independence Hall in Philadelphia, representing the American Revolution; the Capitol in Washington, D.C., with flags of the Union and the Confederacy as a reminder of the Civil War; and a memorial to the dead of World War 1, re-creating Rheims Cathedral out of stones from the battle-scarred cathedral.

Wood panels resting on the parapet show figures of Chaucer, Shakespeare, Dante, and Edward Bouverie Pusey, a leader of the Oxford Movement. Oak carvings on the backs of the choir stalls depict pilgrims kneeling in prayer as Native Americans look on. Small panels on the front row show the achievements of the Brooklyn Bridge, the automobile, and the steam engine.

The European tradition of church as teacher to the community is very evident throughout this sanctuary. Historical references and biblical stories are too numerous to mention, but as you walk around you will discover images that will stir your mind and radiate your spirit.

ADDRESS: *1 West 53rd Street (at Fifth Ave.), New York, NY 10019*
PHONE: *212-757-7013*
HOURS: *Mon.–Fri.: 7:00 A.M.–7:00 P.M. Sat.: 8:00 A.M.–2:00 P.M.*
   Sun.: 7:00 A.M.–7:00 P.M.
   Tuesday Evening Concert Series 7:00 P.M.
WEB SITE: *www.saintthomaschurch.org*
LANDMARK DESIGNATION

FIFTH AVENUE PRESBYTERIAN CHURCH

GUIDANCE VIA THE TELEPHONE

On posh Fifth Avenue this brownstone Presbyterian church hangs out a welcome sign for all who have shopped too much, walked too many miles, or visited too many New York City landmarks. This church, largest of all the Presbyterian churches in the city, has charted a course through the rough seas of modern Christianity by offering, since the 1940s, recorded messages of spiritual guidance twenty four hours a day over the telephone — popularly known as Dial-A-Prayer.

HISTORY

Presbyterianism grew out of the sixteenth-century Reformation, specifically from John Calvin. It arrived in the American colonies in 1611, mainly through Scottish immigrants. In 1707 the Reverend Francis Makemie held a meeting in New York on Pearl Street. Mr.

Makemie, who came with his credentials, saw no reason to get permission to hold services, but the English governor, Edward Hyde, would not allow preaching to more than five people without additional approval. Mr. Makemie was thrown into jail, and his trial became a cause for establishing religious liberty in New York.

In 1717 the Presbyterians dedicated their first church on Wall Street, but their finances were controlled by Trinity Church, which levied a tax on all churches. The First Presbyterian Church did not

receive a charter until after the treaty of 1784, which formed a new American government.

This congregation first assembled in 1808 on Cedar Street in Lower Manhattan and was called the Fourth Presbyterian Church. It had grown out of the First Presbyterian Church, which was once known as the Wall Street Church. Twenty-six people were led by Archibald Gracie, a merchant whose mansion is now the official residence of the mayor of New York City; Richard Varick, leader of the Bank of New York and former mayor; and Oliver Wolcott, Jr., former U.S. secretary of the Treasury and a governor of Connecticut.

Dr. John B. Romeyn, the first minister, who served the congregation until 1825, founded the American Bible Society and established the church's commitment to education. He also headed the General Assembly, causing the congregation to be known as "the cathedral church of the Presbyterians." Dr. James Alexander, serving as minister from 1846 to 1859, helped reestablish Princeton Theological Seminary in New Jersey.

The parish moved north three times before settling on the present site in 1875. Since Presbyterian congregations usually named their churches to reflect locations, the parish officially took the avenue's name when they moved to Fifth Avenue and 19th Street in 1851.

The entire Presbyterian community was shaken to its roots in 1922 in the battle between fundamentalists and modernists. The Reverend Harry Emerson Fosdick, a Baptist who preached at the First Presbyterian Church and was brought to trial by the church's General Assembly, was asked to leave because he would not temper his liberalism or convert to Presbyterianism. (see Riverside Church). "Sin," Fosdick preached, "is simply living in the present age upon ideals and standards of an age gone by." In 1996, Dr. Thomas K. Tewell began the Center for Christian Studies, which features over seventy adult education classes on the Bible, theology, and church history.

ARCHITECTURE

Carl Pfeiffer designed this Gothic Revival brownstone building with an 85-foot-high main sanctuary, adding a stenciled ceiling to resemble the inverted hull of a sailing ship (he was also a shipbuilder). This vaulted wooden masterpiece gives warmth to a nave that seats over 2,000 worshipers. Pfeiffer formed the nave as an auditorium with a wood-faced gallery circling the clerestory level. Twelve softly colored stained-glass windows line the gallery's smooth plaster walls and pierce the paneled ceiling with their Gothic arches. The choir loft is placed on the wall above the minister's podium, where about seven thousand organ pipes ascend to the ceiling. No pillars obstruct the view of the raised pulpit, for the focus is on the minister and his sermon. Look for a prickly-leaf thistle carved into the pulpit as a symbol of the Presbyterian connection to Scotland.

By the 1920s, the congregation included many successful businessmen who wanted a new parish house and a grander entrance on Fifth Avenue. Led by Edward Harkness, one of the founders of Standard Oil, the group financed James Gamble Rogers, who had designed the Butler Library at Columbia University, to create the additions that smoothly harmonize with Pfeiffer's original structure.

ADDRESS: 7 *West 55th Street (at Fifth Ave.), New York, NY 10019*
PHONE: 212-247-0490; 212-246-4200 *(Dial-A-Prayer)*
212-246-4204 *(Thought Line)*
HOURS: *Mon.–Fri.*: 8:00 A.M.–9:00 P.M. *Sat.–Sun.*: 8:00 A.M.–6:00 P.M.
WEB SITE: *www.fapc.org*

EROL BEKER CHAPEL
OF THE GOOD SHEPHERD

AT ST. PETER'S CHURCH — "A PLACE OF PURITY"

The renowned American sculptor Louise Nevelson (1900–1988), when commissioned to design a chapel for St. Peter's Evangelical Lutheran Church, envisioned a "place of purity, an environment for the spirit." She also viewed the project as "a major breakthrough for a Jew to design a chapel for Christian use." To underscore her theme, Nevelson created white wooden sculptures displayed against walls of white plaster. The result is spectacular: a place of peace that transcends organized religion.

HISTORY

St. Peter's was founded in 1862 by German immigrants who had first worshiped in a small loft on Third Avenue and 49th Street. A Victorian Gothic church preceded the present building. When real estate developers set out to build Citicorp Center, St. Peter's negotiated an interesting deal — the corporation agreed to build and sell back to St. Peter's a new church on the same site, thereby creating the first condominium church in the country. The church makes a simple, forceful statement: Any house of worship built nowadays must be as up-to-date as the latest news bulletin, as well as a space for New Yorkers to get together and celebrate "life at the intersection." That means big.

The gray granite church, designed by Hugh Stubbins and Associates, opened in 1977. It contains a soaring 85-foot-high sanctuary, an intimate chapel, theater, music room, and studio — all within 56,417 square feet. These elements are essential parts of St. Peter's spiritual link to Manhattan's artistic community. Many unsung artists, both visual and performing, are invited to present their work to large, appreciative audiences.

St. Peter's Erol Beker Chapel designed by Louise Nevelson

The chapel, named for its patron, the industrialist Erol Beker, was dedicated on December 13, 1977. Its innovative, modernistic nature mirrors the ambience of the church as well as the ultramodern Citicorp complex.

ARCHITECTURE

Louise Nevelson conceived this intimate chapel as a major artwork: a five-sided sanctuary with six abstract wood sculptures filling most of the plaster walls. The sculptor named the panels *Cross of the Good Shepherd* and *Trinity*, (three wooden panels on the north wall); *Frieze of the Apostles*, which holds 12 square boxes filled with wooden pieces (east wall); *Cross of the Resurrection* (southeast wall); *Grapes and Wheat Lintel*, abstract forms representing bread and wine (over the entrance); and *Sky Vestment — Trinity* representing vestments worn at services (west wall).

A frosted white window and skylight on the north wall illuminate the pentagonal room, which measures nearly 28 feet long and 21 feet wide. The 9-foot-high *Cross of the Good Shepherd* is mounted on a gilded wooden slab and placed above the simple Parsons table that is used as an altar. There is seating for 28. Visitors may relax in bleached ash pews set diagonally to the center aisle, planned by Nevelson so that different views of the sculptures could be experienced depending on the direction one is facing.

Don't leave St. Peter's before going into the main sanctuary, affectionately called the granite tent, and marveling at its creative design by Massimo and Lella Vignelli. Artwork from many talented artisans hangs throughout this huge space. Look for the flowery blue "Persians," glass sculptures by Dale Chihuly, the world's foremost glass artist. A free-standing sixteenth-century Dutch cross dominates the space.

Jazz vespers, a tradition begun in 1965 by the Reverend Dale R. Lind, are conducted in the sanctuary every Sunday at 5:00 and have made St. Peter's world-famous for its jazz ministry. Duke Ellington, for whom the jazz center is named, and his collaborator Billy Strayhorn ("Take the A Train"), donated the piano that sits beside the pulpit in the main sanctuary. It stands as a symbol of gratitude from "people of the night" to whom St. Peter's reached out, including John Coltrane, Max Roach, and Dizzy Gillespie. Many musicians have been eulogized within its walls, and Lester Young, undisputed master of the tenor saxophone, is remembered with an annual celebration that began in 1994. It attracts jazz stars from "elder statesmen to the young burners."

As you leave the building, be sure to see the exterior cross, designed by Arnaldo Pomodoro of Milan. This majestic dark bronze sculpture, 8 feet tall and 6 feet wide, is a remarkable presence on busy Lexington Avenue.

ADDRESS: *619 Lexington Avenue (at 54th St.), New York, NY 10022*
PHONE: *212-935-2200*
HOURS: *Daily: 8:00 A.M.–9:30 P.M.*
WEB SITE: *www.saintpeters.org*

CHRIST CHURCH

BRILLIANT MOSAICS AS A MAJOR DESIGN ELEMENT

Of all the spectacular sights in Manhattan, none is more daz-zling than the mosaics that this United Methodist church uses as a major design element to inspire spirituality. Seven million tiny tiles glitter on interior walls, depicting images of Christianity. Tiles of stone or glass, known as tesserae, cover 14,000 square feet. Bruno De Paoli of Long Island City, master of the mosaic tradition, and his craftsmen executed all the designs from sketches by the architects. Application of the tesserae began in 1931, was interrupted by World War II, and would not be completed until 1951. The work is said to be equal to the finest Byzantine art in any museum.

HISTORY

Christ Church traces its roots to 1881 with a congregation of sixty families who lived in the developing residential area on the east side of Central Park. Outgrowing their building at Madison Avenue and 60th Street, the group united with another Methodist church on 61st Street, which had begun quite humbly in 1863 as a Sunday school over a Third Avenue saloon known as Dingledein's. The merged congrega-tion dedicated a new building in 1883 on Madison and 60th Street. The present Park Avenue site was acquired in exchange for that Madison Avenue property, and Christ Church was dedicated in 1933.

ARCHITECTURE

Ralph Adams Cram and Samuel Ferguson, the Boston architectur-al team, used older Byzantine and Romanesque churches of the Mediterranean area as their guides for Christ Church. They were influ-enced by the early and undivided Christian Church, with Constantinople as its center. Cram, who did not live to see Christ

Church completed, has been quoted as saying, "This earliest Christian art was the combination of the Greek intellectual qualities of the West expressing themselves in form, and the emotional qualities of the East expressing themselves in color." The Nobel prize-winning poet William Butler Yeats saw the Byzantine Empire as one of the great civilizations that "spoke to the multitude and the few alike."

The exterior of Christ Church is simple brick and stone, accented with columns of figured marble and inlays, and detailed with a round entrance and a circular stained-glass window, known to be a prototype for rose windows of later Gothic churches.

The narthex, with dark marble walls and golden mosaic ceiling, leads into the nave, where glittering tiles and colorful medallions cover round arches and a vaulted ceiling. The design of the nave is typically early Christian, with a line of marble columns and square piers leading to an intimate apse holding the altar table. A checkered floor of antique pink and dark green marble squares paves the entire sanctuary; more than thirty-two varieties of marble can be found throughout the interior.

High above the altar, a semidome holds the early Christian figure of the Pantocrator (Greek, meaning "all-sovereign Ruler of all") or Christ as Judge, with the symbols IC and XC (Alpha and Omega). In a band above the dome, seven medallions represent gifts of the Christian Spirit: the sun (understanding), a book (counsel), a lion (fortitude), a dove (wisdom), a lamp (knowledge), a cross (piety), and a crown (spiritual reward). Below the dome is written the summary of the law that unites the Old and New Testaments: "Thou shalt love the Lord with all thy heart and with all thy soul and with all thy mind: Thou shalt love thy neighbor as thyself."

The reredos holds sixteenth-century icons on panels of wood and a pair of ancient doors decorated in the Russian tradition. They were known as holy doors because only the clergy were privileged to pass through them.Look closely at two icons placed above the center of the altar. They are from Czar Nicholas II and his wife, Alexandra, and were used in the Winter Palace at St. Petersburg. Other icons pay homage to fifteenth- and sixteenth-century images.

Stop by the intimate chapel, which opens from the north aisle; it is a miniature version of the nave and has its own semidome holding a traditional mosaic Byzantine cross. The chapel's colorful wood ceiling

Mosaic of The Pantocrator, Christ as Judge

is reminiscent of medieval Spain. Mosaic medallions are placed throughout the church. Be sure to look for two peacocks, an ancient symbol of immortality, and Noah's Ark, a metaphor for survival.

THE ART OF MOSAICS

The history of mosaic art celebrates the era of Emperor Constantine I, who rebuilt Byzantium as Constantinople in A.D. 330 and made it the capital of the Roman Empire. Until the Turks conquered Constantinople in 1453, Byzantine artisans created many of the world's mosaic masterpieces. They achieved natural bright light by tilting and slanting the tesserae to reflect from many angles.

Glass for enamel tesserae is heated and melted. The liquid is cast into forms known as pancakes, which are then broken into pieces, and the vibrant inner edges are used as the faces for the individual tesserae in a mosaic design.

Tesserae are also cut from thick sheet glass, upon which gold or silver leaf has been applied. A thin covering of glass is fused to the face to protect the metals.

ADDRESS: 520 Park Avenue (at East 60th St.), New York, NY 10021
PHONE: 212-838-3036
HOURS: Mon.-Fri.: 9:00 A.M.-5:00 P.M. Closed Sat.
Sun.: 8:00 A.M.-1:00 P.M.

CENTRAL PRESBYTERIAN CHURCH

DISTINGUISHED MINISTRY OF MUSIC

Glorious choral music has always been an outstanding tradition of Central Presbyterian Church. At the turn of the twentieth century Charles Ives (1874–1954), the highly accomplished

American composer, was Central's organist and choirmaster—he wrote several of his major works expressly for the parish. Since Ives was heavily involved in the life insurance business, most of his works were not published until after 1939. He did receive the public recognition he deserved in 1947, winning the Pulitzer Prize — an accolade he disdained — for his Third Symphony. The Musica Sacra, a professional choir now a permanent part of Lincoln Center, was founded in 1966 by Richard Westenburg when he was serving as Central's organist and choirmaster. Central City Chorus, a fifty-member volunteer group, continues the church's ministry of music by presenting lively seasonal concerts in the sanctuary.

HISTORY

The congregation began in 1821 on Broome Street in Lower Manhattan and had four other homes before moving to its present site. Central Presbyterian Church held the first service in the present sanctuary in September 1929. The building was purchased from Park Avenue Baptist Church. It had been erected for the ministry of the Reverend Harry Emerson Fosdick, a liberal progressive preacher who left a mark on twentieth-century Christianity. Fosdick was a central figure in the fundamentalist versus modernist battle that rattled both Presbyterians and Baptists (see Riverside and Fifth Avenue Presbyterian Churches).

The building, largely financed by John D. Rockefeller, Jr., became overcrowded, and the congregation moved on to the new Riverside Church in Upper Manhattan. Left behind were many artifacts now cared for by the present congregation. The oak screen showing the twelve Apostles was carved by five members of the famous Oberammergau Passion Players from Bavaria. Originally the screen covered the Baptist baptismal tank; the Presbyterian congregation uses it as the chancel's centerpiece, a communion table surrounded by ivy and grapes. Evergreen ivy represents everlasting life; grapes are a symbol of the communion wine and the blood of Jesus.

A memorial chapel was built on the south side of the sanctuary by Presbyterians in 1945 to remember the son and namesake of their pastor the Reverend Theodore Cuyler Speers, who had been killed in

World War II. In 1983 two major streams of Presbyterianism, from North and South, joined to become the United Presbyterian Church of America. To commemorate this event, Central Presbyterian displays a charming needlepoint banner of the partnership in the Speers Chapel.

Turmoil engulfed the church in 1972, when developers from the Asia Society wanted to build a museum on the site to house artifacts of John D. Rockefeller III. After many emotional meetings, the Asia Society retreated to 70th Street, the Rockefeller artifacts ended up at the Metropolitan Museum of Art, and the church where John D. Rockefeller, Jr., had conducted Sunday Bible classes for many years was saved from the wrecker's ball.

ARCHITECTURE

This Neo-Gothic church, designed by Henry C. Pelton in association with Allen & Collens, was built between 1920 and 1922; five row houses were originally on the site. The exterior of gray granite blocks with limestone detail has two entrances: Park Avenue, where the Great Seal of the United States is carved into a corner of the facade, and 64th Street, where the seal of New York State is above the door. Asymmetrically designed, the Park Avenue frontage holds an office tower that is topped off by a parapet, a Gothic bell tower, and a peaked roof covering the nave. The eight-story bell tower has been vacant since the fifty-three-bell carillon was moved to Riverside Church (see entry) in 1930.

Study the carvings on the exterior — pelican for piety, rose for love, unicorn for chastity, and peacock for immortality. Above the towering stained-glass windows are wolves attacking sheep and vultures attacking doves, symbolizing the constant struggle between good and evil.

Inside, stained-glass windows tell biblical and modern stories. The twelve windows on the north and south walls represent the twelve Apostles. At the top of each window a quatrefoil (a four-piece flower) indicates the Four Gospels; at the center of each is a symbol of the Apostle.

The east window, above the chancel, was commissioned by the Presbyterians in 1929 as a memorial to their pastor of thirty-one years, the Reverend Wilton Merle-Smith. David as the psalmist is shown with Moses the lawgiver and Jesus. Study the west window above the rear balcony. Six historic figures relevant to Baptist tradition are shown: John Milton, the seventeenth-century English poet carrying his epic poem *Paradise Lost*; John Bunyan, holding his book *Pilgrim's Progress*; William Carey, a British missionary from 1794 who built a church in India; Roger Williams, the English clergyman who defended religious freedom and founded the colony of Rhode Island; Adoniram Judson, the first foreign American missionary who worked in Burma (see Judson Memorial Church); and Francis Wayland, a religious educator and early-nineteenth-century president of Brown University, who carries the inscription "Respect your own conceptions."

ADDRESS: **593** *Park Avenue (at East 64th St.), New York, NY 10021*
PHONE: *212-838-0808*
HOURS: *Mon.-Fri.: 10:00 A.M.–4:00 P.M. Sun.: 10:00 A.M.–2:00 P.M.*
   Worship at 11:00 A.M. Closed Sat.
Enter through office building if doors are locked

TEMPLE EMANU-EL

WORLD'S LARGEST SYNAGOGUE

The name itself, Emanu-El — Hebrew for "God is with us" — underscores the atmosphere of reverence and awe inspired by this huge temple of Reform Judaism. Dedicated on January 10, 1930, the sanctuary soars to the height of a ten-story building. It is as long as half a city block and as wide as a football field with seating for 2,500. The building is complemented by a temple within a temple. Beth-El (House of God) Chapel takes its name from a congregation that merged with Emanu-El in 1927. Look for the Tiffany stained-glass window that graces the chapel's area above the Moorish Ark; both artifacts are from Emanu-El's former site on 43rd Street.

HISTORY

In 1845 thirty-three German immigrants established Cultus Verein, a cultural society to adapt to their new country. They rented a room at the corner of Grand and Clinton Streets in Manhattan's Lower East Side and started to hold religious services under the name Temple Emanu-El. As the congregation grew they occupied a Methodist church on Chrystie Street and the Baptist church on East 12th Street (see St. Ann's Armenian Cathedral) before building their first place of

worship at the northeast corner of Fifth Avenue and 43rd Street in 1868. Because extreme noise from commercialism had invaded their vicinity, the lay group, under the leadership of the famous jurist Louis Marshall, planned to relocate. The congregation worshipped at Temple Beth-El on 76th Street and Fifth Avenue and moved to the present site just before the Depression of 1929. Incidentally, Emanu-El's new home on upper Fifth Avenue once held the mansions of Caroline Astor and her son, John, where social events were held for The 400, an elite group of New York City society.

The freedom in America had created an environment that allowed Congregation Emanu-El, which began as a Conservative synagogue, to make meaningful changes in long-standing European traditions. In 1856 Dr. Samuel Adler, a leader of the Reform movement in Germany, arrived to lead the congregation. For the first time families sat together to worship and music was added to accompany prayers. Felix Adler, son of Dr. Adler, would leave his father's followers to start the nonsectarian group the Society for Ethical Culture (see entry).

In 1873 the first permanent English-speaking rabbi, Dr. Gustave Gottheil, was appointed to accommodate the children of the original congregants. Confirmation services were begun for girls. In 1945 the temple began broadcasting part of the Friday evening service on WQXR-FM (96.3). Broadcasts still attract a large audience and now can be accessed on the radio station's Internet site.

ARCHITECTURE

No one style is attributed to this limestone building. Two architectural firms participated: Kohn, Butler & Stein for its understanding of the spiritual needs of Jewish community, and Bertram Goodhue's associates at Mayers, Murray & Philip for their expertise in creating unobstructed sanctuary space.

A Romanesque archway dominates Emanu-El's facade, which holds a circular stained-glass window representing the twelve Tribes

of Israel. Three decorative bronze doors lead into the Art Deco lobby, reflecting the newest design of the 1930s. Upon entering the sanctuary, you will be overwhelmed by the spacious interior, blazing with colors streaming through the majestic stained-glass windows. Walk around the ambulatory, filled with old memorial plaques, and see the small windows holding charming images of the temple's three predecessors.

Most impressive is the sacred Ark on the eastern wall. It is set within an arch that mirrors the temple's entrance. Byzantine mosaic tiles created by Hildreth Meiere (see St. Bartholomew's Church), fill the wall and sparkle with color in the style of Gustav Klimt, the Viennese painter who was admired by many of the founding members.

Rabbi Ronald B. Sobel set a priority for the congregation to preserve objects from its own history and from centuries of Jewish culture. Over many years Reva Godlove Kirschberg and Cissy Grossman nurtured and cataloged the treasures. The Herbert and Eileen Bernard Museum, in the 65th Street Community Center, opened in 1997 and contains over 250 items. Be sure to see the Venetian hanging Sabbath lamp designed like a Baroque fountain. Jews were welcomed into Italy's guilds, and the lamp is a charming example of Italian design applied to traditional household objects.

When you leave the synagogue, look for the engraved stone bench in the Garden of Freedom, near the exterior entrance to Beth-El Chapel. The garden is a bicentennial tribute to the people of the United States "in grateful recognition of 200 years of precious liberty, 1776–1996."

ADDRESS: *1 East 65th Street (between Fifth & Madison Aves.)*
New York, NY 10021
PHONE: *212-744-1400*
HOURS: *Daily: 10:00 A.M.–5:00 P.M. (Enter on 65th St.)*
WEB SITE: *www.emanuelnyc.org; www.wqxr.com*

CHURCH OF
ST. VINCENT FERRER

"WHERE HEAVEN AND EARTH ARE JOINED AND UNITED"

The master builder Bertram Grosvenor Goodhue was once quoted in *The New York Times* as saying, "I think St. Vincent Ferrer is my best work . . . it fulfills the age-old ideal of a consecrated church . . . that is, a place where heaven and earth are joined and united." The late actress Claudette Colbert, who received her first communion and confirmation in this church, often returned to rest in its comforting solitude. Another neighbor, the pop artist Andy Warhol, frequently attended Sunday services, always sitting in the last pew.

The Great Rood Facade of St. Vincent Ferrer

HISTORY

The church was dedicated on May 5, 1918, the third building for a growing Roman Catholic parish. It was close to both the residences of wealthy Fifth Avenue and the huge number of Irish immigrants living in Third Avenue tenements, who were employed in the nearby homes as cooks and housekeepers. The cost of the present church was largely borne by these working women, who donated a major part of their small wages to the construction fund. Their names are immortalized on a stone tablet at the shrine of St. Vincent near the entrance. The congregation is cared for by the Dominican Order, formally known as the Order of Preachers. Its patron, Vincent Ferrer, was a fourteenth-century Spanish preacher of the Dominican Order who evangelized throughout Spain and Europe.

ARCHITECTURE

The architect Bertram Goodhue's building plan is simple: the random ashlar and limestone church is fourteenth-century French Gothic with echoes of Norman Romanesque. It rises to 77 feet from floor to vault. Designed on a Latin cross plan, the church is 221 feet long with 95-foot transepts and seats 1,500 worshipers. But there is nothing simple about the magnificent west front on Lexington Avenue. Goodhue placed the Crucifixion, or Great Rood, on the exterior—something never done before in church architecture. This stone masterpiece was carved by Lee Lawrie, who included a panoply of saints, popes and theologians. The Gothic rose window dominating the facade holds nine choirs of angels, each associated with a Dominican saint. Fifteen scenes in the lower section represent the mysteries of the Rosary, which tell the life of Jesus and his mother, Mary.

Interior walls and Gothic pillars in the nave are of sandstone with Guastavino acoustic tiles lining the walls and arches. Most of the stained-glass windows tell stories of the Dominican Order and were created by Charles Connick, under the direction of Goodhue. The chancel is a masterpiece, with the Great Rood, a richly polychrome wooden image of the Crucifixion, high above the entrance and acting as a mirror for the exterior Rood. An elaborate carved oak reredos reaches 44 feet. The screen holds three paintings by Alfredo Mira illustrating miracles attributed to St. Vincent, as well as twenty-four statues of saints, thirty angels, and an 8-foot figure of Christ the King. The golden tabernacle is covered with enamel images from the Old and New Testaments.

You'll see three symbols constantly repeated throughout St. Vincent's: a dolphin, a dog, and a pelican. The dolphin, a kinglike image among fish, was said to bear the souls of the righteous across the sea to the land of the blessed. The origin of the dog lies with St. Dominic's mother, Jane of Aza. While she was pregnant she dreamed of a dog with a blazing torch in its mouth setting fire to the world. Along came Dominic. A more amusing pun is the word *dominicans*— when divided it becomes *domini canes*, which translates from Latin as "watchdogs of the Lord." The pelican symbolizes redemption or the Blessed Sacrament. It is said that the bird pierces its own breast in time of famine to feed its young.

The chapels in St. Vincent's are surrounded by floor-to-ceiling wrought-iron grillwork designed by Samuel Yellin. The gates add an intimate touch to small shrines within this large medieval nave. Bertram Goodhue's attention to detail can be fully appreciated when viewing the Stations of the Cross, painted by Telford and Ethel Paullin. He varied the sizes and shapes of the canvases so they would look like a fine art collection. Study these museumlike renditions to see how heaven and earth are truly joined and united.

ADDRESS: 869 Lexington Avenue (between 65th & 66th Sts.)
New York, NY 10021
PHONE: 212-744-2080
HOURS: Daily: 9:00 A.M.–6:30 P.M.
LANDMARK DESIGNATION

ST. JOHN NEPOMUCENE

FOR SLOVAKS, A PLACE TO WORSHIP IN FREEDOM

For more than a century this Roman Catholic church has attracted Central European immigrants from throughout New York
City and became known affectionately as the Slovak Basilica.
The Slovakian language is used in the liturgy as well as in song, causing many worshipers to feel as if they were back in "the old country."

HISTORY

This congregation, calling itself the Society of St. Matthew, was
founded in 1895 by immigrants who wanted their own center of worship and space for cultural activities. Parishioners subsequently purchased a former synagogue in the East Village on 4th Street. By 1908
the congregation had outgrown that space and moved to another synagogue, on East 57th Street. Finally, in 1924, the group built its own
church, with rectory and elementary school, on present site. The parish
expanded with every new wave of immigration from the then-Com-
munist countries of Eastern Europe and held many social events in its
auditorium and basement cafeteria.

Over the years, though, the congregation dwindled. The number of
children dropped, and the school was closed in 1987. But new waves
of Eastern Europeans started to arrive in the 1990s and, like their predecessors, discovered that St. John's is a warm haven not unlike their
homeland church.

ARCHITECTURE

John Van Pelt designed this Romanesque church true to its
European heritage. The red-brick and limestone exterior holds a circu-
lar central window bordered with terra-cotta symbols of the four
Evangelists: Matthew as an angel; Mark as a winged lion; Luke as an

ox; and John as an eagle. Round arches and columns abound, while an asymmetrical tower anchors the corner of 66th Street.

All the stained-glass windows tell one story — the life of Jesus and Mary (the memorials written on the windows are in Slovakian). The sky blue ceiling, brass chandeliers, and gargoyles on limestone columns

add interest to the nave. The chancel holds the focal point, a richly polychrome image of Jesus on the cross. The vaulted ceiling is filled with mosaic images of the Trinity — the Father, as a full-length figure; the Son, represented by a triangle; and the Holy Spirit as a dove. Angels, in oil paintings, kneel in adoration. An altar with a rounded baldachin (marble canopy) was added in 1956 and rests on a deep green marble podium. Brown marble pillars support the mosaic-lined canopy which tells the story of St. John Nepomucene (c. 1345–1393).

John served as vicar-general to the archbishop of Prague. He was martyred by King Wenceslas IV because he refused to reveal what the queen had told him in confession. The king had him thrown to his death from the Charles Bridge. By the seventeenth century John had been canonized and become patron of bridges and protector against floods.

When you leave the church, look up at the detailed tympanum, a terra-cotta panel over the main entrance. St. John is holding his fingers to his lips while his torturers wait on either side. The twelve Apostles are carved in a line under John's image. A typical New Yorker might think he was asking for a little less noise on First Avenue.

ADDRESS: *411 East 66th Street (at First Ave.), New York, NY* 10021
PHONE: 212-734-4613/ 212-734-4370
HOURS: *Daily:* 8:00 A.M.–8:00 P.M.

❖ ❖ ❖ ❖

UNITARIAN CHURCH OF ALL SOULS

"THE BOSTON RELIGION"

U nitarianism was the nineteenth-century brainchild of William Ellery Channing, a minister of the Federal Street Church in Boston whose sermon "Unitarian Christianity" was the foundation on which the faith rested. Lucy Channing Russel, William's sister, had invited about forty people to her home in Lower Manhattan to hear her brother preach that the Bible must be interpreted by reason and, since it "proclaims the unity of God, . . . we object to the doctrine of the Trinity." The Trinity maintains that one God exists in three divine figures: God the Father, Jesus the Son, and the Holy Spirit. The dogma, stated in the Nicene Creed, cannot be explained by reason but is accepted by faith as the center of Christian theology. Channing's sermon, reprinted in pamphlet form, became a best-seller, leading his adherents to establish a Unitarian congregation whose charter dates from 1819.

HISTORY

This congregation's first church was built on Chambers Street and dedicated in 1821 before a minister could be found for "the Boston religion." The Reverend Henry Whitney Bellows (1814–1882), a New Englander right out of Harvard Divinity School, joined All Souls in 1839. He would devote his entire life to the church, guiding the congregation as well as contributing to city and national life. In 1861 Bellows founded the United States Sanitary Commission, precursor to the Red Cross, which treated and cared for Union soldiers wounded in the Civil War. At one of the commission's fund-raising efforts, he sponsored a fair that featured private collectors' works of art. Noting the popularity of the exhibit, he encouraged the creation of a public art institution through the Union League Club, which he had also organized. The Metropolitan Museum of Art evolved from Bellow's vision. Most important, Bellows organized the Unitarian denomination. He was editor of *The Liberal Christian*, published in New York City, and after the Civil War he founded the National Conference of Unitarian and Other Christian Churches.

Notable members of the congregation included William Cullen Bryant, poet and editor of *The Evening Post*; Peter Cooper, businessman and founder of the Cooper Union for the Advancement of Science and Art; Herman Melville, author of *Moby Dick*; Louisa Lee Schuyler, an organizer of the Sanitary Commission and founder of the Bellevue School of Nursing; Nathaniel Currier, renowned lithographer (with James Ives); Dorman Eaton, U.S. commissioner of civil service who helped crush William "Boss" Tweed; and many prominent bankers and businessmen.

When Bellows died after serving the Unitarians for forty-three years, the congregation commissioned Augustus Saint-Gaudens to create a bas-relief memorial, which is in the chancel. Don't miss this masterpiece on your visit.

In 1932 All Souls opened its present site (its fourth home), as FDR was elected president; unlike his mother, who was a Unitarian, the new chief executive attended an Episcopal church. In 1961 the Unitarians consolidated with the Universalists, who date back to 1793, to form the Unitarian Universalist Association. The group maintains offices at the United Nations headquarters (see Tillman Chapel) and in Washington, D.C. Today this congregation is involved in a church school and the popular Musica Viva concert program.

ARCHITECTURE

Hobart Upjohn, architect and grandson of the architect Richard Upjohn (see Trinity Church), created this traditional New England meetinghouse of red brick and limestone in a distinctive American style. The squarely centered central tower, reminiscent of many colo-

nial and Georgian buildings, acts as a beacon.

The colonial interior is simple, with plain white pillars supporting rounded arches. Brass and crystal chandeliers hang from a vaulted ceiling, and pristine white pews are trimmed with mahogany. The raised pulpit, with a twin stairway, rests against the rear wall of the chancel, while Palladian-style windows with clear glass flood the sanctuary with natural light. There is seating for 600 parishioners in the main sanctuary and 600 more in the community hall beneath.

Be sure to see the Theodore Chickering Williams Memorial by E. B. Longman—a marble bas-relief for All Souls' third minister, who is enfolded in the wings of his guardian angel.

ADDRESS: *1157 Lexington Avenue (at 80th St.), New York, NY 10021*
PHONE: *212-535-5530*
MUSICA VIVA CONCERTS: *212-794-3646*
HOURS: *Daily: 9:00 A.M.–4:00 P.M. Enter through the side garden*
WEB SITE: *www.allsoulsnyc.org*

CHURCH OF
ST. THOMAS MORE

JACKIE'S CITY HAVEN

Former First Lady Jacqueline Kennedy Onassis, who lived nearby, was a frequent midday visitor to this Roman Catholic church. The widow of America's thirty-fifth president, like many worshipers before her, found solace in this charming sanctuary, which seems to have been moved intact from the English countryside and hidden away in the shadows of posh Park Avenue co-ops. The small-town atmosphere is further enhanced twice a day — at noon and six in the evening — when a three-minute Angelus rings from the tower. This old tradition, a tribute to Mary, the Mother of Jesus, calls all to prayer before meals. As you hear the bells toll, recall the French artist Jean-François Millet's painting, The Angelus, which hangs in the Louvre and portrays two peasants at prayer in a field. For a few moments the serenity that graces Millet's pastoral scene is felt on 89th Street as St. Thomas More's bells remind all to stop for quiet contemplation.

HISTORY

In July 1950 the parish of St. Thomas More began on this site in a building that had been home for two previous groups. When the present congregation moved in, they worked with their guiding force, Bishop Philip Furlong, and the interior architect William Boegel to gently alter the sanctuary, which seats over three hundred. The church was erected in 1870 as the Episcopal Church of the Beloved Disciple for residents at St. Luke's Home for Indigent Christian Females next door. A small chapel was added in 1879 to the west side, and the rectory and parish house in 1893 to the east side. All were gifts from Caroline Talman. The Episcopal congregation departed in 1929, merging with the Church of the Heavenly Rest on 90th Street (see entry). In the same year the Dutch Reformed Church of Harlem relocated to this site, bringing along their stained-glass windows (see Ephesus Seventh-Day Adventist Church). They remained until 1949. Look for the oak plaque just inside vestibule that acknowledges the Dutch Reformed parishioners who donated the original windows.

The patron, St. Thomas More (1478–1535), was an English politician and an Oxford scholar well known for his essay *Utopia*, published in 1516. In 1532 More resigned his post as Lord Chancellor of England, refusing to recognize Henry VIII's authority over the pope and Henry's divorce from Catherine of Aragon. More was arrested and imprisoned in the Tower of London. In 1533 the English Reformation began; two years later Sir Thomas More was beheaded for treason. The Catholic Church bestowed sainthood on him four hundred years after his martyrdom, and today he is honored as a patron of the legal profession.

Inside the parish house is a copy of the famous portrait of Sir Thomas as Lord Chancellor, painted in 1527 by Hans Holbein the Younger. You can see the original oil in the nearby Frick Collection at Fifth Avenue and 70th Street.

ARCHITECTURE

Four architects — Louis A. Osborne, Thomas M. Fanning, and the firm of Hubert, Pirsson & Co. (who also planned the Chelsea Hotel on West 23rd Street) — are credited with designing the many elements of this picturesque Gothic Revival church. The exterior of gray sandstone is set off by a striking tower that rises eight stories. It holds a well-used bell from 1878, arched windows, and a parapet crowned with three pinnacles. Just under the top dormer is an empty roundel that was to encase a clock like those found on English village churches.

The Gothic frame that holds the entrance doors was etched with fitting words — "We love him because he first loved us." Directly over the entranceway is a stained-glass window from the early 1900s showing the Resurrection of Jesus. It was a memorial to the beloved Dutch Reformed pastor Dr. Joachim Elmendorf, who has a church in Harlem named after him (see Elmendorf Reformed Church). To the left of the entrance a window dating to 1910 is a copy of the famous picture in the Bodleian Library at Oxford that shows Jesus knocking on a stranger's door. Be sure to glance up to the clerestory level to see the softly colored windows that the original Episcopal congregation left.

Architectural changes were made by each group that resided in this small sanctuary. The rehearsal room of the Dutch Reformed choir is now the Foley Chapel, a cozy nook dedicated to Mary. It is filled with warm woodwork and has a minia-ture Great Rood beam at the entrance. Old stained-glass win-dows from the Episcopal parish resembling handcrafted Byzantine medallions grace the east and west walls. A charming polychrome stat-ue of Mary is tucked into a corner niche.

In the main sanctuary the sense of intimacy is heightened by the chancel's only stained-glass win-dow. It is a triptych of the Nativity with a graceful angel, seemingly in flight, guarding the Holy Family. Beneath the window a simple reredos of wood and brocade encircles the tabernacle.

Pure white statues by the sculptor Harry Donohue decorate each side of the chancel. Joseph, Mary's consort, and Mary holding the Infant Jesus are framed in decorative Gothic arches with gilded panels. Banks of candles glow in front of Mary's image. Stop here and light a candle for Jackie and her family. Her son, John, his wife, Carolyn, and her sister, Lauren, were memorialized at St. Thomas More in July 1999 after a plane crash claimed their lives.

ADDRESS: 65 East 89th Street (between Madison & Park Aves.)
New York, NY 10128
PHONE: 212-876-7718
HOURS: Mon.–Fri.: 7:00 A.M.– 7:00 P.M. Sat.: 8:00 A.M.–7:00 P.M.
Sun.: 8:00 A.M.–8:00 P.M.
Enter through the parish house when the main entrance is closed

ISLAMIC CULTURAL CENTER OF NEW YORK

MASTERWORK OF MODERN DESIGN

This opulent house of worship, covering an entire city block, is an architectural masterpiece, a monument to the second largest faith in the world next to Christianity. More than 1.1 billion people practice Islam. New York City claims sixty mosques and an estimated 400,000 to 600,000 worshipers. This mosque sits cater-corner on its site so that it faces the qiblah, the ancient Kaaba shrine within the Grand Mosque in the Saudi Arabian city of Mecca. Mecca is the center of the Muslim world because it is the birthplace of Muhammad, Islam's revered prophet.

Administrators of the Islamic Center welcome groups from all educational and religious institutions. A bookstore has a wide collection of books and tapes to explain the principles of Islam. Note the electronic screen placed on the gate at 96th Street. Besides directing visitors to the entrance on 97th Street, the narrow screen highlights a daily message. Take care to abide by Islamic custom and remove your shoes before entering the prayer room. A rack is at its entrance to hold your footwear.

HISTORY

This congregation had worshiped since the 1960s in a converted building on 72nd Street at Riverside Drive. The faithful planned the new mosque as the first building in New York City specifically designed for Islamic worship. The governments of Saudi Arabia, Malaysia, Kuwait, and Libya provided financing to purchase the site. Kuwait donated $17 million for construction costs. The board of trustees that maintains and supervises the center consists of Muslim ambassadors to the United Nations. The center, which officially opened on September 25, 1991, counts more than nine hundred members from the metropolitan area, many who are African Americans from Harlem.

Islam, whose name means "peace," is based upon the teachings of the prophet Muhammad (570?–632), who believed in one God, Allah. At the age of forty Muhammad, a wealthy merchant in Mecca, experienced a revelation. He believed himself to be called by Allah to be the Arabian prophet of the true religion. Muhammad's life was filled with many revelations and visions, collected in the Koran, Islam's holy book. The Prophet's basic teachings include belief in one God, that humankind must submit to God's teachings, that heaven and hell await the present generation, and that the world will end one day with a great judgment. Muslims are

from two principal sects, the Sunni and the Shí'ite. The Islamic Center belongs to the Sunni sect, which represents about 84 percent of Muslims in the world. The Sunni follow orthodox tradition and accept the four caliphs (heads of the Muslim state) as rightful successors to Muhammad. The Shí'ite split from the Sunnis by rejecting this oral tradition.

ARCHITECTURE

The architectural firm Skidmore, Owings & Merrill—creators of Lever House in mid-Manhattan and the landmark Chase Bank at 43rd Street—designed the Islamic Center as a masterwork of modern building. The complex also includes a lecture hall, school, museum, and residence for imams (prayer leaders).

Etched on the limestone exterior of the main edifice is a traditional Islamic design. Since the religion forbids the use of figurative design, all motifs are in geometric patterns. The base of the building is tan-colored granite, supporting an impressive copper dome. On the exterior of the dome the name Allah (Arabic for God) is written four times. The towering minaret, thrusting 130 feet skyward from the southeast corner, was designed by Swanke, Hayden & Connell. A circle of black wrought iron on the minaret surrounds an opening used by an imam to call followers to prayer. The points of the crescent moon atop the minaret indicate the direction of the Kaaba shrine in Mecca.

The focus of the interior is a pale green prayer hall, which rises to 80 feet and measures a perfect square. It has a balcony reserved for women and a *minbar*, the pulpit for the imam. The *mihrab*, a niche representing the presence of the Prophet Muhammad, is surrounded by a handsome bronze frame as well as inscriptions from the Koran. It also points toward Mecca. An inner dome, acting as a skylight, is encircled by a gold-leafed stone rim etched with verses from the Koran. Natural light pours in through twelve huge clerestory windows covered with a lattice pattern. A circle of electric lights, 18 feet off the ground, hangs from the drum of the dome. Sea foam green carpeting with colorful rectilinear patterns covers the floor of the prayer hall. Since this hall is open only on Friday evenings, there is a richly carpeted room on the lower level that is used for daily visits. You will see a partition in the downstairs room since in this orthodox tradition men and women worship separately.

ADDRESS: 1711 *Third Avenue (between 96th & 97th St.)*
    Enter on 97th Street
PHONE: 212-722-5234
HOURS: Daily: 9:00 A.M – 5:00 P.M. *Main prayer service Friday evening*

BY THE WAY

As you make your rounds in EAST SIDE MANHATTAN, you may wish to visit other spiritual places. Some are public, others are open at special times. Be sure to call ahead.

ST. MARY'S CATHOLIC CHURCH OF THE BYZANTINE RITE: 1964. This church was designed by the Franciscan architect Brother Cajetan Baumann for a congregation established in 1912. The modern design in white concrete holds huge stained-glass windows and colorful exterior mosaics. When the sanctuary is illuminated, the building glows like a massive candle. The iconostatis and enormous mosaic of the Risen Christ are impressive contemporary interpretations of ancient Byzantine symbols.

246 East 15th Street (at Second Ave.) 212-677-0516

FRIENDS MEETING HOUSE: 1861. This Quaker meetinghouse and seminary is attributed to Charles T. Bunting. This is one of the first buildings in Stuyvesant Square Historic District, where most houses were built in the late nineteenth century. The austere red-brick Greek Revival **landmark** with white trim is surrounded by a black wrought-iron fence. Students from the next-door Friends Seminary play in the churchyard. The interior space used for weekend worship is sparsely furnished, in keeping with Quaker tradition. This Christian group, well-known as pacifist, emphasizes service to others and the Inner Light, a feeling within each body of God's guiding spirit.

15 Rutherford Place (between 15th & 16th Sts.) 212-673-5750

ST. GEORGE'S EPISCOPAL CHURCH: 1846. A brownstone built by Otto Blesch and Leopold Eidlitz in early Romanesque Revival style. The **landmark** exterior design is attributed to Blesch's Bavarian roots. *Rundbogenstil*, the round-arched style from Germany, had an enormous impact on American design. St. George's was one of the first

Romanesque buildings in America. The interior was rebuilt by Eidlitz after a fire in 1866. The congregation, dating from 1749, included the financier J. P. Morgan, who actively participated in church government. The sanctuary is now shared with **Manhattan Cornerstone Presbyterian Church**, which holds Sunday worship services and weekday gatherings in the chapel. The property was once part of the Peter Stuyvesant colonial farm, now called Stuyvesant Square Historic District. The neighboring park was laid out in 1836 and is still surrounded by its original cast-iron fence.

209 East 16th St. (between Second & Third Aves.) 212-475-0830

CALVARY EPISCOPAL CHURCH: 1848. This design by James Renwick, Jr., is English Gothic Revival style (with twin spires that were removed) holds an unusual five-sided apse. All forty-eight clerestory stained-glass windows are from the nineteenth century. This is only the second home for a congregation active since the Revolutionary War. Records show that the former First Lady Anna Eleanor Roosevelt was baptized in her home in 1884 by Calvary's rector, with her uncle, the former President Theodore Roosevelt, as godfather. In her later years Mrs. Roosevelt often visited the church. The author Edith Wharton also grew up in the parish and was said to have used Rector Edward Washburn, her best friend's father, as a prototype for Dr. Ashmore in *The Age of Innocence*.

61 Gramercy Park North (at 21st St. & Park Ave. South) 212-475-1216

LUTHERAN CHURCH OF GUSTAVUS ADOLPHUS: 1887. This Gothic Revival church is built on a site established by Swedish immigrants in 1865. The exterior rose window has a unique center—a Byzantine hexagram often referred to as a Star of David, a symbol of Judaism, which causes many inquiries. Byzantine stars were commonly used as good omens. The church was named for Gustav II Adolph (1594–1632)—Gustavus Adolphus in Latin—a popular Swedish king who died as a champion of Protestantism in the Thirty Years' War. Be sure to visit the exquisite interior with its Tiffany-like skylight and original gas chandeliers. An active senior center is open daily, and the "22 Below" cabaret for young adults takes place on Saturday evenings.

155 East 22nd Street (between Lexington & Park Aves.) 212-674-0739

ST. STEPHEN'S CHURCH: 1848. The Romanesque Revival design was created by James Renwick, Jr., for the Roman Catholic congregation. The church was extended in 1865 by Patrick C. Keely and restored in 1940. Don't miss the more than forty interior murals from the 1870s by Constantino Brumidi, who also painted the frescoes on the dome, walls, and ceilings of the Capitol in Washington, D.C. The Carmelite Friars care for the parish, which merged with **Our Lady of the Scapular** in 1990.

142 East 29th Street (between Lexington & Third Aves.) 212-683-1675

CHURCH OF THE GOOD SHEPHERD: 1902. This red-brick church was designed by Henry Vaughn, who worked on the National Cathedral in Washington, D.C. It is an homage to a fourteenth-century chapel in East Anglia, and was a gift from the Houghton Family of Corning glassworks. The Episcopal parish was founded in 1858 as a mission chapel of the Church of the Incarnation and continues to thrive in Kips Bay, which derives its name from the seventeenth-century landowner Jacobus Henderson Kip. Be sure to see the window of the Good Shepherd designed by the English artisan Frederick Cole.

236 East 31st Street (between Second & Third Aves.) 212-689-1595

CHURCH OF THE INCARNATION: 1864. **Landmark** Episcopal church was designed by Emlen T. Littell, with additions and restorations by D. & J. Jardine to the east end of the building following a fire in 1882. The parish began in 1850 as a mission chapel of Grace Church and was located at 28th Street and Madison Avenue. The Gothic Revival brownstone church was built as part of the elite residential Murray Hill neighborhood. The interior artwork is outstanding. Be sure to see the designs of Louis Comfort Tiffany, John La Farge, William Morris, and Edward Burne-Jones in the stained-glass windows; sculptures by Augustus Saint-Gaudens and Daniel Chester French; and a monument by Henry Hobson Richardson. In 1991 the architect Jan Hird Pokorny began a major ongoing restoration. The church takes an active role in the community and serves as meeting place for local groups.

209 Madison Avenue (at 35th St.) 212-689-6350

CHURCH OF OUR SAVIOUR: 1959. This smooth stone Roman Catholic basilica is by Paul W. Reilly. The interior was designed by the Viggo Rambusch Company with a glorious baldachin in the chancel and an impressive stained-glass window of Our Saviour by Per Bergethon. Founded in 1955 by Francis Cardinal Spellman, the group had worshiped in a nearby brownstone razed to make way for the Doral Hotel. A 7-ton statue of St. Patrick rises above the facade's rose window, while the four Evangelists hold up the bell tower.

59 Park Avenue (at 38th St.) 212-679-8166

CHURCH OF ST. AGNES:  1997. This Italianate-style structure by Acheson Thornton Doyle was built after fire destroyed the previous church. The Roman Catholic congregation founded in 1873 is now mainly commuters using nearby Grand Central Station. Look for Agnes, a fourth-century adolescent martyr, in the sanctuary mural created by Sean Delonas, a *New York Post* artist. A street is named for Archbishop Fulton J. Sheen (1895–1979), charismatic preacher and early television star of *Life Is Worth Living*, who often spoke in the sanctuary. A Latin Mass is celebrated every Sunday at 11:00 A.M.

143 East 43rd Street (between Lexington & Third Aves.) 212-682-5722

UNITED NATIONS MEDITATION ROOM: 1952. "We all have within us a centre of stillness surrounded by silence. It has been the aim to create in this small room a place where the doors may be open to the infinite lands of thought and prayer." These are the words of the UN secretary-general Dag Hammarskjöld (1905–1961), who planned every detail of this simple V-shaped room. After his death in a plane crash in the Congo, staff members and the artist Marc Chagall donated the design on a 15-foot-wide and 12-foot-high royal blue glass panel that sits outside the entry. The stained glass depicts mankind's yearning for peace, alongside prophets, symbols of motherhood, and victims of war. When Chagall unveiled the panel with secretary-general U Thant on the third anniversary of Hammarskjold's death, he said, "The main thing is not to see it, but to feel it."

First Avenue & 46th Street, west side of the General Assembly lobby.
212-963-4475

UNITED NATIONS GARDENS: These gardens hold gifts symbolizing man's quest for peace. The huge bronze statue by Evgeniy Vuchetich, *Let Us Beat Our Swords into Plowshares*, was given by the Union of Soviet Socialist Republics in 1958. *Good Defeats Evil*, (St. George slaying a dragon), by Tsereteli Zurah, is also from the Soviet Union and commemorates the signing of a nuclear treaty in 1987. Its base holds missile shells from the United States and Russia. The nearby bronze

equestrian statue *Peace*, by Antun Augustincic, is a gift from Yugoslavia. Be sure to see the man who helped formulate modern international law, Padre Francisco de Vitoria; his bust is a tribute from his countryman King Juan Carlos of Spain. In 1998 a bronze African elephant sculpture from the governments of Kenya, Nepal, and Namibia was installed near the First Avenue fence on 48th Street. The statue is 11 feet high and weighs 7,000 pounds, but it can easily be missed in the summer months, when it is engulfed by surrounding trees and shrubs. In 2000 Ireland's Prime Minister Bertie Ahern presented *Arrival*, created by the Irish artist John Behan to represent the Irish diaspora. A mighty bronze ship holds 150 immigrants while several travelers disembark.

First Avenue & 46th Street. Public Space

RAOUL WALLENBERG MEMORIAL: 1998. Five black shafts mined from Swedish bedrock stand over 12 feet high in this tribute by Gustav Kraitz. They are inscribed with the Wallenberg history. A blue globe tops the center column, and a life-size briefcase or diplomatic pouch with the initials RW stands apart on paving stones from the Jewish ghetto in Budapest, Hungary. Raoul Wallenberg, a Swedish diplomat stationed in Budapest, saved the lives of 100,000 Hungarian Jews during World War II by issuing passports to neutral Sweden. He was imprisoned by the Soviet government and disappeared in 1945.

First Avenue & 47th Street, opposite the United Nations. Public Space

CHURCH OF HOLY FAMILY: 1965. This contemporary church was designed by George J. Sole. In 1924, when a Roman Catholic church was founded on this site for Italian immigrants, the Turtle Bay area was filled with factories and tenements. In 1947 construction of the United Nations dramatically changed the neighborhood and Holy Family became a spiritual home for diplomats from many nations. Services are conducted in many languages, and themes of peace and universality fill the church walls. After Pope Paul VI addressed the UN in 1965, he held an ecumenical meeting for peace in the sanctuary. In commemoration a bronze bas-relief portrait of the pontiff was placed above the cornerstone. Also see the medallion of the cherubic Pope John XXIII on the exterior. The austere nave is dominated by a huge aluminum sculpture of the Risen Christ surrounded by a crown of lights. Stained-glass windows depict modern-day refugees with "Hope" written in many languages, while three ceramic groups show the Holy Family in flight to Egypt. The artisan Jordi Bonet created all the windows and ceramics as well as the Stations of the Cross painted on a horizontal panel. The side altar of St. Joseph was a gift from Italy; Joseph is holding a replica of the church. Look for the free-standing bronze John the Baptist guarding a black-granite baptismal font; the haunting image is by the American artist Frederick Shrady. Once outdoors, visit the Garden of Mary, a quiet oasis with ponds and floral displays created by the parishioner Christian Blake.

315 East 47th Street (between First & Second Aves.) 212-753-3401

CHURCH OF SWEDEN: 1870. This former private home was donated by James Talcott to the New York Bible Society in 1920 and purchased by Swedish Lutherans in 1978. The congregation was founded in 1873 as the Swedish Seaman's Church at 5 Water Street. The serene white chapel on the upper floor has antique ceiling beams and original leaded windows. The library on the main floor is filled with Swedish books and usually lots of Swedish visitors. Services are held in their language.

5 East 48th Street (between Fifth & Madison Aves.) 212-832-8443

CENTRAL SYNAGOGUE: 1870. This Moorish Revival sandstone **landmark** by Henry Fernbach has copper domes and banded arches modeled after those of the Doma Synagogue in Budapest. Note the exterior lamp fixtures, echoing the shape of the twin domes. This Reform congregation, founded in 1846 by immigrants from Bohemia, has the distinction of worshiping in the oldest building in continuous use as a synagogue in New York. The group, first known as Ahavath Chesed on Ludlow Street, merged in 1898 with Shaar Hasomayim and renamed the synagogue in 1920. The ornate interior was badly damaged by fire in August 1998 while the building was undergoing restoration, but it has been re-created and updated by Hardy Holzman Pfeiffer Associates.

123 East 55th Street (at Lexington Ave.) 212-838-5122

L'EGLISE FRANÇAISE DU SAINT ESPRIT (THE FRENCH CHURCH OF THE HOLY SPIRIT): This former private home, purchased in 1941, is the church's eighth location. A nursery school entrance shares the doorway, but slim glass doors at street level allow a peek into the small sanctuary. Antique prayer boards and over forty coats of arms from colonial families like du Pont, Delancy, Ruyon, and Jay, line the white stucco walls. Clear leaded-glass windows serve as a reredos and hold a blue-and-gold cross as well as the seal of the Protestant Huguenot Society. Services in French use the same hymns that were sung on Easter Sunday in 1628 during the founding ceremony. Back then New Amsterdam's multilingual minister, Jean Michel, of French descent, who Latinized his name to Jonas Michaelius (see Marble Collegiate Church), conducted Dutch services on Sunday mornings and French services in the afternoons. In 1804 the Huguenots joined the Episcopal diocese with an endowment that continues to support a French-speaking pastor. Annual remembrances are held for the Edict of Nantes in April, which granted full liberty to Huguenots, and for Bastille Day in July. The Edict's annulment in 1685 caused a flight to the American colonies.

109-111 East 60th Street (between Lexington & Park Aves.) 212-838-5680

TRINITY BAPTIST CHURCH: 1931. Scandinavian Modern design is by Martin Gravely Hedmark. The congregation was founded in 1867 as the First Swedish Baptist Church of New York and began to use English instead of Swedish for services in 1942. A towering exterior wall of yellow ombré brickwork ascends into the shapes of old Hansa gables found in churches around the Baltic Sea. Two tall black columns from Sweden act as cornerstones, while miniature iron steeples representing two areas of Sweden are placed on either side of the main tower. Wrought-iron appliques and grills called the Angel Forest, cover the entrance doors and narthex window. The square sanctuary has a central dome and eight slender columns covered with hand-modeled terra cotta. Orrefors glass fixtures light the pulpit. The main window over the baptismal platform shows Jesus preaching the parable of the sower. Be sure to look above the balcony for a charming symbol of peace, a small white bird in stained glass sleeping with his head tucked under his wing. On the round window overlooking the street an inscription in Swedish reads, "God Bless You." Symbolism abounds in the windows designed by the architect, on the iron baptismal gates, and on the ends of the birch pews.

250 East 61st Street (between Second & Third Aves.) 212-838-6844

OUR LADY OF PEACE CHURCH: 1886. Victorian Gothic design was by Samuel Warner for the German Presbyterian Church of the Redeemer. In 1918 the building became the National Italian Parish, founded by the Reverend Philip Leone from St. Lucy's Roman Catholic Church in East Harlem for immigrants who had settled in the factory-filled area. An extension to the red-brick church was added in 1921. Murals, oil paintings, and statues are tributes to the culture of Italy. Be sure to see the full-length portrait of a white-robed Pope John XXIII in the balcony and the Venetian chandeliers. Two intimate side chapels honor Our Lady of Romitello from Sicily and Our Lady of San Marco. Encased in the back of the sanctuary is a richly adorned statue of Santa Fara of Sicily, who holds symbols of her restored sight.

237 East 62nd Street (between Second & Third Aves.) 212-838-3189

PARK EAST SYNAGOGUE (Congregation Zichron Ephraim): 1889. The red brick and granite structure was designed by Ernest Schneider and Henry Herter in Moorish Revival style. The heavily ornamented facade holds horseshoe arches, symmetrical towers with completely different details, and a rose window set into the triangular gable. A granite plaque is inscribed in Hebrew with lines from Psalm 100: "Enter into His gates with thanksgiving and into His courts with praise." This **landmark** was built by the founding German congregation, headed by Rabbi Bernard Drachman and his father-in-law, Jonas Weil, for "harmonious combination of Orthodox Judaism and Americanism," and to protect Orthodox tradition. Its official name, meaning "Memorial of Ephraim," is a tribute to Weil's father. The synagogue community center and school, with an entry into the sanctuary, is on Third Avenue.

163 East 67th Street (between Lexington & Third Aves.) 212-737-6900

ST. JOHN THE MARTYR: 1888. Brownstone Romanesque Revival design with asymmetrical tower was built for Knox Presbyterian Church, which deserted the building because of fire damage. The Roman Catholic Czechoslovakian congregation dedicated the church in 1904 to the patron John Nepomucene. Across town would be another church to the same patron, but a Slavic congregation met there (see entry). The small, austere interior was renovated in the 1950s. A polychrome rood screen and gilded baldachin fill the chancel. See the row of angels holding the shields of eight Anglican cathedrals at roof level. Every Tuesday at 10:30 A.M. the church has a cable variety show on channel 57: *Waiting for God—Oh!*

259 East 72nd Street (between Second & Third Aves.) 212-744-4880

ST. JAMES' CHURCH: 1884. Neo-Gothic brownstone building was renovated by Ralph Adams Cram in 1922 from the original French Gothic structure designed by R. H. Robertson. Cram closed the

Lexington Avenue entry and placed a rose window and terra-cotta carv-ing of the Nativity above the new entrance on Madison Avenue. Because this Episcopal church was dedicated on Christmas Day, the carving acts as a gentle reminder that every day is Christmas in this haven. Its congregation has been in the forefront of outreach programs, with members working in shel-ters for the homeless, as men-tors in the public school sys-tem, and as volunteers in com-munity centers. Don't miss the gilded wooden reredos created

Nativity Typanum at St. James

by Cram. As you study the design with the Risen Christ in center, look for the patron James holding a pilgrim's staff and the church logo, a scal-lop shell. High above the main altar, ten stained-glass windows by the Henry Wynd Young Studio show those who defended their faith. Look for Joan of Arc, Alfred the Great, Martin of Tours, and archangels. In the south transept a life-size St. George clad in armor is sculpted in relief on the chancel wall; it commemorates over six hundred parish-ioners who served in World War II. In the north transept visit a small chapel that holds the original altar and polychrome reredos from 1884. Two Tiffany windows, also from the old building, parallel a fifteenth-century image of the Madonna and Child. Most stained-glass windows were replaced in 1924 by the Charles Connick Studio of Boston. This church was founded in 1810 as a summer chapel to escape the oppres-sive heat of Lower Manhattan. A handbell choir of children and adults rings out joyful music at Sunday services.

865 Madison Avenue (at 71st St.) 212-288-4100

MADISON AVENUE PRESBYTERIAN CHURCH: 1899.
Neo-Gothic church with a smooth corner tower was built by James E. Ware for two congregations that merged. Madison Avenue Church traces its roots to 1834, when it was known as the Church in the Swamp, near the Lower Manhattan shipyards on Avenue D and West 4th Street. Philips Church, which was on the present site, evolved

from a congregation in 1844 who built on land donated by James Lenox, a member of the congregation whose family owned the thirty-acre farm from which the area derives its name (Lenox Hill). The focus of the sanctuary, a huge Celtic cross suspended from a sea green ceiling, reminds the congregation of its Scottish roots. Be sure to see ship wheels in three corners and elegant oak screens placed over interior balconies running the length of the nave. The X-shaped carvings, representing St. Andrew's cross, were uncovered in 1999, when the interior was remodeled by Page Ayres Cowley Architects. St. Andrew was martyred on an X-shaped cross and became patron saint of Scotland when some of his relics arrived in the country. Dr. Fred Anderson, pastor, community activist, and well-known writer of hymns, composed "Surely, the Lord Is in This Place" with John Weaver, music director, to celebrate the dedication of the newly completed sanctuary on October 1, 2000. Weekly meetings of the St. Andrew's Music Society feature chamber music and keyboard recitals. Stop by the Alice Abigail Dana Chapel for a more intimate spot to reflect.

921 Madison Avenue (at 73rd St.) 212-288-8920

CHURCH OF THE RESURRECTION: 1862. English country design by Joseph Sands and James Renwick, Jr., has a distinctive steep roof and charming nave that seats about 275. It was built as the Church of the Holy Sepulchre by an Episcopal group who soon renamed it. The apse holds a sculptured stone reredos with the scene of Mary Magdalene meeting the Risen Jesus outside his tomb. The Beaux-Arts architect Cass Gilbert, Jr. (see National Museum of the American Indian) served as a vestryman here from 1919 to 1922.

115 East 74th Street (between Park & Lexington Aves.) 212-879-4320

TEMPLE ISRAEL: 1966. This modern design by Schuman & Lichtenstein is the seventh home for a German congregation founded in 1870 on 125th Street in Harlem (see Mount Olivet Baptist Church). The austere eight-story limestone building has a sanctuary that seats 1,000. A free-standing, 30-foot-high circular Ark that holds the Torah is placed on a rock from Mount Sinai. This Reform group has been a leader in defining modern American Judaism.

112 East 75th Street (between Park & Lexington Aves.) 212-249-5000

ST. JEAN BAPTISTE CHURCH: 1910. Italian Mannerist design is by Nicholas Serracino. The French Canadian Roman Catholic parish was founded in 1882 as the Shrine of St. Anne Mission Chapel by St. Vincent de Paul Church on West 23rd Street (see entry). A dance hall on 86th St. and Park Avenue was rented for services while ground was broken to build the first church on this site. The congregation soon outgrew that building, and plaques in the narthex thank parishioner Thomas Fortune Ryan for his "princely generosity" and the Reverend Arthur Letellier for masterminding the construction of the new church. The **landmark's** gray limestone facade has Corinthian columns, gallant angels, and a dome that rises thirteen stories. The interior, measuring 22,000 square feet, is filled with French stained glass by Charles Lorin, son of Nicholas Lorin, who created windows at St. Patrick's Cathedral (see Lady Chapel). The majestic main altar rises 55 feet and is a favorite spot for weddings. There is daily exposition of the Blessed Sacrament in a 6-foot monstrance (a sunburst-shaped receptacle with a small center window that holds consecrated bread, the body of Christ).

184 East 76th Street (at Lexington Ave.) 212-288-5082

HOLY TRINITY GREEK ORTHODOX CATHEDRAL: 1931. Grand Byzantine design is by Thompson, Holmes & Converse. The congregation was formed in 1892 by Greek immigrants who worshiped in several locations before purchasing in 1904 an Episcopal church that was eventually destroyed by fire. The merger of Holy Trinity Church and the Church of the Annunciation on West 54th Street allowed the purchase of the present site. In 1972 interior renovation added a marble altar and iconostatis (altar screen), Byzantine-style windows from Florence, and mosaics by Sirio Tonelli. Be sure to see the enormous marble panels inscribed with the Decalogue of Moses and the Nicene Orthodox Creed. The Chapel of St. Nicholas, named for the Greek patron of seafarers, is a quiet spot for contemplation. The cathedral is the seat of the Greek Orthodox Church in North and South America and its red-brick and limestone complex includes an office center and meeting space.

319 East 74th Street (between First & Second Aves.) 212-288-3215

ST. MONICA'S CHURCH: 1907. French Gothic design is by Schickel & Ditmars. The opening of the George Erhert Hell Gate Brewery in 1866 started major development of the village of Yorkville. The Roman Catholic parish was founded in 1879, and services were held in the present-day auditorium, which was completed in 1883. The patron Monica is the mother of St. Augustine of Hippo (354–430), author of *City of God* and *Confessions*. Be sure to see the stained-glass window that has been placed at eye level for contemplation. Ambrose, bishop of Milan, stands between the repentant son Augustine and a joyful Monica, an encounter that mothers can appreciate. A white Carrara marble altar that ascends 40 feet high holds a carved image of Monica flanked by the Archangels Gabriel and Michael. Light filters into the sanctuary from twenty-six figurative stained-glass windows commemorating biblical events. In 1954 the church was restored after fire damaged the roof and interior.

413 East 79th Street (between First & York Aves.) 212-288-6250

ZION-ST. MARK'S LUTHERAN CHURCH: 1888. This church by J. F. Mahoney was built by Beyer & Tivy of Hoboken, New Jersey for the German Evangelical Church of Yorkville. "Deutsche Evangelische Kirche von Yorkville" is carved above the entrance. The building was purchased by Zion Lutheran in 1892. St. Mark's Lutheran Church, founded in 1848 (see Community Synagogue/Max D. Raiskin Center), merged with Zion in 1940 and brought along the Black Forest altar, pulpit, and lectern now in the chancel. Bigotry toward Germans was rampant as World War II began, and church bulletins reported hard times for most families, who had members fighting on both sides. In 1990  Hurricane Hugo blew out four German stained-glass windows, but with help from the community they were restored. See *Jesus at the Stranger's Door* from the Dorcus Society for a skillful repair. This bilingual community holds services in German and English.

339 East 84th St. (between First & Second Aves.) 212-650-1648

ST. IGNATIUS LOYOLA CHURCH: 1895–1898. This Italian Renaissance **landmark** was designed by the firm of William Schickel and Isaac Ditmars for the Society of Jesus (Jesuits). The parish was founded in 1851 as the first Roman Catholic church in Yorkville and served a huge area of the East Side until St. Joseph's opened in 1873 (see entry). The foundation of a former church, named for St. Lawrence O'Toole, an Irish martyr, is still visible on the site. The limestone facade is unadorned, but the barrel-vaulted interior is lavishly decorated from a restoration in 1947. This church held the funeral for the former First Lady Jacqueline Kennedy Onassis, who was christened in the chapel of St. John the Baptist. The baptistry, separated from the sanctuary by a semicircular wrought-iron gate, is filled with mosaics illustrating John's life. Above the lavish main altar, the patron Ignatius (1491–1556), is portrayed in three Venetian mosaics. Look for him as a wounded soldier in the Battle of Pamplona in 1521. He founded the Jesuit Order (see St. Francis Xavier Church) and today the Ignatian Lay Volunteer Corps from the church share the spirit of their patron with those in need.

980 Park Avenue (at 84th St.) 212-288-3588

PARK AVENUE UNITED METHODIST CHURCH: 1927. This Gothic design is by Henry C. Pelton (see Riverside Church and Central Presbyterian Church). It is the fourth home for a congregation founded in 1837 as a local Sunday school and known also as the Yorkville and Harlem Heights Mission. The present name was adopted in 1883. An intimate interior focuses on a stone baldachin (altar canopy) with a stained-glass rose window in the chancel wall. Note the wooden pulpit, styled after an eleventh-century design from the Church of San Miniato al Monte in Florence. This serene haven is a welcoming respite from the noisy thoroughfare.

106 East 86th Street (between Lexington & Park Aves.) 212-289-6997

PARK AVENUE SYNAGOGUE (Agudat Yesharim, the Association of the Righteous): 1927. Moorish design is by Walter Schneider. In 1882 German immigrants worshiping on 86th Street merged with several groups to form this major Conservative synagogue. The sanctuary, with Moorish-style Ark and octagonal domed ceiling, seats 1,200. Works of Jewish art fill the lobby and public areas. A school extension was added in 1980 and dedicated "to the Sacred Memory of the Million Jewish Children Who Perished in the Holocaust." On the school's facade, two bronze sculptures by Nathan Rapoport echo the theme, *Tragedy and Triumph*. Dr. Janusz Korczak of Warsaw is seen protecting the orphans he cared for as they were marched to the Treblinka death camp, while another bronze portrays the Menorah being carried back to Israel by three men who rescued it from the destroyed Temple of Jerusalem. Engraved is the Hebrew word *Zakhor* (Remember). Be sure to see the American painter Adolph Gottlieb's stained-glass windows from 1954, which were moved into the school building. Abstract forms are in colors that were commanded to Moses: purple, scarlet, blue, gold, and white. Try to identify traditional emblems, biblical stories, rituals, and holidays.

50 East 87th Street (between Park & Madison Aves.) 212-369-2600

ST. JOSEPH'S CHURCH OF YORKVILLE: 1894. Romanesque Revival design by William Schickel & Co. is the second Roman Catholic church to be built on this site. The smooth limestone exterior holds a circular stained-glass window surrounded by iconography of the four Evangelists. A statue of the patron is tucked into a niche under the gable. The parish was founded in 1873 by Archbishop John McCloskey for German immigrants who were worshiping in the chapel of the nearby St. Joseph's Orphanage, which had been opened by the Church of the Most Holy Redeemer on East 3rd Street (see entry). Most of the congregation worked at two neighborhood breweries or at the Steinway Piano Factory in Queens, easily reached by a ferry from East 92nd Street. The monochromatic interior has been renovated several times but architectural details of the Romanesque style are intact. The nave is basilica shaped with arched colonnades. Six murals painted on a barrel-vaulted ceiling are attributed to an artist identified only as Schmalzl. He included the Annunciation, the Nativity, and the Finding of Jesus in the Temple. The reredos, designed by Donald Berg and installed in 1997, echoes the shape of the Romanesque arches and focuses attention on the simplicity of the apse. Stained-glass panels over the narthex doors hold a wreath of acanthus leaves, a symbol of victory over death. Mass in German is cel-

ebrated once a month. When the doors are closed, enter through the rectory.

404 East 87th Street (between First & York Aves.) 212-289-6030

CHURCH OF THE HOLY TRINITY: 1889. French Gothic **landmark**, built by Barney & Chapman, was a gift from Serena Rhinelander in memory of her father and grandfather. The family owned farmland here dating back to 1798. This Episcopal church was founded by clergy of St. James' on Madison Avenue to care for immigrants who were flooding into the Yorkville area. Don't miss the romantic bell tower, rising 150 feet and shaped like a filigree castle. The English artisan Henry Holiday designed vivid stained-glass windows showing intricate biblical scenes and armies of saints. Look above the main door to the tympanum by Karl Bitter, who sculptured the Trinity accompanied by those who made it to the heavenly kingdom. A high wrought-iron gate surrounds the chestnut-brick complex, which includes the parish house of St. Christopher.

316 East 88th Street (between First & Second Aves.) 212-289-4100

IMMANUEL LUTHERAN CHURCH: 1886. The gray stone Gothic design was built on the present site by German immigrants who listed the congregation's founding date of 1863 on the cornerstone. The 200-foot-high bell tower holds a gift of three bells from Augusta Victoria, empress of Germany (wife of the last emperor, William II). They are inscribed *Glaube* (Faith), *Hoffnung* (Hope), and *Liebe* (Charity). Side windows in the nave were all destroyed when the 86th Street corner site was blasted for the now-defunct Gimbel's East department store. They were replaced in 1978, when the Belgian sculptor Benoit Gilsoul (see Tillman Chapel), created ten glorious modern windows. Faceted chunks of colorful glass represent the seventeenth-century Christian hymn "Te Deum Laudamus" (Praise to the Lord). An oil painting, *The Transfiguration of Jesus*, is placed high on the wall of an intimate chancel filled with Black Forest wood. Look above the main entry for an old window holding Byzantine stars commonly referred to as the Star of David. Hexagrams are omens of good fortune found on many Christian churches.

122 East 88th Street (at Lexington Ave.) 212-289-8128

CHURCH OF THE HEAVENLY REST: 1926. Mayers, Murray & Philip designed the unique thirteenth-century Gothic building with a twentieth-century Art Deco limestone facade. Exterior sculptures of Moses and John the Baptist are by Lee Lawrie. The austere sandstone interior has a stone reredos with Latin cross and an adoring angel sculptured by Malvina Hoffman. Look up to the carved molding that extends around the sanctuary. Hand-carved lettering, with no spacing between words, spells out the entire seventeenth chapter of the Gospel of John. The exquisite Chapel of the Beloved Disciple (see Church of St. Thomas More) with stenciled beams is a quiet spot for meditation. This Episcopal parish, originally at 45th Street and Fifth Avenue, was founded in 1865 by Civil War veterans. Louise Whitfield Carnegie (Mrs. Andrew Carnegie), wife of the steel magnate, sold the site to the church while insisting on, but not getting, final approval of building plans. She lived across the street in what is now the Cooper-Hewitt Museum and did not want her view obstructed.

2 East 90th Street (at Fifth Ave.) 212-289-3400

BRICK PRESBYTERIAN CHURCH: 1938. This red-brick and limestone Georgian design by Adams and Woodbridge was constructed by York and Sawyers. The spire holds a bell and weather vane from 1767, when Brick served as a chapel on Spring Street for the First Presbyterian Church. To distinguish between the two buildings, worshipers would say, "Let us go to the brick church." Hence its name. Pace University is now on that site. Brick merged with Park Avenue Presbyterian and built this third church, which seats 800. Louise Whitfield Carnegie, wife of Andrew, was an active and generous member. So was Thomas Watson, founder of IBM, who is remembered with a meeting space designated Watson Hall. Don't miss the sanctuary's nineteen chandeliers—blue, coral, and gold-leaf metal tiers of "petal-carved shells" (the same motif runs along the ceiling). A wrought-iron pulpit and chancel rail, designed by Samuel Yellin, look like black lace. Stop by the narrow, walnut-paneled chapel completed in 1950. Its novel seating plan holds only 64 worshipers and was inspired by the Virginia Chamber of Deputies in Colonial Williamsburg. Colorful flags and inlaid crests on the floor represent countries where the Reformed Presbyterian Church took hold. Three windows from the family of Mary French are placed in rounded bays and add delicate beauty to the small space. Be sure to read the church reformers' names engraved in the chancel: Augustine, John Calvin, John Knox, Columba, Bernard of Clairvaux, and Jerome. On the back wall another list recognizes, among others, Martin Luther, Roger Williams, Abraham Lincoln, and Woodrow Wilson, an active layman who served as twenty-eighth president of the United States. Enter through the parish house on 92nd Street.

1140 Park Avenue (at 91st St.) 212-289-4400

ST. NICHOLAS RUSSIAN ORTHODOX CATHEDRAL:

1902. Designed by the architect John Bergesen, this cathedral echoes a seventeenth-century Baroque church in Moscow. In 1895 the congregation, led by the Reverend Alexander Hotovitsky, began to worship at 19th Street and Second Avenue in a private home. This red-brick and terra-cotta **landmark**, which has five cupolas, each topped with a gilded cross, was funded by Emperor Nicholas II and Russian citizens and became the seat of the diocese in 1905. It was the first Orthodox church built in New York City. Following the Bolshevik Revolution in 1917, the cathedral was taken over by clergy of the "living church" or "renovationists," who were controlled by the Soviet Communist government. The founding congregation, who recognized the Patriarch of Moscow and his Metropolitan Council, rejected the civil government. They would lose St. Nicholas from 1926 to 1952, when the U.S. Supreme Court ruled that the cathedral belonged to the Russian Orthodox Church and their leaders in America (see Russian Orthodox Cathedral of the Holy Virgin Protection). In the semicircular sanctuary, which holds 900 worshipers, be sure to see the cross that was rescued from the Russian battleship *Retvizan* as it sank in a Japanese attack on Port Arthur in 1904. The cross was donated by Captain M. E. Osipov in memory of his sailors who were among the first parishioners of St. Nicholas. Port Arthur was named for the Russian Ambassador to Washington, Count Arthur Paul Cassini who was instrumental in the building of the cathedral and who signed the Sino-Japanese Peace Treaty. His portrait hangs in the home of his grandson, the international designer Oleg Cassini.

15 East 97th Street (between Fifth & Madison Aves.) 212-289-1915

UPPER MANHATTAN AND HARLEM

❖ ❖ ❖ ❖

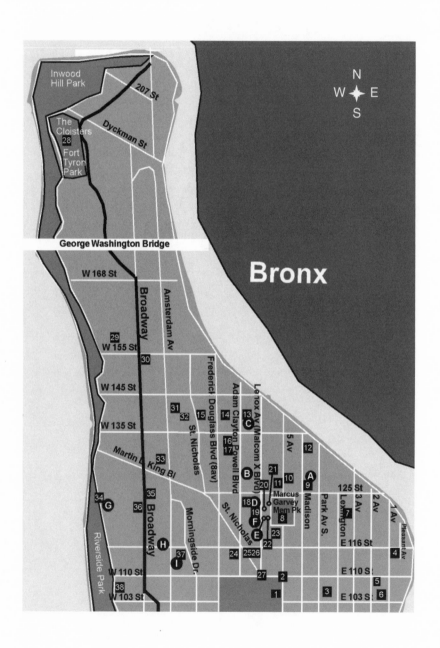

UPPER MANHATTAN & HARLEM

FEATURES:

A. *All Saints Church*
B. *Metropolitan Baptist Church*
C. *Mother AME Zion Church*
D. *Ephesus Seventh Day Adventist Church*
E. *St. Martin's Episcopal Church*
F. *Mount Olivet Baptist Church*
G. *Riverside Church*
H. *St. Paul's Chapel at Columbia Univ.*
I. *Cathedral of St. John the Divine*

BY THE WAY:

1. Central Park Conservatory Garden
2. Duke Ellington Memorial
3. St. Cecilia's Church
4. Our Lady of Mt. Carmel
5. St. Ann's Church
6. St. Lucy's Church
7. Elmendorf Reformed Church
8. Marcus Garvey Park
9. Metropolitan United Methodist Church
10. *St Andrew's Episcopal Church*
11. *Mt. Moriah Baptist Church*
12. *Abraham Lincoln*
13. *Abyssinian Baptist Church*

14. Victory Tabernacle Church
15. St. Mark's United Methodist Church
16. St. Philip's Church
17. St. Aloysius' Church
18. Greater Metropolitan Baptist Church
19. Ebenezer Gospel Tabernacle
20. Bethelite Community Church
21. Ethiopian Hebrew Congregation
22. Mt. Morris Church
23. Emanuel AME Church
24. First Corinthian Baptist Church
25. Memorial Baptist Church
26. Canaan Baptist Church
27. Malcolm X Plaza
28. The Cloisters
29. Our Lady of Esperanza Church
30. Church of the Intercession
31. Our Lady of Lourdes Church
32. St Luke's Church
33. St. Mary's Church-Manhattanville
34. Grant's Tomb
35. Jewish Theological Seminary
36. James Memorial Chapel
37. Eglise de Notre Dame
38. N. Y. Buddhist Church

REMEMBER AS YOU TOUR:

Malcom X Boulevard is the same as Lenox Avenue & Sixth Avenue.
Adam Clayton Powell Boulevard is the same as Seventh Avenue.
Frederick Douglass Boulevard is the same as Eighth Avenue.
Martin Luther King Boulevard is the same as 125th Street.

ALL SAINTS' CHURCH

JAMES RENWICK, JR.'S, LAST MASTERPIECE

A pair of stars prominently carved on the twin towers of this Roman Catholic church have prompted visitors to ask the clergy if this haven had once been a synagogue. The motif dates to the Byzantine era, when celestial symbols were believed to be marks of rank and omens of destiny. Historians report that Polish Jews adopted the hexagram in the early 1800s as a sign of their faith, naming it the Star of David for the biblical king. The architect James Renwick, Jr., like artisans of ancient Byzantium, may have wanted a emblem of good fortune on the French Gothic facade of All Saints', his last great masterpiece, for it would take ten years to build.

HISTORY

Harlem was sparsely settled in 1879 when a group of Irish immigrants met at 129th Street and Third Avenue in a city-owned barn to solemnize the founding of their new parish. They were led by the Reverend James Power (1849-1926), who named the congregation after his boyhood parish. In 1883 the group laid a cornerstone, which cannot be located, on the present site and three years later opened a basement church. After years of financial delays the upper church was dedicated on December 10, 1893, by Archbishop Michael Corrigan. In the early 1900s Father Power, a firm believer in education, opened a primary school for boys and girls, a kindergarten and day nursery for children of working mothers, a large high school, and a settlement house on 125th Street for children's recreation. He enlisted the help of the Christian Brothers of Ireland, who arrived in 1906 to teach the boys, and the Sisters of Charity from Baltimore as teachers for the girls (see Shrine of St. Elizabeth Ann Seton).

While the parish has seen many demographic transformations since the beginning of the twentieth century, All Saints remains a source of strength in its neighborhood. The primary school is still open, a living testament to Father Power, who served the parish for over forty-five years until his death. Today parishioners are active in neighborhood groups, working on health initiatives and programs on behalf of incarcerated mothers.

ARCHITECTURE

James Renwick, Jr. (1818–1895), with his nephew William of the firm Renwick, Aspinwall & Russell, designed All Saints with the same architectural elegance bestowed on St. Patrick's Cathedral and Grace Church (see entries). The exterior tan-colored bricks hold inlays

of beige accents and lots of terra-cotta trim. The central gable is dominated by a glorious rose window whose shape is echoed in a charming series of small clerestory windows. Niches running across the facade and under the rose window were originally designed to hold statues of saints the church honored, but they remain empty. Decorative spires on the peaked roofs, which proclaim the structure's French Gothic heritage, have lost much elegant trim.

Unobstructed light from two tiers of stained-glass windows pours into the huge cruciform interior with fan-vaulted ceiling and a wide open view to the hand-carved high altar. Traditional murals unveiled in 1917 surround the apse and tell of the life and Passion of Jesus. Overhead is a Bernini-like icon of Jesus on the cross accompanied by a pair of angels. The golden sculpture evokes the emotion of Jesus' death and the Christian message that he died to give his believers life.

Six tall Victorian candelabra, with an angel at each base, add a soft glow to the apse. The altar and the many statues in the chancel were all designed by V. A. Fucigna, who was listed among those who attended the dedication ceremony.

A free-standing oak altar was crafted in 1990 by William Steele, parishioner and retired carpenter. He used wood from sixteen countries to create an inlaid panel of the Last Supper. Nearby stands "Big Pole," similar to a totem pole, which was a gift to the congregation from visiting Asmat people of Indonesia. Once a month members of the Ibos, a tribe from Nigeria, hold a spectacular Sunday service—all arrive in gorgeous native dress.

Before leaving, rest in one of the handsome mahogany pews that together can seat more than 1,500. They are said to have been hand-carved in Ireland's County Cork. Look closely at the mahogany pulpit covered with intricate carvings of the Apostles and Evangelists, all identified by name. Also take time to climb to the loft for a wide-angle visual treat. See the innovative polygonal ends of the transepts and the original stenciled walls that surround the choir.

ADDRESS: *47 East 129th Street (between Madison & Park Aves.)*
New York, NY 10035
PHONE: *212-534-3535*
HOURS: *Daily: 9:00 A.M.–4:00 P.M. Enter through the office*

METROPOLITAN BAPTIST CHURCH

FIRST AFRICAN AMERICAN CHURCH IN HARLEM

Unlike established churches that moved to Harlem from locations in Lower Manhattan, Metropolitan Baptist was always part of this neighborhood. It was formed in 1912 by the merger of two local churches: Mercy Seat Baptist Church and Zion Baptist Church.

HISTORY

In the early 1900s Harlem underwent a dramatic change as the bottom fell out of the real estate market. Speculators had built town houses and apartments that they could not rent. The housing glut coincided with the construction of Penn Station, which left black families from the Tenderloin District around 34th Street dispossessed. They streamed uptown to Harlem.

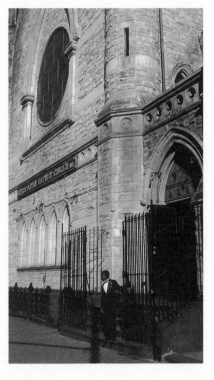

Metropolitan Baptist's congregation worshiped in three Harlem locations as its membership grew. By 1914 fifty thousand people had moved to the neighborhood, and the church became a stable institution. To accommodate its growth Metropolitan purchased New York Presbyterian Church, its fourth and final home.

Construction of the present building was started in 1884 by a congregation of Scotch-Irish immigrants living in the then-fashionable suburb. Completion took six years, probably because of financial restraints. The Presbyterians remained until 1918, when the building was sold to Metropolitan, led by the Reverend Dr. W. W. Brown, a powerful preacher and visionary leader. By 1930 the church had 5,500 members and a Sunday school for 1,000 children.

James McBride, author of *The Color of Water*, writes affectionately of his parents' membership in this church in the early 1940s. Every Sunday the Reverend Abner Brown (son of Dr. Brown) attracted huge crowds. McBride remembers, "That man was the finest preacher I've ever heard to this day. He could make a frog stand up straight and get happy with Jesus. . . . He brought God into your everyday life in a way that made you think heaven was right next door. Harlem loved him. . . . [My father] was a deacon and he sang in the church choir. And it was a mighty, mighty choir, too. What a time it was." The church, still well-known for its inspiring choir, is often visited on Sundays by bus-loads of European and Asian tourists.

ARCHITECTURE

John Rochester Thomas (1848–1901), the architect most famous for designing the Surrogate's Court on Chambers Street in Lower Manhattan, constructed the church's first section from 1884 through 1885. It faces West 128th Street. The rough-faced limestone structure blended Gothic and Romanesque styles and held a small chapel used as a lecture room. The main auditorium structure was planned for a later date, but by then Thomas had moved on. From 1889 through 1890, Richard R. Davis, a Harlem architect, designed the second section: the Seventh Avenue facade and northern area of church. Davis used many of Thomas's details but the designs of both architects were merged skillfully. Romanesque features, using squat columns and round towers, combine with Gothic pointed arches and a single flying buttress. The 128th Street facade, two and a half stories high, is dominated by a huge slate roof shaped as a partial cone. Its main gable is distinguished by a rose window flanked by small granite columns and placed over five Gothic windows. The west side of the church uses these same elements.

Architectural experts say that Davis appears to have plagiarized his design from the nearby Reformed Low Dutch Church, on Lenox Avenue and West 123rd Street, which was designed by Thomas in 1885. Nevertheless, Davis was so proud of his creation that he claimed the entire building as his own, ignoring John Thomas's contribution (see Ephesus Seventh-Day Adventist Church). It is to the congregation's credit that the church's handsome exterior remains little changed on its corner site.

Entering, the visitor is reminded of the many years this church has been in the community. Low ceilings, narrow passageways, and old stained-glass transoms lead into the main auditorium. The original lecture room, which is used for smaller meetings, has messages in stained glass high on its wood-paneled walls: "Search the Scriptures" is one suggestion left by the original congregation. The smooth cream-colored walls of the main sanctuary hold many colorful windows. Stop and rest in the arc-shaped pews and, if you're fortunate, you might hear one of the fine choirs practicing.

ADDRESS: *151 West 128th Street (at Adam Clayton Powell, Jr., Blvd.) New York, NY 10027*
PHONE: *212-663-8990*
HOURS: *Tues.–Fri.: 10:00 A.M.–3:00 P.M. Enter through 128th Street office Sun.: 10:00 A.M.–3:00 P.M. Closed Sat. & Mon.*
LANDMARK DESIGNATION

MOTHER AFRICAN METHODIST EPISCOPAL (AME) ZION CHURCH

NEW YORK STATE'S OLDEST AFRICAN AMERICAN CHURCH

The congregation of New York State's oldest African American church vigorously promotes "the freedom tradition" in the spirit of its eighteenth-century founders. This house of God is known far and wide for its social programs and as a champion of civil rights.

HISTORY

In 1796 a handful of black members of the predominantly white John Street Methodist Church (see entry) broke away to form their own house of worship, naming it the African Chapel, and then Zion, the biblical designation of the church of God. The dissidents were led by James Varick, who decreed that there was to be no distinction of

race, color, or economic condition in the new church. Reformers established their church on Leonard Street and in 1822 appointed Varick
the first bishop. A chapel, called Little Zion, was opened in 1822 to
serve black workers in the farm community of Harlem. The founding
church on Leonard Street became known as Mother Zion.

As organizer of the African Methodist Episcopal Zion Conference
of Churches in 1820, Mother Zion nurtured the association as it spread
throughout the United States and Canada. The conference used many
of its churches as stations on the Underground Railroad, giving safe
passage to slaves escaping to freedom. Sojourner Truth, born a slave,
spoke often at the Leonard Street church. Harriet Tubman and
Frederick Douglass, leading abolitionists, were both members of the
Zion Conference. Douglass, who arrived in New York City as a fugi-
tive slave in 1838, was sheltered near the church by David Ruggles,
who published the black magazine *Mirror of Liberty*.

Mother Zion's strong leadership continued into the twentieth century with a civil rights crusade led by its pastor the Reverend Dr.
Benjamin C. Robeson, brother of Paul Robeson, famed singer and actor.
He was joined in the pulpit frequently by his brother in espousing the
need for racial equality in America. Dr. Robeson's preaching attracted
Langston Hughes, novelist and poet; the educator W. E. B. Du Bois, a
founder of the National Association for the Advancement of Colored
People in 1910; the opera contralto Marian Anderson; and the world
heavyweight boxing champion Joe Louis. Paul Robeson, whose last
American concert was held at the church in 1958, also played an
important part in the Harlem Renaissance, a literary and artistic movement that drew black artists from many states to New York City.
Robeson, greatly loved by the community, died in 1976, and huge numbers attended his funeral at Mother Zion.

An interesting side story: A pocket in Central Park known as
Seneca Village, alongside the Great Lawn at West 85th Street, was
discovered to have been the neighborhood of freed slaves and European
immigrants. The area held schools, homes, and three churches, each
with a graveyard. One church was identified as Mother Zion, which
is believed to have held services there from 1853 to 1856. The Zion
congregation also owned one of the graveyards, which had been used
by its downtown members since 1825. In the development of Central

Park, city officials evicted Seneca Village residents and destroyed all property, including the graveyards. Visit the New-York Historical Society to see a collection of newspaper accounts and petitions from residents who protested the action. The society is anxious to locate families whose ancestors were part of the village.

In 1972 the congregation built the James Varick Community Center behind the church. It is here that Mother Zion, led by Dr. Alvin T. Durant, runs its outreach programs, stating that they are "continuing in the tradition of the founding fathers who sought to address not only the spiritual needs of their members, but their temporal needs as well."

ARCHITECTURE

George Washington Foster, Jr. (1866–1923), one of the first black architects registered in the United States, died shortly after he completed his Neo-Gothic plan, never seeing the impressive Mother Zion Church, which was built between 1923 and 1925 at its sixth location. The exterior of the symmetrically designed building is made of rough gray stone blocks trimmed in white terra cotta and set above a smooth granite base. The wide central gable is dominated by a stained-glass window filled with ornate tracery. The triple-arched portico, with bright red doors, takes up most of the 95-foot-wide lot.

As you enter the narthex, the Zion legacy is very much in evidence. Be sure to see a charming window holding a stained-glass image of the first church, occupied from 1800 to 1864, on Leonard Street. On one wall is a marble plaque commemorating the first Board of Trustees: James Varick along with Peter Williams, Francis Jacobs, George Collins, George E. Moore, Thomas Cook, David Bias, Thomas Sipkins, George White, and William Brown. Another plaque details the founders of the AME Zion Conference.

The sanctuary layout is a popular style from the mid-nineteenth century—the auditorium plan, in which seats are arranged in arcs, as in a theater. The pulpit is raised on a platform to indicate the importance of the pastor's sermons. The shallow space has a central aisle and two side aisles, with a curving balcony whose back wall holds a huge stained-glass window of the Nativity. There is seating for over 1,000 members. The walls of the sanctuary hold portraits of some of the twenty-eight pastors who have guided this flock through the years. Bishop James Varick, who died in 1827, is buried in an open crypt below the sanctuary. Stop by for a visit and see a cameo painting of the Zion leader.

ADDRESS: *146–148 West 137th Street (between Adam Clayton Powell, Jr., & Malcolm X Blvds.), New York, NY 10030*

PHONE: 212-234-1545

HOURS: *Daily: 9:00 A.M.–4:00 P.M. Enter through the Varick Center on West 136th St.*

LANDMARK DESIGNATION

EPHESUS SEVENTH-DAY ADVENTIST CHURCH

"AND GOD BLESSED THE SEVENTH DAY"

A spirit of community service touches every aspect of this Harlem church. The atmosphere of "good neighbor" springs from a time in the late nineteenth century when the building housed the Dutch Reformed congregation that had established the Pleasant Sunday Afternoon Club. Its 300 members were trained for community service and noted for good deeds. The Ephesus congregation proudly carries on this tradition. Incidentally, Seventh-Day Adventists celebrate their Sabbath on Saturday, which they count as the seventh day of Creation. Bible School also meets on the Sabbath. Its tradition springs from a Bible school that was organized in 1739 by Ludwig Hacker for German immigrants in Ephrata, Pennsylvania.

HISTORY

This church was built in 1885 for the Reformed Low Dutch Church of Harlem, which had been organized in 1660 by the largest landowner in the community, Captain Johannes Benson. The congregation outgrew the First Reformed Church, which they had built in 1873, but kept the parish house at 121st Street and Third Avenue as Elmendorf Reformed Church. It is still there.

The present building was constructed as the Second Reformed Church but formally designated Collegiate Reformed Church of Harlem. As Harlem's demographics changed, the sect moved downtown to 89th Street (see Church of St. Thomas More) and leased the Second Reformed Church to Ephesus Seventh-Day Adventist in 1930. The

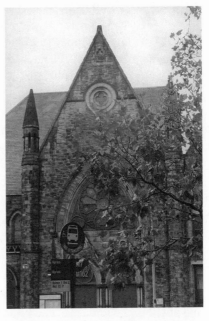

Ephesus group is the result of a recent merger between two of New York City's oldest black Adventist assemblies. The name Ephesus, that of an ancient city in western Turkey, is from the New Testament letters of Paul to the Ephesians. The congregation purchased this building in 1939.

The internationally famous Boys Choir of Harlem was founded in this church in 1968 by Walter Trumbull, who used music as a tool for children's social development. The independent choir, with the addition of a girls' section in 1986, now occupies its own building. In keeping with a long tradition of joyful music, Ephesus choral groups begin with four-year-old children and encompass all age-groups. On the Sabbath the choral group occupies a prominent position in the balcony above the pastor's podium and fulfills its traditional role—singing the good news of the Bible.

A fire destroyed the church's interior in 1969. A dramatic 20-foot spire that could be seen for miles had to be removed from the tower. The rest of the exterior, but little of the original stained glass, survived. The congregation worked for nine years to restore the sanctuary at a cost of several million dollars, while St. Andrew's Episcopal

Church invited them to share its space until Ephesus could return to its historic home.

ARCHITECTURE

John Rochester Thomas, a prominent architect (see Metropolitan Baptist Church), built this Neo-Gothic church in 1885 and the church hall in 1894. The facade is beige Ohio sandstone with charming carved gargoyles, chubby angels, and enhanced columns. A head of a man with a mustache is placed between a double set of red wooden doors at the main entrance. Could it be the architect leaving his image behind, as the medieval church builders did? Thomas designed more than 150 churches before he died at the age of fifty-three.

The restored interior uses the original layout. Its main focus is the wood-paneled central stage, holding a choir loft, pulpit, chairs for the elders, and a recessed baptistry. Some parishioners miss the slanted floor of the former sanctuary, which afforded better views in the arc-shaped auditorium. Soft light filters in through new multicolored stained-glass windows in the balcony. Two large windows in the sanctuary hold the only figurative art left by the Dutch congregation: Jesus being baptized by John, and Jesus as the Good Shepherd.

Tucked behind the main sanctuary is an intimate chapel for the Bible school. This modern space is filled with blond wood and cream walls in an octagonal layout. Here study groups keep their historic sanctuary alive with energy, music, and song.

ADDRESS: *267 Lenox Avenue (Malcolm X Blvd.) at 123rd St.*
  New York, NY 10027
PHONE: *212-662-5536*
HOURS: *Daily: 9:00 A.M.–5:00 P.M. Enter through 123rd Street office*
  Saturday Sabbath Services at 11:00 A.M.

ST. MARTIN'S EPISCOPAL CHURCH

"A SINGING TOWER"

L ocated in Mount Morris Park Historic District, St. Martin's is neighbor to scores of handsome brownstone residences—remnants of the days when Harlem was home to a wealthy and powerful elite. While the history of the area is fascinating, so is the story of St. Martin's bells. With limited financial means a spirited congregation donated to the church an outstanding carillon, affectionately called a singing tower, which became the neighborhood symbol of hope and joy. It was blessed by the Reverend John Howard Johnson on December 18, 1949. An engraving unseen by the public on the carillon's large bell depicts St. Martin sharing his cloak with a suffering stranger. This act of charity fittingly represented a congregation who knew that the only poor person was one who was poor in spirit.

HISTORY

Plans in 1878 for an East Side subway line to Harlem resulted in the speculative building of elegant row houses and apartment buildings throughout this five-square-mile area. Churches were also built as part of the real estate boom. Holy Trinity Episcopal Church, built by a congregation of English, Irish, and German immigrants, was completed in 1888. It was designated St. Martin's in 1925, and the park was renamed Marcus Garvey Park in 1973.

The interior of St. Martin's was twice ravaged by fire, in 1925 and 1939, and rebuilt both times. Pastor John Howard Johnson (1897–1995), who had led the congregation since 1928, was installed as the first rector when St. Martin's was officially incorporated as an independent parish in 1940. A socially conscious clergyman, Mr. Johnson was a leader of the Citizens League for Fair Play, the first group to picket the 125th Street business area in 1933 in an effort to persuade white merchants to employ black workers. Johnson was a trustee of the National Negro Baseball League and the New York Public Library, and a chaplain appointed by Mayor Fiorello La Guardia to the New York City Police Department. Look for a memorial to the left of the high altar saluting two Harlem police officers, John Holt and Emmett Cassidy, who were killed in the line of duty. To the right is a fitting memorial to Reverend Johnson.

Record-breaking crowds turned out at St. Martin's whenever royalty paid a call. Queen Juliana of the Netherlands came in 1952 to hear the carillon made by her countrymen; Queen Mother Elizabeth of Britain visited in 1954 on her way to worship at the Cathedral of St. John the Divine. The Reverend David Johnson, son of John Howard Johnson, was installed in 1961 as the second rector of St. Martin's. He persevered in the mission of social advocacy established by his father, and passed the leadership of the congregation to his brother, the Reverend Johan Johnson, in 1998. The pastor also cares for and shares activities with St. Luke's Church on Convent Avenue (see entry).

ARCHITECTURE

The architect William A. Potter used rough, rock-faced sandstone blocks on the exterior of the church and parish house to create a Romanesque Revival complex filled with gables, spires, and the famous ninety-foot tower. The church tower is capped with a copper-covered steeple that holds forty-two bronze bells. The carillon, recognized as one of the finest in the city, has a range of three and a half octaves, from low C to high G. It was made by the van Bergen foundry in the Netherlands and weighs more than 9 tons.

The cream-colored interior of St. Martin's is a cruciform with two transept galleries. Intimate chapels are placed along the side walls, while a 500-pound limewood cross, made in England, hangs over the chancel's entrance. Look in the south transept for St. Martin's Chapel. It holds the first altar used by the congregation in 1928. A bronze pulpit in the sanctuary was a gift from the Church of the Heavenly Rest (see entry) when it moved to Fifth Avenue and 90th Street. An inscription notes that it was made in 1888.

Most impressive is St. Martin's artwork, a reminder of the important role the Christian Church played in the arts. Mosaic copies of well-known masterpieces fill the sanctuary. Works of Raphael, Michelangelo, Fra Lippi, Botticelli, and El Greco are splendidly reproduced by Mellini of Florence. They were installed from 1956 through 1961. Especially beautiful is the mosaic of the patron Martin (316-397), a convert to Christianity who evangelized peasants, founded a seminary, and was made bishop of the French city of Tours. His mosaic pays homage to the original rendering by the Spanish artist José Ribera. St. Martin is attired in a vivid bishop's cloak and seems to be blessing all who pass by. An insert on his cloak recalls the story of an earlier cloak that he shared with a poor stranger.

ADDRESS: *230 Lenox Avenue at 122nd St. (Malcolm X Blvd.)*
   New York, NY 10027
PHONE: *212-534-4531*
HOURS: *Mon.–Thurs.: 10:00 A.M.–3:00 P.M. Enter through rectory on*
   122nd St.; Sun: 8:00 A.M.–2:00 P.M. Closed Fri. and Sat.
LANDMARK DESIGNATION

MOUNT OLIVET
BAPTIST CHURCH

CLASSIC SANCTUARY DEDICATED TO GOOD WORKS

This unique building, standing majestically on a corner lot and emblazoned with a festive banner reading, "Bring your family back to God," is a testimony to Harlem's cultural treasures and spiritual life. On Mount Olivet's facade two icons represent congregations that worshiped in its sanctuary: the Star of David, symbol of Judaism, and a Cross, symbol of the religion that was built upon Judaism, Christianity.

HISTORY

In 1876 twenty-one black Baptists calling themselves Gethsemane Mission began holding meetings at 112 West 26th Street. Two years later members officially organized in the nearby Fifth Avenue Baptist Church and named themselves after Jerusalem's Mount of Olives, site of the agony of Jesus in the Garden of Gethsemane. As Mount Olivet's congregation continued to increase, parishioners moved in succession to three midtown Manhattan spaces before purchasing the present site in 1924. Like those of other black churches, Mount Olivet's move uptown paralleled the relocation of its members to Harlem, where the overbuilt housing market was opening up to black families.

This building had been erected in 1907 by Temple Israel, a synagogue founded in 1870 as Congregation Yod b'Yod (Hand in Hand) above a print shop on 125th Street. German Jewish families had moved into nearby brownstones formerly occupied by English and Irish tenants. The congregation relocated downtown in 1920 (see Temple Israel) but not before the synagogue evolved from traditional Jewish practices to progressive Judaism. The First Church of the Seventh-Day Adventists used the Harlem building for three years until Mount Olivet took possession.

The Reverend Charles Walker, an early activist and pastor of a former Mount Olivet location on 53rd Street and Seventh Avenue, helped form the first black YMCA in 1900 and the first black militia in New York State, which marched in the funeral procession for President Ulysses S. Grant. The YMCA branch, which followed the northward migration in 1919, is currently named for Jackie Robinson, the Brooklyn Dodgers player who broke the color barrier in major league baseball. The Y was an important meeting place for black intellectuals, writers, and artists who were responsible for the flourishing cultural life of the Harlem Renaissance.

Between 1925 and 1929 the Harlem Renaissance was in full swing, led by Countee Cullen (1903–1946), poet and novelist who grew up in the community (the local branch of the New York Public Library is named for him). Artists were pouring into Harlem from all over America and participating in the life of its mainstays, the church-es. Zora Neale Hurston, who came from Florida, dedicated a copy of her first novel, *Jonah's Gourd Vine*, to "the first and only real Negro poets in America—the preachers, who bring barbaric splendor of word and song into the very camp of the mockers. Go Gator, and muddy the water."

For years as the population swelled, Harlem developed a vibrant economy, including prosperous banks and scores of small businesses. But the Great Depression took a devastating toll on the area, and it never fully recovered.

ARCHITECTURE

This neoclassical structure, completed in 1907, was designed by Arnold Brunner, well-known for both his ecclesiastical buildings and the original buildings of Mount Sinai Medical Center on upper Fifth Avenue. The granite temple sits atop a horizontal stairway with four Corinthian columns dominating the entrance. Three huge stained-glass windows are placed above the triple opening of the portal.

Eight pairs of round arch windows surround the sanctuary and enhance the classical design of the interior. The upper wall of the chan-cel is graced by white marble pillars, while the lower portion holds an Ark with gilded doors. The white marble baptistry, a sacred location for the Baptist church, is placed within the Ark, which once held sacred Torahs. Lions of Judah still stand guard on either side.

Mount Olivet holds other symbols of the former Temple Israel. Look for the Star of David enshrined in the top portion of the sanctuary's jewel-toned windows and cast in green metal on the exterior.

Don't miss a stained-glass skylight set like a jewel in the center of the blue-toned ceiling—a memento of a temple once illuminated by gas light. The decorative-faced gallery, supporting original brass candelabra, encircles apricot-colored walls.

Mount Olivet is a peaceful house of God that has comforted many people. It sponsors a food pantry, clothing distribution program, and senior citizen groups.

ADDRESS: *201 Lenox Avenue (Malcolm X Blvd. at 120th St.)*
  New York, NY 10027
PHONE: *212-666-6890/ 212-864-1155*
HOURS: *Mon.–Fri.: 10:00 A.M.–7:00 P.M. Sat.: 10:00 A.M.–4:00 P.M.*
  Sun.: 8:00 A.M.–2:00 P.M. Enter through office

RIVERSIDE CHURCH

SACRED HOUSE THAT ROCKEFELLER BUILT

This interdenominational church features one of New York City's most spectacular treasures: a tower, rising to almost 400 feet, whose top six stories are filled with a carillon of seventy-four bronze bells. They weigh more than 100 tons. Since the bell tower also contains a winding staircase leading to an observation platform, visitors can survey a gorgeous panorama of New York City from this lofty perch—but it is not for the fainthearted.

HISTORY

Riverside Church, financed by John D. Rockefeller, Jr. (1874–1960), from the huge oil fortune amassed by his father, was completed in 1930 and became known as the Protestant Cathedral for the many faiths represented at its services. The south wing, dedicated to Dr. Martin Luther King, Jr., was opened in 1955 to support the church's expanding community services. Riverside had humble beginnings, dating back to a Baptist congregation in 1841 on Norfolk Street in Lower Manhattan, then to the Fifth Avenue Baptist Church from 1860. In 1921 the congregation relocated to Park Avenue and 64th Street (see Central Presbyterian Church) but outgrew that space.

The Resurrection Angel at Riverside Church

Rockefeller purchased the present site in spacious Morningside Heights and built Riverside in a neighborhood that includes Columbia University, Grant's Tomb, and Union Theological Seminary.

The Reverend Harry Emerson Fosdick (1878–1969), controversial and influential clergyman, was the founding minister. He was famous for his forceful sermons, which were broadcast nationwide. Mr. Fosdick challenged millions with his liberal view of racial and economic justice, and his calls for world peace. He was also a professor at Union Theological Seminary. But in 1922 his much publicized sermon "Shall the Fundamentalists Win?" led the First Presbyterian Church, where he was preaching, to expel him for heresy. Rockefeller, one of Fosdick's many adherents, took up his cause and offered him the pulpit of Park Avenue Baptist Church. As his popularity grew and the church became too congested, the charismatic minister was given Riverside as his permanent pulpit.

Today Riverside's congregation hails from more than forty national, ethnic, cultural, and denominational backgrounds, and the church has continued to act as a safe haven for all of them. Here on April 4, 1967, Dr. Martin Luther King, Jr., delivered his famous sermon "Beyond Vietnam," in which he questioned why black men could serve in the United States military and be denied basic rights when they returned to civilian life. He was assassinated exactly one year later.

Stop by the bookstore for a copy of the church's history with details of its artifacts, and browse through it while relaxing downstairs at the Riverside Café.

ARCHITECTURE

This steel-frame Gothic building by the architect Henry C. Pelton in association with Allen & Collens is modeled after the thirteenth-century cathedral at Chartres. The main sanctuary, 215 feet long and 89 feet wide, soars to 100 feet. Beautiful artifacts, too numerous to count, can be seen throughout the building. The clerestory level of the nave is filled with images of saints and Bible personalities in French stained glass; they are duplicates of windows at Chartres. The lower aisle windows salute contemporary musicians, scholars, reformers, and builders.

Highlighting the chancel, which holds the altar, is a fascinating stone screen. It identifies seventy figures who have made outstanding contributions to society in both ancient and modern times. Remembered are teachers (Socrates, Erasmus, Thomas Aquinas); artists (Michelangelo, John Milton, J. S. Bach); healers (Hippocrates, Louis Pasteur, Joseph Lister); humanitarians (Booker T. Washington, Abraham Lincoln, Florence Nightingale); reformers (John Calvin, John Wesley, Martin Luther); missionaries (David Livingstone, John Eliot, William Carey); and, at each center, Jesus, who personified every role. As you leave the nave, look up to the choir loft for the 20-foot gilded mold of *Christ in Majesty* by Sir Jacob Epstein. The original cast is at Llandaff Cathedral in Wales. The mold is placed above *Trompeta Majestatis* (The Majestic Trumpets), a wooden sculpture that seems to be resounding in tribute to Epstein's ascending Christ.

Outside the main sanctuary is Gethsemane Chapel, specially built to hold the Heinrich Hoffman painting *Christ in Gethsemane*. The picture is overwhelming in this tiny space. Be sure to see the secluded Christ Chapel, off the narthex, which holds sixteenth-century Flemish stained-glass windows. Designed in eleventh-century Romanesque style, the chapel has an exquisite rose window with a Paschal Lamb and symbols of the Apostles.

But there is no question about it, the dominant feature of Riverside is the twenty-four-floor tower. It rises between the nave and the south wing, built with some of the heaviest steel columns and beams ever used in a skyscraper. At the tower's west base is the main entrance, elaborately decorated like the portals of Chartres Cathedral. Be sure to see the Resurrection Angel, poised on the nave's vaulted roof with trumpet in hand, joyfully accompanying the carillon's music.

THE LAURA SPELMAN ROCKEFELLER CARILLON

Named in honor of Laura Spelman Rockefeller (1839–1915), mother of John Jr., the carillon is remarkable for its 20-ton bourdon, the largest and heaviest tuned carillon bell ever cast. It sounds on the hour every day of the year, and the drum mechanism automatically plays the "Parsifal Quarters" from Richard Wagner's opera *Parsifal*. The carillon was originally installed in 1925 at the Park Avenue Baptist Church.

Back then it had fifty-three bells and a bourdon of 10 tons. When the congregation moved to Riverside, the carillon was dramatically enlarged by its originators, Gillett & Johnston Foundry of England, to become the first carillon to surpass five octaves. In 1956 the upper range of bells was replaced by the van Bergen Foundry of Holland. Enjoy the free concert —thanks to Mr. Rockefeller—while sitting in nearby Riverside Park.

ADDRESS: 490 *Riverside Drive (at 122nd St.), New York, NY 10027*
PHONE: 212-870-6700
HOURS: Daily: 9:00 A.M.–4:00 P.M.
CARILLON CONCERTS: *Sun.:*—10:30 A.M., 12:30 P.M., *and* 2:30 P.M.
WEB SITE: *www.theriversidechurchny.org*
LANDMARK DESIGNATION

ST. PAUL'S CHAPEL

AT COLUMBIA UNIVERSITY
WITNESS TO STUDENT LIFE

Hundreds of thousands of students have walked through the portico of this interdenominational chapel, which bears the words "Pro Ecclesia Dei" (For the Assembly of God). The university's motto—"In Lumine Tuo Videbimus Lumen" (In Thy Light, We See Light)—is also inscribed under the doorway. Although this small space has many Christian symbols, most students use the haven for services, music programs, and noontime organ recitals. In January 2000 Jewish students moved to the new Robert K. Kraft Family Center for worship and social events.

HISTORY

The Columbia Lion has roared from three sites since the school was founded in 1754 as Kings College in British colonial New York. The

Sanctuary of St. Paul's Chapel

first location was in Lower Manhattan, near Trinity Church. The present campus, designed by Charles McKim, dates from 1897 and was built on the site of an insane asylum. The chapel was a memorial gift by the daughters of James Stokes and his wife, Caroline Phelps. It opened in 1907.

An inseparable part of the chapel's personality is its music programs. A popular organ recital series sponsored by the Earl Hall Center is presented twice a month at noon during academic semesters. It is free to the public. The chapel holds professional recitals because of an outstanding Aeolian-Skinner pipe organ from 1938. To complement the organ, a Baroque tracker pipe organ arrived in 2001.

ARCHITECTURE

The architects, I. N. Phelps Stokes and John Mead Howells, combined elements of Byzantine, Gothic, and Italian Renaissance design to produce a red-brick and limestone building that is widely admired as an architectural gem. St. Paul's is laid out in the form of a Latin cross (122 feet by 77 feet). It is extended at the east end by a semicircular apse and at the west end by a vaulted portico. Look up before entering the chapel to see the unique capitals on the portico's four columns—these winged cherubs are the work of Gutzon Borglum, sculptor of the presidential heads on Mount Rushmore. Closely study the bronze torchères that flank the portico's columns and discover a sculptured image of the patron, Paul, nestling in the base. St. Paul's outstanding feature is its stately Byzantine dome, whose design was inspired by St. Mark's Church in Venice. The dome holds sixteen windows representing old-line New York families associated with the history of Columbia: the DeWitt Clintons, the William Rhinelanders, the Gerald Beekmans, the Philip Van Cortlandts, and Nicholas Fish, a trustee of the university from 1817 to 1833. Look for each family's coat of arms on the interior windows. The dome caps the crossing and fills the chapel with natural light; it is 48 feet wide and 91 feet high. Crowns of the arches supporting the dome are adorned with terra-cotta symbols of the four Evangelists designed by the sculptor Adolph Weinman. The interior vaults and arches are made of Guastavino tiles, which give the chapel outstanding acoustical quality.

Small marble fragments from a demolished early Christian church in Rome are set into the nave's marble terrazzo floor. Stop by the artist George Nakashima's Peace Altar, a memorial to Columbia's alumni who died in America's wars. The altar's honey color and unique natural shape add a special aura to the sanctuary.

In the apse three stained-glass windows by John La Farge show St. Paul preaching to the Athenians. Note the Parthenon in the background. Paul, who was called Saul, was born in southern Turkey. The son of a Jew who had become a Roman citizen, he persecuted many of Christianity's followers. While on the road to Damascus, Paul was struck blind and speechless by a flashing light. Upon his recovery he converted to "the Way"—a term used before Christian—and celebrated in a local synagogue, where he proclaimed Jesus the Son of God. Paul's great legacy is the record of his missionary adventures: the Epistles and Acts of the Apostles recorded in the New Testament. He is a fitting role model for students at Columbia beginning their own adventures.

ADDRESS: *Amsterdam Avenue and 116th Street, New York, NY 10027*
PHONE: *212-854-1540*
MUSIC PROGRAM: *212-854-0480 "Thursday Noon Series"*
HOURS: *During academic year Mon.–Fri. 10:00 A.M. to 10:00 P.M.*
WEB SITE: *www.columbia.edu/cu/earl/stpauls*
LANDMARK DESIGNATION

CATHEDRAL CHURCH OF ST. JOHN THE DIVINE

WORLD'S LARGEST HOUSE OF WORSHIP

This massive Episcopal church has the distinction of being the world's largest house of worship. It is longer than two football fields and high enough to hold the Statue of Liberty (with room to spare). St.

John's covers 121,000 square feet. Some of the fourteen bays or altars that line the interior pay tribute to American history, the arts, medicine, law, sports, education, and the environment. Movable chairs, instead of pews, can be configured to face any of the bays. Twenty-five hundred people can be comfortably seated. Everyone is welcomed into this diverse community, including two peacocks that roam the gardens.

HISTORY

In 1887 the Episcopal diocese chose the highest point in New York City as the site for a cathedral (from the Latin *cathedra* meaning "bishop's seat"). Thirteen acres were purchased from Leake and Watts Orphan Asylum, whose Greek Revival building from 1843 remains on the grounds. A design competition in 1889 was won by Christopher Grant La Farge (son of the artist and stained-glass innovator John La Farge) and his cousin George Heins. St. John's opened in 1892, but a curtain was used to separate the sanctuary from its unfinished space. The curtain was not removed until 1941. Heins died in 1910, and the cathedral hired Ralph Adams Cram, first as a consultant, then two years later as the architect of record.

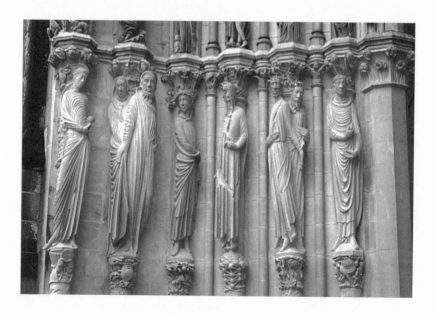

All building stopped when the United States went to war in 1941, and work was not resumed until 1979. With the arrival of Bishop Paul Moore and Dean James Morton in 1972, a renaissance took place that set St. John's on its current path. Plans for refurbishing decayed housing in the neighborhood were established with the city government, and a stoneyard was opened to train and employ local young people in stonecutting. Artists were invited to participate in worship services, and the cathedral became truly a house of God dedicated to human endeavors.

In 1982 a third cornerstone, given by the then-mayor of Jerusalem, Teddy Kollek, was laid and celebrated by a performance of the daredevil Philippe Petit. He walked a tightwire strung high above Amsterdam Avenue and presented a silver trowel to Bishop Moore. A new competition to build the dome of the cathedral

Sculptor Simon Verity

was held in 1991. Look at prototypes on display showing the submissions of Philip Johnson, I. M. Pei, and the winner, Santiago Calatrava, whose soaring glass-and-stone transept is topped with a solar bioshelter filled with greenery. In June 1997 work on St. John's central portal was completed by the master sculptor Simon Verity, assisted by Jean Claude Marchionni and a team of carvers. Look for interesting faces in the crowd: Nelson Mandela and the dragon of apartheid; Lily Auchincloss, a trustee who is immortalized as a baby emerging from a lily blossom; the retired Dean Morton as Noah, with Pepe, the dean's faithful dog, and Dean Morton's wife, Pamela, as Deborah.

ARCHITECTURE

When the cathedral opened in 1892, the design was a composite of Romanesque, Byzantine, and Gothic elements with a cruciform interior. Heins and La Farge placed in the chancel eight massive granite columns, each 55 feet high, to support a mosaic-covered dome above the high altar. The dome's interior design was never executed. Ralph Adams Cram (1863-1942) took over the cathedral's plan in 1912 and created a Gothic nave with graceful stone arches, along with an impressive entrance. He widened the original floor plan from three to five aisles because he did not want to use the cruciform shape. He was unsuccessful, however, and left behind the 100-square-foot transept, unfinished on its south side and still topped with a temporary dome. The crossing tower is not yet built and, in fact, one-third of St. John the Divine remains to be completed after more than one hundred years of building. The chancel's high altar well-represents the diversity of the church. Placed there are icons of several sects: a Moslem prayer rug; two huge brass menorahs, each weighing more than a ton, given by the *New York Times* publisher Adolph Ochs; and twin aqua blue Shinto vases, gifts from Emperor Hirohito of Japan. In the ambulatory behind the high altar are seven "chapels of tongues" circling like rays from a brilliant sun. A different ethnic group is celebrated in each.

St. James Chapel highlights Spanish mystics, artists, and saints. Look for Cervantes, St. Teresa of Ávila, and El Greco in stained-glass windows. The Reverend Henry Codman Potter, seventh bishop of New York, is entombed here (see Grace Church). St. Ambrose Chapel is filled with Italian Renaissance artwork. The decorative wrought-iron gates that enclose the chapel are topped with a gilded representation of seven scenes in the life of Ambrose, a fourth-century Italian bishop. Legend has it that when he was an infant Ambrose's mouth was covered with a swarm of bees but never harmed. Look for his symbol: a beehive. The Celtic Chapel, named after St. Columba and dedicated to the Irish, Scottish, Welsh, and English, holds an enameled stone cross with an ancient design. Gold leaf on the ceiling is in honor of the Celtic monks who created gilded manuscripts. In 1994 Keith Haring's gleaming triptych *The Life of Christ* was dedicated in the Chapel of St. Savior, honoring Eastern cultures. Haring (1958-1990), who began his career with subway graffiti, is fittingly remembered for his unique talent. For details on other chapels, pick up Howard Quirk's guide in the cathedral bookstore.

Walk over to the Gothic baptistry, whose focus is an elaborately carved white marble font. The eight-sided marble chapel was donated by the family of Peter Stuyvesant, last Dutch colonial governor of New

Netherland. Note the governor himself in a colorful frieze by the sculptor John Angel. Stop by the Poet's Corner and read dedications to
American poets. Look for Hippocrates and Florence Nightingale in the
stained-glass window of the Medicine Bay honoring St. Luke, patron
of medicine.

The American History bay window, donated by the family of John
Jacob Astor, who perished when the *Titanic* went down, contains an
interesting pictorial. Some images are of English origin: the Magna
Carta, the forty-fourth archbishop of Canterbury, the capture of
Quebec, and John Smith, the English soldier who founded Virginia and
was involved with the Native American Pocahontas. Also pictured are
the American Liberty Bell, the inauguration of George Washington,
Thomas Jefferson celebrating the Louisiana Purchase, Benjamin
Franklin, and Alexander Hamilton, the first U.S. secretary of the
Treasury, as well as Abraham Lincoln's Gettysburg Address; Henry
Clay, political leader during the Civil War who sought compromise
between the North and South; and the Supreme Court Justice Oliver
Wendell Holmes. At the base of the window, medallions immortalize
Henry Hudson, the explorer who first sailed into New York Harbor;
Betsy Ross sewing the first American flag; Francis Scott Key, writing
"The Star-Spangled Banner" during the War of 1812; and the *Titanic*
disaster in 1912. Notice at the floor level of the American bay the mar-
ble tomb of the tenth bishop of New York, William Thomas Manning,
who worked with Cram, the architect.

Jazz fans must see the tribute to the saxophonist John Coltrane,
who died in 1967; it is next to the Muriel Rukeyser Poetry Wall,
which holds the work of prisoners, children, and visitors. Feel free to
leave your own contribution.

In medieval times the cathedral was the center of civic life, and The
Right Reverend Mark S. Sisk, bishop of New York, is keeping the tradition alive. For a dramatic evening, stop by any Sunday at 7:00 P.M.
for choral vespers by candlelight.

ADDRESS: *1047 Amsterdam Avenue (at 112th St.), New York, NY 10025*
PHONE: *212-316-7540*
HOURS: *Mon.-Sat.: 7:00 A.M.–6:00 P.M. Sun.: 7:00 A.M.–8:00 P.M.*
WEB SITE: *www.stjohndivine.org*

BY THE WAY:

As you make your rounds north of 103rd Street through HARLEM and UPPER MANHATTAN, you may wish to visit other spiritual places. Some are public, others are open at special times. Be sure to call ahead.

CENTRAL PARK CONSERVATORY GARDEN: 1936. This 6-acre garden, which once held greenhouses to supply plants to city parks, was designed by Thomas Price. It is known as "the bridal spot" because so many wedding parties stop here for photos. Note the Vanderbilt gate by the Paris firm Bergeotte & Davvillier at the entrance. It is a remnant from the family mansion at Fifth Avenue and 58th Street—now Bergdorf Goodman. The *Fountain of the Three Dancing Maidens* graces the northerly site, while *The Secret Garden*, a statue of two children from Frances Hodgson Burnett's book of the same name, sits in

the south garden. Maintenance of this haven is a gift from the Weiler-Arnow family.

Fifth Avenue and 104th Street Public Space

DUKE ELLINGTON MEMORIAL:

1997. This bronze statue of Edward Kennedy "Duke" Ellington (1899–1974) rises 25 feet. The designer Robert Graham has placed the jazz luminary beside a grand piano resting on statues of the nine Muses. Duke moved to Harlem in 1923 and was famous for working at the Cotton Club. He composed more than one thousand songs, including "Satin Doll," "Sophisticated Lady," and, with Billy Strayhorn, "Take the A Train." The prolific Duke also wrote

Duke Ellington Ascends

three Sacred Concerts from 1965 to 1973. While resting on nearby benches, you can almost hear Duke saying, "I love you madly"—a line used to close his shows—as the elegant impresario, clad in formal dress, seemingly ascends into jazz heaven.

Fifth Avenue and 110th Street Public Space

ST. CECILIA'S CHURCH: 1887. Roman Catholic church by Napoleon LeBrun is dedicated to the patron saint of music. The elaborate red-brick and terra-cotta facade flanked by two octagonal towers holds a bas-relief on the center gable of St. Cecilia playing an organ. Seven windows sit on ornate columns above the three-arched portico. This Romanesque Revival **landmark** has a basilicalike interior with arches, murals and rich mosaics. The baptismal pool is placed near the entrance, signifying the rite of entry into the Christian faith. Restoration of the cream-colored interior was completed in 1997 by William J. Hughes. This church was founded in 1873 by the Reverend Hugh Flattery for an Irish congregation who worshiped in a nearby hotel and opened the lower church on the present site in 1884. The legacy of the founding congregation is continuing with Hispanic parishioners actively participating in community events.

125 East 105th Street (between Park & Lexington Aves.) 212-534-1350

OUR LADY OF MOUNT CARMEL: 1884. Romanesque building was constructed in white limestone with a decorative interior designed in the tradition of Italy's churches. Roman Catholic immigrants from Sicily who founded the Society of Madonna del Carmine in 1881 saw their group evolve into a large parish. The congregation began worshipping in a rented store at East 111th Street near the East River and its descendants still lead a procession through the East Harlem streets every July 16th to celebrate the feast of Our Lady of Mount Carmel. Most of the church members no longer live in the area, but they return for the celebration. Read *The Madonna of 115th Street* by Robert Orsi for the Italian history of East Harlem. Two nearby churches that partici-

pate in the annual procession were outgrowths of Mount Carmel parish. **St. Ann's Church**, founded in 1911, has an intimate interior filled with huge stained-glass windows, each with a decorative border and signed by A. L. Brink of West 23rd Street. Be sure to visit the grief-stricken Good Friday Madonna dressed in black. **St. Lucy's** was founded in 1900 in a nearby warehouse. A pastel rose window shows

Skylight at St. Lucy's

the patroness, an early Christian martyr, holding her eyes on a plate as a reminder of her blinding. Two patterned skylights fill the ceiling while small stained-glass windows, with saintly images well-known in the Italian European community, encircle the nave. Today all three parishes serve Hispanic, African American, and longtime Italian American members. Enter through the rectories.

Our Lady of Mount Carmel: 448 East 116th Street (East of First Ave.)
212-534-0681

St. Ann's Church: 312 East 110th Street (east of Second Ave.)
212-534-3856

St. Lucy's: 344 East 104th Street (between First & Second Aves.)
212-534-1470

ELMENDORF REFORMED CHURCH: 1908. A Dutch congregation from 1660 used this small site as the First Reformed Church Parish House. It was rebuilt, dedicated as a chapel, and named for their beloved pastor, the Reverend Joachim Elmendorf, after he and his flock moved to a new church in 1885 (see Ephesus Seventh-Day Adventist Church). There is still a Dutch shield over the limestone entranceway that faces Harlem Courthouse from 1893.

171 East 121st Street (between Lexington & Third Aves.) 212-534-5856

MARCUS GARVEY MEMORIAL PARK: 1840. A little over 20 acres was purchased by New York City for Mount Morris Park, which defines Mount Morris Historic District. In 1973 the park was renamed for the community activist Marcus Moziah Garvey (1887–1940), who led a back to Africa movement and founded the United Negro Improvement Association in his native Jamaica. Be sure to see the octagonal cast-iron tower from 1856. This 47-foot **landmark**, which once helped villagers watch for fires in the Harlem countryside, is the only survivor of its kind and sits atop 70-foot rocks. In 1960 the park added a recreation center, but it remains a peaceful oasis.

Between 120th and 124th Streets/ Fifth, Madison, & Lenox Avenues. Public Space

METROPOLITAN COMMUNITY UNITED METHODIST CHURCH: 1871. Gothic Revival building, by the architect Rembrandt Lockwood, was constructed for a Harlem congregation that originated in 1830 as St. James' Methodist Episcopal Church. A group from nearby Emanuel AME Church moved into the space in 1942, formed a new congregation, and renamed the facility. Surrounded by a low wrought-iron railing that fronts a green garden, the brownstone facade and corner tower is filled with Victorian gables and lancet windows. Be sure to see the 46-foot-high Gothic ceiling.

1975 Madison Avenue (at 126th St.) 212-289-6157

ST. ANDREW'S EPISCOPAL CHURCH: 1891. This Victorian Gothic landmark is by Henry M. Congdon. The congregation moved the church from Park Avenue because it was in the path of the planned Grand Central Railroad, now Metro North. The architect rebuilt and enlarged the granite building on this site. A steep-pitched slate roof, recessed portal arches, and clock tower add to the church's dignity. The huge Gothic interior can seat 1,600 and has a few original name plates attached to the oak pews. A graceful black iron grille frames the high altar. An oil painting by Richard Creifelds (1853–1939), *The Calling of St. Andrew*, dominates the apse, which has a symbol of Andrew, an X-shaped stone cross, embedded in the tile floor. Look for a variety of stained glass, said to be from Germany and Italy, filling the cruciform-shaped nave. Two huge round windows reign within the transept walls. Opalescent windows featuring the archangels Michael and Gabriel are Tiffany-style, while the clerestory openings are filled with an antique stenciled design.

2067 Fifth Avenue (at 127th St.) 212-534-0896

MOUNT MORIAH BAPTIST CHURCH: 1887. Gray stone edifice was built by Henry F. Kilburn for Mount Morris Baptist Church, which left this building to join the newly opened Riverside Church (see entry). The present congregation, a merger of Peach Tree Mission and Mercy Seat, was named after Moriah, the Old Testament site of King Solomon's Temple. Softly colored stained-glass windows with roundels of lilies and the original skylight add subtle beauty to a well-preserved nave. Soul-stirring gospel music for *Gospel in Harlem* is telecast from the sanctuary on channel 67 in Manhattan at 7:30 on Sunday mornings.

2050 Fifth Avenue (at 126th St.) 212-289-9488

ABRAHAM LINCOLN AND CHILD: 1948. This life-size bronze statue by Charles Keck, a student of Augustus Saint-Gaudens, is a fitting tribute to Lincoln (1809-1865), the American president whose moral commitment led to the Thirteenth Amendment of the Constitution, forbidding slavery. The sculpture sits within the Abraham Lincoln Houses, designed by a group that included the black architect Vertner W. Tandy.

On Madison Avenue and 133rd Street at Lincoln Housing Complex. Public Space

ABYSSINIAN BAPTIST CHURCH: 1922. This congregation's fourth home is a combination Tudor and neo-Gothic design by Charles W. Bolton & Son of Philadelphia. The fieldstone-faced **landmark** has square towers topped with notched parapets that flank a central gable. The spacious auditorium-style interior can seat over 1,000 worshipers. In 1808 about thirteen black merchants from Ethiopia were relegated to balcony seats in First Baptist Church on Gold Street in lower Manhattan. They fought segregation by forming Abyssinia, the ancient name for Ethiopia, on Worth Street. Adam Clayton Powell, Jr. (1908–1972), the 18th pastor and U.S. congressman from Harlem, succeeded his father, and led the congregation in the civil rights battle. In 1987 Abyssinian Development Corporation was organized to secure homes for seniors, middle-income people, and homeless families.

132 West 138th Street (between Malcolm X & Adam Clayton Powell, Jr., Blvds.) 212-862-7474

VICTORY TABERNACLE SEVENTH-DAY CHRISTIAN CHURCH: 1895.

Marble and limestone mini-temple was built by Jardine, Kent & Jardine as a sales office for Equitable Life Assurance Company. The building is on Strivers' Row, the popular name for a street of handsome town houses and apartments erected in the late 1890s for wealthy white owners, which later attracted successful black tenants. The Coachmen's Union League Society, a group of chauffeurs and coachmen, purchased the small, three-story building in 1923 and remained until 1928. The present congregation moved into the space in 1942. A long, rectangular sanctuary holds over 200 worshipers, who celebrate the Sabbath on Saturday.

252 West 138th Street (between Adam Clayton Powell, Jr., & Frederick Douglass Blvds.) 212-926-6222

ST. MARK'S UNITED METHODIST CHURCH: 1924.

Neo-Gothic stone church was built by Sibley & Fetherston for a parish established in 1871 on a site in Lower Manhattan by the Reverend William E. Butler and former members of Mother AME Zion Church. The black congregation built this fifth home in a northerly move from West 53rd Street. In 1902 the group organized a mission chapel in Harlem that evolved into the independent **Salem United Methodist Church** at West 129th Street and Adam Clayton Powell, Jr., Boulevard. The beige stucco sanctuary, which holds over 1,500 worshipers, is filled with small blue-glass lancet windows installed in

1940 by J. R. Lamb Studios. Each panel is centered with a different icon: the shell of baptism, a dragon of temptation, the harp of David, and the keys of Peter. Huge figurative windows of the Nativity and the Good Shepherd with Children further enhance the auditorium-style nave. Down the street the tower of its sister church, **Mount Calvary United Methodist Church**, dominates the neighborhood. That former Presbyterian church from 1897 has original brass light fixtures and mahogany pews that seat 400.

55 Edgecombe Avenue (at West 138th St.) 212-926-4400

ST. PHILIP'S CHURCH: 1910.

Neo-Gothic design by black architects Vertner Tandy and George Foster, Jr., is this church's fourth home. The salmon-colored brick **landmark** holds almost 1,000 worshipers. The Episcopal congregation evolved from a Sunday school for black children at Trinity Church, where their families could worship only on Sunday afternoons. In 1809 the group formed the Free African Church of St. Philip, named for the Apostle who converted an Ethiopian to Christianity. The parish was officially organized in 1818 by the Reverend Peter Williams, Jr. (1780–1840), the first black priest ordained by Bishop John Henry Hobart. He was the son of Peter Williams (1750–1823), a freed slave, a sexton of John Street Methodist Church (see entry), and a successful businessman who helped found Mother AME Zion Church (see entry). In 1834 St. Philip's was almost destroyed because of Pastor Williams's involvement in the abolitionist movement. Segregation was a major issue when the present site was purchased by the Reverend Hutchens Chew Bishop from property owners who had mistaken him for white. Be sure to study the elegant stone reredos, which was brought from the previous building on West 25th Street. The central gable has an engraved hexagram, an omen of good fortune, on the facade and twin angels tucked under its spire. Look for the bronze plaque from 1878 that credits Joseph Ten Eyck for erecting the former chancel.

210 West 134th Street (between Adam Clayton Powell & Frederick Douglass Blvds.) 212-862-4940

ST. ALOYSIUS' CHURCH: 1910.

This church was built by William Whetton Renwick, who carried on the architectural business begun by his uncle James Renwick, Jr. The AIA Guide to New York says that the Italian Renaissance structure is in the style of the Charterhouse, a fifteenth-century monastery north of Pavia (Certosa di Pavia) known for its relief work and colored decorations. The gray brick and terra-cotta facade is profusely decorated with filigreelike carved bands, fluid statues, putti (angels) faces, and multicolored glazed bricks. A sculpture of the suffering Christ crowned with thorns is placed high on the facade, while the patron, Aloysius, is shown in the tympanum with Mary and the Child Jesus. Glazed purple bricks are a backdrop for praying angels set within lavish frames. This Roman Catholic congregation was founded in 1899 and named for the Jesuit priest Aloysius Gonzaga (1568–1591), who died while tending plague victims. The interior holds a Renwick sculptured fresco of the Risen Christ high above the main altar, while original chandeliers hang from a dark brown sculptured tin ceiling. Golden scagliola (artificial marble) columns are crowned with gilded putti.

219 West 132nd Street (between Adam Clayton Powell, Jr. & Frederick Douglass Blvds.) 212-234-2848

GREATER METROPOLITAN BAPTIST CHURCH: 1897.

Neo-Gothic design is by the architects Ernest Schneider and Henry Herter. Built as St. Paul's German Evangelical Lutheran Church, the **landmark** structure replaced a frame building from 1865 that served the growing German immigrant community. The symmetrical facade of gray Vermont marble has twin towers with finial-capped spires and a central gable holding an opalescent glass rose window from Munich. Be sure to see the cornerstone with the German inscription *Christus Unser Eckstein* (Christ Our Cornerstone). This group left the church in 1939 and moved to Grace Lutheran Church on West 71st Street. In 1940 the Twelfth Church of Christ, Scientist, and its first African American congregation owned the building; the present group separated from Metropolitan Baptist Church (see entry) and took possession in 1985.

147 West 123rd Street (between Adam Clayton Powell, Jr. & Malcolm X Blvds.) 212-678-4284

EBENEZER GOSPEL TABERNACLE: 1891. Gothic Revival

red-brick church was built by Charles Atwood as the Third Unitarian

Church. It is the former home of an Orthodox Jewish congregation, who left a Star of David in stained glass. The present congregation purchased the building in 1942.

225 Malcolm X Blvd. (at West 121st St.) 212-222-0470

BETHELITE COMMUNITY CHURCH: 1889. Romanesque

Revival design by Lamb & Rich was built as the Harlem Club for prosperous families living in nearby brownstones. The four-story building became a sacred haven in 1947 for a nondenominational Christian group. The long rectangular sanctuary with oak pews and central pulpit holds 300 worshipers. A television broadcast is held every Sunday at 5:00 A.M. and Wednesday at 7:30 A.M. on WLNY-NY 55.

36–38 West 123rd Street (between Mt. Morris Park West & Malcolm X Blvd.) 212-427-2839

NEW COMMANDMENT KEEPERS ETHIOPIAN HEBREW

CONGREGATION: 1890. Italian Renaissance design by Frank H. Smith was built as a private residence for John Dwight of the Arm & Hammer Baking Soda Company. The gold brick synagogue has its original arched entrance with pillars. In 1962 the present congregation purchased the building from a medical group and converted the interior for religious purposes. The original black Jews were mainly from the West Indies and had organized in Harlem during the 1930s.

1 West 123rd Street (at Mt. Morris Park West) 212-534-1058

MOUNT MORRIS-ASCENSION PRESBYTERIAN CHURCH:

1906. This classic design by Thomas H. Poole has a rough granite facade with accents of yellow brick. See its hidden copper-clad dome from Marcus Garvey Park. The group that built the church was founded in 1844 as the Harlem Presbyterian Church; they merged with the local New York Presbyterian Church in 1915. That congregation moved in to the Rutgers Presbyterian Church on West 73rd Street in 1942. Black worshipers then took over the church and continue to worship in a gracious sanctuary surrounded with original stained glass.

15 Mount Morris Park West (at 122nd St.) 212-831-6800

EMANUEL AME CHURCH: 1900s. Neo-Gothic gray stone church with central gable and twin towers was built for a German congregation. The present group was organized in 1914 as Bethel AME Church on West 62nd Street, but in 1917 it regrouped under a new name led by the Reverend D. Ward Nichols, who purchased this site in 1926. A marble plaque lists the founding trustees and stewards. Look up to the top of the huge Gothic window that dominates the southern wall and see symbols of the Bible, the covenant given to Abraham, and the crown of Christ. Geometric designs fill ten stained-glass windows in the sanctuary, whose focus is a simple golden cross set in a Gothic arch with pale blue lining.

37 West 119th Street (between Fifth Ave. & Malcolm X Blvd.) 212-722-3969

FIRST CORINTHIAN BAPTIST CHURCH: 1913. Italian Renais-sance design by Thomas Lamb was built as the Regent Movie Theater for the immigrant neighborhood. It was one of the first luxurious theaters in the city, with a single balcony and 1,800 seats. A richly colored terra-cotta facade is adorned with the original centerpiece, scrolls, finials, and a shell sculpture niche. A statue of Jesus Christ now fills the niche. Two roundels hold the symbols Alpha and Omega. The tall central arch is the main entrance. An arcade on ground level holds commercial businesses. A black congregation organized in 1939 purchased this **landmark** building in 1964 from RKO Theaters and lovingly renovated the auditorium for worship.

1912 Seventh Avenue (Adam Clayton Powell, Jr. Blvd. & 116th St.) 212-864-9526

MEMORIAL BAPTIST CHURCH: 1905. This red-brick and limestone Neo-Gothic church was built as the Northminister Presbyterian Church. The sanctuary is filled with light from double tiers of stained-glass windows. Clerestory roundels top twin lancets. The congregation was organized in 1935 by the Reverend Winfred William Monroe and a group from Abyssinian Baptist Church. Monroe was well-known as Harlem's funeral preacher and the first black chaplain to work in the city prison system. The group worshiped above a funeral home and moved to the present site in 1940. The congregation established the Memorial Community Services to develop housing for

Harlem residents and to administer the House of Hope. An energetic gospel choir spreads joy and inspiration at Sunday services.

141 West 115th Street (between Malcolm X & Adam Clayton Powell, Jr. Blvds.) 212-663-8830

CANAAN BAPTIST CHURCH: This former Loew's Movie Theater by Thomas Lamb from the early 1900s occupies a midblock location that extends to West 115th Street. The architect's plans can be found in the Avery Library at Columbia University. The congregation was founded in 1932 by a group from Mount Moriah Baptist Church who wanted to build a new church, "with a warm welcome to all." An inspiring and dedicated pastor, the Reverend E. M. Moore, led the congregation to their third and final home a year before he died. The Reverend Wyatt Tee Walker, an assistant to Adam Clayton Powell, Jr. (see Abyssinian Baptist Church), was installed in 1968 as pastor by Dr. Martin Luther King, Jr., just ten days before Dr. King was assassinated. Walker was an active member of the Southern Christian Leadership Conference and continues to be an inspiring leader. The auditorium-style sanctuary with balcony holds over 1,500. Red-velvet drapes frame the baptistry, located behind the oak podium and choir loft. Stop by the intimate Martin Luther King Chapel in the narthex for a quiet spot to meditate.

132 West 116th Street (between Malcolm X & Adam Clayton Powell, Jr. Blvds.) 212-866-0301

MALCOLM X PLAZA: 2000. Designed by Ken Smith and Zevilla Jackson, this small plaza, 100 by 200 feet, is paved with various colors of slate to form traditional geometric patterns in the Islamic style. Malcolm X (1925–1965), a controversial Muslim preacher in the Harlem community, was murdered while addressing a rally. Read Alex Haley's book *The Autobiography of Malcolm X*, detailing the life of this powerful spokesman who raged about race relations in America. Plants have been selected to bloom after May 19, Malcolm X's birthday.

Northern end of Central Park and intersection of 110th Street, St. Nicholas Ave. & Malcolm X Boulevard Public Space

END OF HARLEM TOUR

THE CLOISTERS: 1934. This museum was designed by Charles Collens for the Metropolitan Museum of Art. Red roof tiles top off the granite medieval building, which is dominated by a four-story tower. Sitting high on a hilltop, the Cloisters impart a sense of spirituality in an ideal setting. The **landmark** takes its name from medieval cloisters (spiritual havens devoted to seclusion) that had covered walks running along the inside walls of their buildings. An open colonnade on one side of the walk faced a quadrangle, usually filled with a garden. Segments of European cloisters, both Romanesque and Gothic, are part of the museum. The medieval art collection housed here was started by the sculptor George Grey Barnard (1863–1938), who began to display his acquisitions in 1914 at 698 Fort Washington Avenue. The Met purchased the collection in 1925 with assistance from John D. Rockefeller, Jr., and kept it in the same location. Fort Tryon Park, a battle site in the American Revolution, was purchased by Rockefeller in 1930 to build a permanent museum. The Cloisters opened in May 1938 on 4 acres, and the rest of the park was given to New York City. Interior galleries hold treasures from A.D. 1000, to Gothic art created in 1520. Be sure to visit the bookshop, where you will find publications detailing the extensive collection. Rockefeller also purchased and donated to the state of New Jersey 700 acres across the Hudson River to protect the serene view.

Fort Tryon Park in Washington Heights 212-923-3700

OUR LADY OF ESPERANZA (Our Lady of Hope): 1912. Italian Renaissance Roman Catholic church is by Charles Pratt Huntington, whose cousin Archer Milton Huntington (1870–1955) donated the land and construction cost. The church building is part of Audubon Terrace, a Neoclassical cul-de-sac built on the farm of the artist John James Audubon. The Huntington name can be found on a tiny brass plaque attached to the first pew on the left side of the nave. A smooth limestone facade and tiled roof were added by Lawrence Grant White of McKim, Mead & White in 1925, when the exterior lateral staircases were brought inside and the nave extended. Look up to the gabled roof and see an ancient wrought-iron Spanish cross, a gift from White that belonged to his father, Stanford. Enjoy rich frescoes, oil paintings of the Stations of the Cross, gilded organ pipes, and red

Sorolla painting of St. Joseph holding the Child Jesus

leather doors embellished with nailheads. A painting of St. Joseph holding the Child Jesus is by J. Sorolla; his other works can be found next door in the museum. Be sure to see the copper-based portrait of Our Lady of Guadalupe in a gilded frame over the nave's entrance. The Reverend Peter O'Donnell, a fine oral historian, is the present caretaker and pastor of over 1,500 Hispanic members.
624 West 156th Street (between Broadway & Riverside Dr.)
212-283-4340

CHURCH OF THE INTERCESSION: 1910. This English Gothic **landmark** was built for an Episcopal congregation by Bertram Goodhue, the master ecclesiastical architect (see St. Thomas Church, Church of St. Vincent Ferrer, and St. Bartholomew's Church). He is buried in the north transept in a monument designed by Lee Lawrie, his favorite sculptor. Its inscription reads: "This tomb is a token of the affection of his friends. His great architectural creations that beautify the land and enrich civilization are his monuments." Be sure to visit the garden cemetery, once the farm of the naturalist-painter John James Audubon. Opened in 1843, it holds many famous citizens, including Audubon, who has the highest cross. Clement Moore (see Chapel of the Good Shepherd at General Theological Seminary), author of "A Visit from Saint Nicholas," is celebrated every Christmas Eve with a gravesite reading of his beloved poem. This church was founded on the present site in 1847 as a chapel of Trinity Church. Be sure to study the symbolic carvings surrounding the main portico and the charming water fountain, watched over by a pair of prayerful angels that sit in an exterior wall.

550 *West 155th Street (at Broadway)*
212-283-6200

OUR LADY OF LOURDES CHURCH: 1902.

Exterior water fountain at Church of The Intercession

This unique **landmark** by the O'Reilly Brothers was built of recycled artifacts. The Victorian Gothic facade from 1863 was moved from Peter Wight's National Academy of Design at East 23rd Street and Park Avenue South. The stone pedestals that flank the front steps were taken from John Kellum's mansion built for A. T. Stewart in 1864. The rear exterior wall was part of the James Renwick, Jr., design for St. Patrick's Cathedral; it was taken down when construction of the Lady Chapel began in 1901. Be sure to study the intricately carved tympanum of the patroness over the center door. The Roman Catholic parish was begun in 1901 by the Reverend Joseph H. McMahon, who would serve the congregation for forty years. He led their first service in a dancing school before the present site was purchased. Today an active Hispanic congregation sponsors a food pantry, youth groups, and a gospel choir.

472 *West 142nd Street (between Amsterdam & Convent Aves.)*
212-862-4380

ST. LUKE'S CHURCH: 1891.

Building was designed by Robert H. Robertson in Romanesque Revival style with an abundance of round entrance arches. Alexander Hamilton's country home, The Grange, built in 1801, was moved next door to St. Luke's and served for a time as its rectory. The Episcopal congregation, founded in 1820 (see Church of St. Luke-in-the-Fields), built the church because Greenwich Village was overcrowded with immigrants. This Hamilton Heights Historic District was a rural area until 1879, when the West Side elevated railroad was extended. Two other Gothic Revival churches were soon built nearby: **Covenant Avenue Baptist Church** in 1897 and **St. James Presbyterian Church** in 1904. A major restoration in the 1960s replaced the windows in the nave with modern interpretations, but original stained glass can still be seen throughout the sanctuary.

285 Convent Avenue and West 141st Street 212-926-2713

ST. MARY'S CHURCH—MANHATTANVILLE 1909.

English Gothic design is by Carrère & Hastings and T. E. Blake. The **landmark** has a red-brick facade with a wide gable that rises to an open bell tower. The exterior stone sill below a huge leaded-glass window is carved "1823 St. Mary's Church Manhattanville 1908," denoting the name of the rural nineteenth-century village near 125th Street and Broadway. This Episcopal parish was founded in 1823 by the Reverend William Richmond as an outgrowth of the affluent St. Michael's Episcopal Church (see entry). Land was donated by a member of the local gentry, Jacob Schieffelin, who is buried with his family in a vault under the church porch. The interior holds memorials to founding members and a baptismal font that was a gift of St. Mary's Girls Friendly Society in June 1910. The Sheltering Arms Asylum was opened in 1864 for orphans, the sick, and the elderly, and lasted until the 1930s. The park next door takes its name from that charitable home. Be sure to see the white frame parish house from 1851 that sits in the garden. Presently the socially minded congregation rings the church bell for two minutes every day someone is executed in the United States.

521 West 126th Street (Amsterdam Ave. & Old Broadway) 212-864-4013

GRANT'S TOMB: 1891–1897. This Neoclassical landmark by the architect John Duncan and the sculptor John Massey Rhind is a memorial for the U.S. President and Civil War General Ulysses S. Grant (1822–1885) and his wife, Julia Dent (1826–1902). The white granite monument rises 150 feet and is styled after Mausoleus's Tomb (350 B.C.) in Turkey. The facade engraving reads, "Let Us Have Peace," words by Grant himself. The president's birthday is celebrated every April 27 by family members, featured speakers, and West Point cadets. Be sure to see the bronze busts of Grant's five generals: William

Tecumseh Sherman, Philip Henry Sheridan, George Henry Thomas, James Birdseye McPherson, and Edward Otho Cresap Ord, as well as battle maps and flags. A mural by Allan Cox of Grant and Robert E. Lee shaking hands at the Confederate surrender ceremony in Appomattox faces the entranceway. Both generals were West Point graduates. This tomb is a silent reminder of a terrible conflict that claimed more American lives than any other war before or since.

Riverside Drive and West 122nd Street 212-666-1640

JEWISH THEOLOGICAL SEMINARY: 1930. Neo-Georgian building by Gehron, Ross & Alley and David Levy is the seat of the Judaic Conservative Movement. Enter through the gate in the corner tower to reach the campus. You will find two spiritual havens: the Women's League Seminary Synagogue, which is egalitarian, and Stein Chapel, which is traditionally Conservative, with separate seating for men and women. The seminary was founded in 1886 and holds the largest library of Judaica outside Israel.

3080 Broadway (between West 122nd & 123rd Sts.) 212-678-8000

JAMES MEMORIAL CHAPEL AT UNION THEOLOGICAL SEMINARY: 1908. Allen & Collens built this Neo-Gothic chapel of Manhattan schist trimmed in limestone, and laid out the interdenominational seminary as a campus on two city blocks. The interior renovation of the chapel in the 1970s by Philip Ives created a flexible environment for worship. Dark paneled walls, pews, and chancel were removed. A raised platform is now the chancel, and the sanctuary with slate floor holds chairs that can be arranged in any configuration. Be sure to look up at the wooden cathedral ceiling and reredos in the balcony; the altarpiece is from the original seminary, founded in 1836 by Presbyterians. Smooth renovated walls hold the original stained-glass windows and are filled with artworks created by neighbors. The **landmark** is host to the seminary's school of sacred music and is named for its patron, D. Willis James of the Phelps-Dodge Company.

3041 Broadway (between Broadway & Claremont Ave.) 212-662-9144

EGLISE DE NOTRE DAME (CHURCH OF OUR LADY): 1910–1928. French neoclassical design with Corinthian portico was built in two sections: the semicircular apse and grotto were completed in 1910 by Daus & Otto; the main body was created from 1914 to 1928 by Cross & Cross and would be expanded continually. The landmark was modeled after the Church of St. Louis in Paris, known as L'Eglise des Invalides, the final resting place of Napoleon I. Plans for a large drum and high dome were never completed; a shallow dome and low roofline replaced them. The Fathers of Mercy from St. Vincent de Paul Church (see entry) began this Roman Catholic congregation in 1908 as a mission chapel for French immigrants in the community. The smooth pale stone interior has a rough stone grotto of Our Lady of Lourdes behind the main altar to honor the appearance of the Blessed Mother in 1858 to St. Bernadette in France. The French artist Edmond Becker created the altar, pulpit, and communion rail in white marble and gilt bronze. An 8-foot crucifix

Garden at Notre Dame

with Mary and the disciple John draws all eyes to the apse, especially when their enameled halos are electrically glowing. The neighborhood is filled with French Beaux-Arts-style homes and St. Luke's–Roosevelt Hospital Center.

405 West 114th Street (at Morningside Dr.) 212-866-1500

NEW YORK BUDDHIST CHURCH: This haven is made up of two buildings in this historic district. Number 331, built in 1902 by Janes & Leo, was the Beaux-Arts town house of Marion Davies, aspiring actress and mistress of the newspaper founder William Randolph Hearst. Number 332 was built in 1963 by Kelly & Gruzen with a landmark bronze statue of Shinran-Shonin (1173–1262), founder of the Jodo-Shinshu Buddhist sect, dominating the exterior. The sculpture originally stood in Hiroshima and survived the first atomic bomb attack of World War II. In September 1955 the statue was placed at the church as a symbol of hope for world peace.

331-332 Riverside Drive (between 105th & 106th Sts.) 212-678-0305

WEST SIDE
AND
GREENWICH
VILLAGE

❖ ❖ ❖ ❖

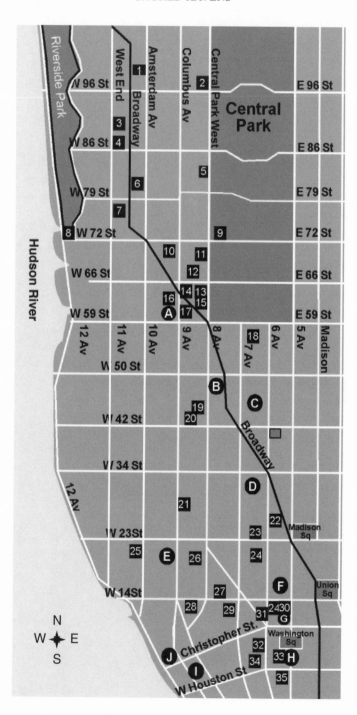

WEST SIDE AND GREENWICH VILLAGE

SOUTH OF 103RD ST. TO W. HOUSTON ST.

FEATURES:

A. St. Paul the Apostle Church
B. St. Malachy's
C. Church of St. Mary the Virgin
D. Church of St. Francis of Assisi
E. Chapel of the Good Shepherd
F. St. Francis Xavier Church
G. Church of the Ascension
H. Holy Trinity Chapel at NYU
I. Church of St. Luke-in-the-Fields
J. Church of St. Veronica-In-The-Village

BY THE WAY:

1. St. Michael's Church
2. First Church of Christ Scientist
3. B'nai Jeshurun
4. Church of St. Paul & St. Andrew
5. Congregation Rodeph Shalom
6. Holy Trinity RC Church
7. West End Collegiate Church
8. Eleanor Roosevelt Memorial
9. Strawberry Fields
10. Blessed Sacrament Church
11. Shearith Israel Synagogue

12. Stephen Wise Free Synagogue
13. Holy Trinity Lutheran Church
14. Church of Latter-Day Saints
15. Society For Ethical Culture
16. Robert Moses Memorial
17. American Bible Society
18. Calvary Baptist Church
19. St. Luke's Lutheran Church
20. Holy Cross Church
21. Church of the Holy Apostles
22. Cathedral of St. Sava
23. St. Vincent de Paul Church
24. Shearith Israel Cemeteries
25. Church of the Guardian Angel
26. Saint Peter's Church
27. Our Lady of Guadulupe
28. St. Bernard of Clairvaux
29. Metropolitan-Duane UM Church
30. First Presbyterian Church
31. Jefferson Community Garden
32. Saint Joseph's Church
33. Judson Memorial Church
34. Our Lady of Pompeii
35. St. Anthony of Padua Church

ST. PAUL THE APOSTLE CHURCH

TRADITION OF REACHING OUT

This Roman Catholic house of worship has roots deeply embedded in the city's melting pot. Waves of German, Irish, Italian, and Hispanic immigrants settled in the neighborhood and struggled to survive. This fortresslike building served as a safe haven for all new arrivals as the Paulist Fathers, in the spirit of brotherhood, gave to all who needed hope.

HISTORY

A convert to Catholicism, the American-born Isaac Hecker (1819–1888) left his family's flour mill business and with five associates founded the Paulist Fathers in 1858. They pledged to "meet the needs of the Church as they arise" and started their work on the present site, once an undeveloped and undesirable piece of property on West 59th Street in Manhattan. A small chapel and convent were built at that time and enlarged twice. On January 25, 1885, the Paulists celebrated the opening of the church seen today, which Father Hecker had modeled after the Cathedral of Santa Croce in Florence. The group had been building the new church since 1876.

Since the majority of the congregation always consisted of newcomers to American society, an elementary school was added in 1886 to ease the children's assimilation. In 1865 Hecker founded the first national Catholic magazine, *The Catholic World*, which grew into the Paulist Press. His vision became an instrument of spiritual transformation for a nation. Today the press catalog lists more than nine hundred books, videos, and audiotapes for adults and children.

The Paulists watched their congregation depart as thousands of homes were razed for the building of Lincoln Center. At their low point in 1973, they considered demolishing the church and relocating it on a lower floor of a high-rise replacement building. Instead, a physical and spiritual renovation began and with it an evolution that again welcomed many newcomers to the parish. Worshipers came from new cooperative apartments and from the campus of Fordham University at the new Lincoln Center. Rooms below the main church were made available for community meetings as well as many self-help groups. From shantytown to tenements to costly condominiums, the church survived the gentrification of its neighborhood. Stop by the bookstore and gift shop in the narthex for more information.

ARCHITECTURE

Jeremiah O'Rourke designed the Gothic exterior, which includes two squat towers that should have been topped off with decorative spires. The building blocks were purchased at public auction by an enterprising Paulist priest, Adrian Rosecrans. The craggy gray blocks are the remains of the Croton Aqueduct on 42nd Street, which was torn down and replaced by the New York Public Library. After 1882 George Deshon, a Paulist who was a U.S. Army engineer and roommate of Ulysses S. Grant at West Point, took over construction of the castlelike church, which measures 284 feet long and 121 feet wide. The recycled stone exterior is not extraordinary, but a beautiful addition was installed in 1958 above the front portal: Lumen Winter's frieze entitled *Conversion of St. Paul*.

However, the interior, created in the Byzantine style favored by early Christians, is remarkable. Both round and octagonal blue limestone columns support decorative arches and line the nave, which soars 100 feet. The dark blue vaulted ceiling is covered with stars representing the midnight sky on the day the church was dedicated. An astrological mural was created by George Searle, an astronomer and also a Paulist priest.

The spacious interior holds an awe-inspiring high altar of marble, alabaster, and onyx designed by Stanford White, Philip Martigny's baroque sanctuary lamp, John La Farge's stained glass and murals, and the marble work of Augustus Saint-Gaudens. Note an original oak pulpit that stands halfway down the nave. In premicrophone days acoustical problems made it necessary to place the pulpit where it would be most efficient. The church attracted huge crowds to hear outstanding preachers. The marble baptistry has been relocated to the back of the nave as a symbol of the belief that baptism is the entry into Christian life. Designed by John La Farge, the font stands in the center of an open pool of water to accommodate the many adults who receive the sacrament of baptism.

Be sure to visit a 20-foot-high sarcophagus dominated by an enormous angel of the Resurrection who envelops both the priestly figure of Isaac Hecker and Paul the Apostle. It is the final resting place for a visionary pastor who created a place of dignity, especially for immigrants looking for the American dream.

ADDRESS: 415 West 59th Street (at Columbus Ave.), New York, NY 10019
PHONE: 212-265-3495; BOOKSTORE: 212-315-0918
HOURS: Daily: 7:30 A.M.–6:00 P.M.
WEB SITE: www.stpaultheapostle.org

ST. MALACHY'S: THE ACTORS' CHAPEL

"THERE'S NO BUSINESS LIKE SHOW BUSINESS"

Located in the heart of Broadway's theater district, this Roman Catholic church has been a stop-off for thousands of entertainers praying that their shows will be smash hits. The list of those

Mural of the Patron

who have worshiped here reads like *Who's Who*—Spencer Tracy, Danny Thomas, Bob and Dolores Hope, Perry Como. While filming *Going My Way*, Barry Fitzgerald and Bing Crosby sparred affectionately on St. Malachy's steps. Joan Crawford and Douglas Fairbanks, Jr., said their "I do's," in the chapel, and Gregory Peck stopped by to light a candle before he made his stage debut. So it seems only fitting that the bells of St. Malachy's can joyfully ring out "There's No Business Like Show Business" (Irving Berlin's famous melody) to remind the neighborhood that this is a special haven on Broadway's backstage. Incidentally, it was Irving Berlin (later joined by Oscar Hammerstein II), who organized the building of the sculpture on Broadway and 47th Street honoring another St. Malachy's parishioner, George M. Cohan, the song-and-dance man who created the American musical. Cohan was antiunion, and Actors' Equity never forgave him.

HISTORY

St. Malachy's, named after a twelfth-century reformer of Ireland's Catholic Church, was founded in 1902, ministering to a congregation of Irish immigrants on the present site. The church began to gain fame in 1920, when the theater district moved uptown to Broadway from 14th Street. Residential blocks were quickly replaced by restaurants and nightclubs catering to theatergoers and tourists. Broadway was booming with 154 productions on the boards, and actors began to establish homes nearby. Realizing the special needs of these new parishioners, St. Malachy's opened the Actors' Chapel, below the main church, and arranged services to accommodate rehearsal and curtain times. Masses were held at midnight, 2:00 A.M. and 4:00 A.M. for standing-room-only crowds.

Beginning in the 1960s the Broadway neighborhood fell prey to prostitution and drug peddling. Tourists avoided the area. St. Malachy's congregation dwindled as members fled to the suburbs, leaving only the poor and elderly. A pastoral team led by the Reverend George Moore participated in local community groups to rescue both church and neighborhood from decay. In 1977 Encore Community Services was established to reach out to the neighborhood's senior citizens. The late comic actor Chris Farley of *Saturday Night Live* was a weekly volunteer at the senior center. Today St. Malachy's, helped by the Shubert Foundation, the Times Square Business Improvement District, and a loyal congregation, remains an important influence on a revitalized Broadway and a lifesaver for senior citizens.

ARCHITECTURE

St. Malachy's gray brick and limestone exterior holds many beautiful elements associated with Neo-Gothic design—filigreed spires and gables, terra-cotta moldings on pointed arch windows, and a dominant stained-glass rose window with intricate stone tracery. The church was designed in 1903 by the New York architect Joseph H. McGuire. In 1923 the rectory, which added 18 feet to the church's frontage, was completed by Adolph P. Wohlpart.

St. Malachy's began a major restoration in 1991. The exterior was capped with a new roof, and the interior was rewired, repainted, and reconfigured. The original baptismal font, resting on a marble runner embedded in the pale wooden floor, was placed at the sanctuary's entrance to signify baptism as entry into Christian life. Honey-colored pews were set at angles to surround the altar. Marblelike pillars, lining the nave and supporting soaring Gothic arches, complement the sense of openness.

Don't miss the fresco of angels rejoicing on the clerestory walls and starry blue ceilings enhancing the vaulted alcoves. Especially beautiful is the painting *The Crucifixion of Jesus* over the high altar. A lively mural of St. Malachy preaching in his bishop's robe harks back to the first congregation. Before you leave visit the handsomely framed portrait of St. Genesius, actor, martyr, and patron of theatricals, which hangs on the west wall. Broadway's old tradition of lighting a candle for a successful show continues at this spot.

ADDRESS: *239 West 49th Street (between Broadway & 8th Ave.)*
   New York, NY 10019
PHONE: *212-489-1340*
ENCORE FRIENDLY VISITORS SERVICE: *212-581-4224*
HOURS: *Mon.-Fri.: 8:00 A.M.–5:00 P.M. Sat.: 4:30 P.M.–6:00 P.M.*
   Sun.: 8:30 A.M.–2:30 P.M.
E-MAIL: *actrchapel@aol.com*

CHURCH OF ST. MARY THE VIRGIN

SEAT OF ANGLO-CATHOLICISM IN TIMES SQUARE

As the best-known Anglo-Catholic parish in the Episcopal diocese, this Times Square church echoes with Gregorian chants, glows with tranquil beauty, and burns incense so freely at Sunday services that it is affectionately referred to as *Smoky Mary's*.

HISTORY

This parish was founded in 1868 at 228 West 45th Street on land donated by John Jacob Astor, Jr., and his wife, Charlotte Augusta

Astor. In 1894 the need for more space led to the purchase of seven lots extending midblock from West 46th to West 47th Street. The original 45th Street site was returned to the Astor family. The Free Church of St. Mary the Virgin opened on December 8, 1895, with great fanfare. As a free church, St. Mary's did not charge for pew rentals and was governed by a lay board of trustees headed by the pastor. The building's rapid completion was thanks to the estate of Sara Louie Cooke and the use of steel framework, the type of construction associated with Chicago skyscrapers.

The congregation was named after St. Mary the Virgin at England's Oxford University, where the Reverend John Keble, Church of England priest and an Oxford academician, urged his church to recover its faith and return to its Catholic roots. The campaign was known as the Oxford Movement (1833-1845). Efforts to revive ceremonial customs that had been abandoned by the established church caused controversy, riots, and even bloodshed because of anti-Catholic prejudices. In New York, St. Mary's congregation was led by its twenty-five-year-old founder, the Reverend Thomas McKee Brown, who followed liturgical ritual as never before seen in an Episcopal church. He instituted daily Mass (previously celebrated only four times a year) and used a choir group with small orchestra during Sunday services. Today St. Mary's carries on what is now considered a traditional ministry, for all Episcopal churches eventually followed its lead. The Mission House next door is leased to charitable groups whose rental fees provide repair funds for the old building.

ARCHITECTURE

Pierre LeBrun, of Napoleon LeBrun & Sons, designed this church in fourteenth-century French Gothic style. The 46th Street Indiana limestone frontage measures 125 feet and that on 47th Street, 95 feet. Exquisitely carved terra-cotta figures grace the facades on both exteriors. Over the 46th Street tympanum, a recessed space above the entrance, is an elaborate representation of the Annunciation. The niche between the dark wooden doors holds J. Massey Rhind's sensitive sculpture of Mary cradling the Infant Jesus. At the 47th Street entrance, no longer in daily use, a smaller relief of the Annunciation and figures of church and civic authorities decorate the facade.

Upon entering the sanctuary, gaze up at the star-filled blue vaulted ceiling, which has been restored to its original grandeur. Twenty-two piers of clustered stone columns support the clerestory walls and separate the nave from the ambulatory. Be sure to see the three-dimensional Stations of the Cross in unusual pastel colors lining the upper walls of the walkway.

The five-sided apse holds the congregation's original high altar and is surrounded by clerestory windows filled with illustrations of the many joys in Mary's life. The stained glass was designed by the English

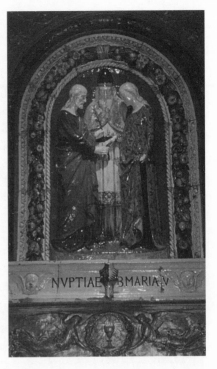

Mary and Joseph celebrate their marriage

artist Charles Kempe and is fascinating for both its artistry and its subject matter. On either side of the 48-foot-deep chancel are carved polychrome statues of Christ the King and Mary, and high above the entrance is the Great Rood beam, depicting the Crucifixion. Nearby a white marble memorial by J. Massey Rhind honors St. Mary's founder, Father Brown, who died in 1898 at the age of fifty-seven. St. Mary's was his only parish.

Don't miss the medieval-style painting of Mary with Sts. Anselm, John, and Dominic, encased in a gilded frame and tucked into the ambulatory behind the high altar. It is by Valentine d'Ogries, who painted most of the murals in the 1920s. The handsome wood statues of the twelve Apostles that line up on the nave's columns and the intricately decorated pulpit are by the Boston artisan Johannes Kirchmayer. He carved all the woodwork, including the angel-filled font cover of the baptistry and the 30-foot-high oak ceiling in the Lady Chapel.

Traditionally placed behind the high altar, the Lady Chapel is modeled after the famous Sainte-Chapelle of Paris from 1247. It was a gift of the Haley Fiske Family and is filled with wood paneling from the Netherlands. Two lavish murals from 1902 depict the Magnificat and the Epiphany; the Assumption is from 1925. St. Joseph's Chapel, in Italian Renaissance style, has a gilded wood-paneled ceiling, marble flooring, and a reredos holding a glazed Della Robbia-style plaque of Mary and Joseph celebrating their marriage. As in all the small chapels in this church, a traditional bell is placed at the entrance to announce the arrival of the celebrating minister.

Come by for organ rehearsal, usually on Friday afternoon around 2:30, for a glorious gift of music.

ADDRESS: 145 West 46th Street (between Sixth and Seventh Aves.) New York, NY 10036

PHONE: 212-869-5830

HOURS: Mon.-Fri.: 7:00 A.M.-9:00 A.M. and 11:00 A.M.-7:00 P.M. Sat.: 11:00 A.M.-6:00 P.M. Sun.: 8:00 A.M.-6:00 P.M.

WEB SITE: www.stmvirgin.com.

LANDMARK DESIGNATION

CHURCH OF
ST. FRANCIS OF ASSISI

AN OASIS OF HOSPITALITY

No one is ever turned away by the Franciscan friars of this Roman Catholic sanctuary that is world-renowned for its bread line, instituted in 1929 at the onset of the Great Depression. In one Depression year more than 1.4 million people were fed by the good friars. Today, rain or shine, seven days a week, priests and volunteers dispense coffee and sandwiches to a line of needy New Yorkers. Equally impressive spiritual programs are also offered: *Come Home*, for alienated Catholics, counseling for separated or divorced couples, activities for senior citizens, and adult education courses. "The Good Word," a two-minute recorded phone message, gives daily thoughts to those needing consolation, encouragement, or a laugh.

HISTORY

This church opened on the present site in 1844 and was replaced in 1891 with the building seen today. During its early days the parish served a German-speaking congregation, but later it cared for Irish immigrants who poured into the neighborhood. In the first thirty years of the twentieth century, many parishioners were pushed out by bars, gambling halls, and bordellos, and the area became derisively known as the Tenderloin District. But the Friars of St. Francis, led by Pastor Anselm Kennedy, persevered. In 1910 Penn Station opened and, while it displaced many residents, the transportation hub attracted a new wave of working people and commuters to the church. The surrounding commercial building boom would also fill the area with offices and department stores. Today few parishioners remain, but the friars graciously accommodate the transient population and see their church evolving, once again, into a busy spiritual haven.

ARCHITECTURE

This Romanesque church designed by Henry Erhardt has a facade of buff-colored brick trimmed with terra-cotta and four colorful mosaics relating to the Franciscans. The church runs through the entire block, and at the back entrance on 32nd Street a courtyard designed in 1958 by the Franciscan architect Cajetan Baumann is a popular spot. Betti Richard was commissioned to sculpt a bronze statue of St. Francis kneeling in prayer, which is placed in front of a huge crucifix carved into the stone portico above the church's back door. Gleaming spots on the statue are evidence of the "fingertip ritual," prayerful touches from thousands of visitors.

The interior of the church is filled with exquisite stained-glass windows, individual shrines, and beautiful wood statues. But the most outstanding feature is the Great Mosaic, completed in 1925 and covering the apse's entire surface (1,600 square feet). It is the work of the Tyrolean artist Rudolph Margreiter. Mary stands in majesty atop the world, crushing a serpent (evil) under her foot and cradling the boy Jesus, clothed in crimson. St. Francis and St. Clare of Assisi are surrounded by twenty-six angels. The lower portion shows the chapel of Portiuncula, birthplace of the Franciscan Order, and the Umbrian countryside, symbolizing the love Francis had for nature. Represented in the mosaic are Columbus, Dante, and

Junípero Serra, holding a replica of the Franciscan mission church he founded in California. Margaret of Cortona, fondly called the *Mary Magdalene of the Franciscan Order*, is shown with a small white dog. A total of twenty-two figures represent the history of the Franciscan friars.

Stop by the lower church, which holds the National Shrine of St. Anthony of Padua, completed in 1931. This popular saint, a contemporary of St. Francis, is often invoked as a healer and a means for believers to find lost or misplaced objects.

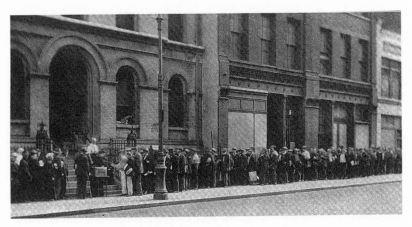

The St. Francis Breadline early 1930's

The patron, St. Francis (1181–1226), who lived and died in Assisi, was the son of a wealthy merchant. After having been a prisoner in a minor civil war, the young man abandoned his worldly life, exchanged his fancy clothes for rags, and became an itinerant preacher. He attracted seven disciples and in 1209, received approval from Pope Innocent III to establish a new religious order. Francis died at the age of forty-five, but not before he created the Christmas crèche, wrote "Canticle of Brother Sun," and miraculously received the stigmata, a duplication of the wounds of Jesus when he was nailed to the cross. To this day the friars of the Franciscan Order emulate St. Francis's life. They wear distinctive brown robes cinched by a white cord with three knots, signifying their vows of poverty, chastity, and obedience. For a heartfelt experience, see Franco Zeffirelli's film *Brother Sun, Sister Moon*, which pictures a young, nature-loving Francis struggling to find his destiny.

ADDRESS: 135 West 31st Street (between 6th & 7th Aves.)
   New York, NY 10001
PHONE: 212-736-8500
THE GOOD WORD: 212-736-9233
HOURS: Mon.-Fri.: 6:00 A.M.–7:00 P.M. Sat.: 7:00 A.M.–7:00 P.M.
   Sun.: 7:00 A.M.–6:00 P.M.
WEB SITE: *www.st.francis.org*

CHAPEL OF
THE GOOD SHEPHERD

AT GENERAL THEOLOGICAL SEMINARY

This seminary, the oldest educational institution for Episcopal priests in the United States, is set in a quadrangle of green lawns and charming red-brick buildings. Old World ambience surrounds this historic campus, befitting the origins of the Anglican Church. Look through the Italianate-style railing on 20th Street and see the Chapel of the Good Shepherd directly in the center. Its tower holds a fine carillon, whose bronze bells ring out a daily call to evensong as night falls on the city.

HISTORY

In 1817 a general convocation of the Episcopal Church announced the founding of the denomination's first American seminary, which originated in New York City, relocated to New Haven, Connecticut, and finally returned to New York, incorporating in 1822. Clement Clarke Moore, whose father, Benjamin, was New York's first Episcopal bishop as well as president of King's College (now Columbia University), donated sixty lots to build the seminary on the present site. Moore is best remembered as the author of "A Visit from St. Nicholas," which begins with the famous words "T'was the night before Christmas, when all through the house . . . " He was a professor at the seminary and is buried in Upper Manhattan (see Church of the Intercession and St. Peter's Church in Chelsea). In 1825, the cornerstone of the East Building was laid. The West Building was added in 1836 near the Hudson River, which once ran through the grounds.

But the seminary as it stands today is credited to Eugene Augustus Hoffman, the third dean, who served from 1879 to 1902. Dean Hoffman carried out his plan to create a campus worthy of its purpose and laid the foundation for the outstanding book collection in the sem-

Chapel of The Good Shepherd at General Theological Seminary

Typanum of Jesus at the Chapel of the Good Shepherd

inary's library. Today the library contains the largest group of Latin Bibles in the world, and one of six Gutenberg Bibles in the United States.

The Chapel of the Good Shepherd was consecrated on November 1, 1888—All Saints' Day. It was the gift of Dean Hoffman's mother, in memory of her husband. The bronze doors, completed in 1899, were a memorial to Dean Hoffman's young son and namesake.

In 1895, as building continued, the quadrangle was enclosed by extending the Ninth Avenue railing along 20th Street and setting it atop a brownstone wall. The footprint was now in place for the seminary to play a continuing role in the Chelsea neighborhood.

ARCHITECTURE

In 1825, Bishop John Henry Hobart, to whom Clement Moore bequeathed Chelsea Square, prevailed upon the planning committee to use the Gothic style for the new seminary. The West Building still stands as a fine example of early Gothic Revival in New York. In 1872, when the architect Charles Coolidge Haight was renovating the West

Building, he was asked by Dean Hoffman to submit a master plan for the entire seminary. Haight's plan was shaped like an 'E', with the back extending along 21st Street, and the southern side of 20th Street opened as a campus. The buildings all had red-brick walls, brownstone trim, and slate roofs. An occasional tower, buttress or chimney added to the charm and unity of Haight's pioneering style, dubbed English Collegiate Gothic.

In 1960 a modern library and dean's house with an entranceway leading to the quadrangle replaced the original main gateway facing Ninth Avenue, but all of Haight's other buildings have survived inside the quad.

The Chapel of the Good Shepherd is at the seminary's center, its prominent tower rising 161 feet. At the entrance, two sets of bronze doors portray scenes from the New Testament, and the tympani above the doors show Jesus as the Good Shepherd and Jesus at the Resurrection. Both were designed by J. Massey Rhind, who also created the 20-foot-wide marble reredos. Carved images of Moses, Matthew, Mark, Peter, Paul, Luke, John, and Elijah dressed in animal skins surround Jesus, who holds a stray lamb. Look for St. Paul with a small Gothic building tucked in his arm. His image is said to resemble the architect.

A Gothic rood screen separates students from visitors in this intimate space, measuring 43 feet wide and 101 feet long. Most of the red- and yellow-brick interior is filled with dark oak choir stalls. Study the ten stained-glass windows created by the Reverend John Henry Hopkins and painted by Lavers and Westlake of London. They are filled with over ninety images from the Old and New Testaments. Try to visit when the seminarians, who number around 150, assemble for evensong. It's about the closest you'll get to heaven here on earth.

ADDRESS: 175 Ninth Ave. (West 20th & 21st Sts., between 9th and 10th Aves.) New York, NY 10011 Entrance on 9th Avenue only
PHONE: 212-243-5150
HOURS: Mon.–Fri.: 12:00 P.M.–3:00 P.M. Sat.: 11:00 A.M.–3:00 P.M. Closed Sun. Evensong 5:30 P.M.
Grounds may be closed for special celebrations or during exam periods.
WEB SITE: www.chapelatgts.edu

ST. FRANCIS XAVIER CHURCH

MONUMENT TO FRIENDSHIP

The spiritual presence of two close friends—Francis Xavier and Ignatius Loyola—is found all over this Roman Catholic church. A remarkable vision of the meaning of life had descended upon these young Spaniards, causing them to found the Society of Jesus. Look for stories of friendship and sacrifice told in frescoes, icons, and other works of art, capturing the faith that Francis and Ignatius ignited in their followers.

HISTORY

In 1847, the Reverend John Larkin of the Jesuit community founded the Church of the Holy Name of Jesus in Lower Manhattan between the Bowery Road and Elizabeth Street. Parishioners included an immigrant population, which was increasing by leaps and bounds. Tragically, the church burned to the ground a few months later, and the congregation moved to temporary space at Third Avenue and 11th Street. Plans were made to replace the parish when the Jesuits purchased ten lots of land that make up the present site. The church and a college building were dedicated on July 6, 1851, by Archbishop John Hughes, who placed the complex under the patronage of the Apostle of the Indies, St. Francis Xavier. An ever-increasing congregation caused the parish to replace the first church and, on December 3, 1882, dedicate the sanctuary we see today. It seats 1,200, with the lower church, now known as Larkin Hall, holding the same number. In 1954, as families left the parish for the suburbs, the lower church was converted to a meeting space.

Today Xavier has become a magnet for artisans and career people. The parish's active lay committee participates in a ministry of social justice. The church sponsors adult education classes, a shelter for the homeless, distribution of food baskets, and literary discussion groups.

Ceiling medallion of the Patron

Note the nearby residence (24 West 16th St.) of William Cullen Bryant, poet, orator, and editor of *The Evening Post,* who lived in the neighborhood for eleven years until his death. He belonged to the Unitarian Church (see Unitarian Church of All Souls).

ARCHITECTURE

The architect Patrick C. Keely is said to have used the floor plan of the Cathedral of Pisa (1063–1272) in Italy as his model. The design is referred to as Classical Roman and the shape as the basilica plan. An ornamental arcade typically characterizes the facade. The church extends from the main entrance on 16th Street through to 15th Street, about 190 feet. The exterior rises 104 feet to the top of the cross on the granite facade.

The large, graceful interior is a visual treat. On either side of the nave, round arches are supported by pilasters veneered with Italian marble. Glistening marble columns are topped with Corinthian cornices, and carved oak pews are bordered by cream-colored terrazzo aisles. Stained-glass windows deliberately lack figures because of the lavish frescoes that fill the walls. These frescoes were sketched and painted by William Lamprecht. At the intersection of the nave and transept, the ceiling is adorned with a central medallion of Francis Xavier surrounded by four smaller medallions of angels. Each holds a symbol of his virtues. Eleven other angels throughout the vaulted ceiling also extol the saint's life. Five frescoes over the marble altar depict

the life of Jesus and Mary. Beneath those works are sandstone statues of five Jesuit saints: Peter Claver, apostle of Africa; Francis Jerome, evangelizer of cities; Francis Borgia, organizer of foreign missions; Francis Regis, missionary to peasants; and Peter Canisius, apostle of Germany.

Many small altars surround the sanctuary. One holds a mosaic image of the first Jesuit missionary to America, Isaac Joques, in prayerful supplication while the Native Indians who martyred him quietly keep watch.

The simplicity of the Mary Chapel contrasts with the grandeur of the church. Red-brick walls hold stained-glass windows celebrating the blessings in Mary's life. This serene space is used for weekday services.

The patron Francis Xavier (1506–1552), was a college roommate in Paris with Ignatius Loyola. He joined Ignatius and five others in founding the Society of Jesus in 1534. Francis left Ignatius in Rome and traveled in the Indies, Japan, and to the coast of China, where he died on a desolate island. His body rests in a cathedral built by the Jesuits in Goa, a Portuguese colony in India. Legend says that Francis was always seasick on his voyages and spent most of the time hanging over the ship's railing. On one journey, so the story goes, his crucifix fell overboard, but it was returned to him by a kindly lobster. That may explain why he is seen firmly grasping his crucifix above the church porch.

ADDRESS: *46 West 16th Street (between Fifth & Sixth Aves.)*
New York, NY 10011
PHONE: *212-627-2100*
HOURS: *Daily: 7:30 A.M.–6:00 P.M. Use church office at 55 West 15th St.*
if closed
TOURS: *Saturday after 5:00 P.M. Mass, Sunday after Noon Mass.*
Must sign up before services begin.
WEB SITE: *www.rc.net/newyork/stfrancisxavier*

CHURCH OF THE ASCENSION

FIFTH AVENUE'S FIRST CHURCH

Like the phoenix, the legendary bird that threw itself upon a fiery pyre and rose reborn from the ashes, this Episcopal church recovered from a devastating fire and, as a result, became the first house of worship built on Fifth Avenue. Several decades later a well-known group of artisans updated the interior and created a fashionable haven for the congregation to carry on its ministry.

HISTORY

This parish was established in 1827, when the French Huguenot Eglise du Saint Esprit, having no pastor, invited the Reverend Manton Eastburn, from Christ Episcopal Church, to start a new congregation. At first Ascension occupied a building on Canal Street, but it was destroyed by fire in 1839 (see St. Vincent de Paul). Determined parishioners rented a nearby room for services and drew up plans for a new church.

New York City in the early 1800s was still a small town emerging from meadows and fields. Fifth Avenue was unpaved and ended abruptly at a wooden fence across 23rd Street (the boundary between city and suburbs); the avenue was neither a popular residential district nor a good location. Indeed, it was a daring step when the clergy and con-

Church of the Ascension

gregation dedicated Ascension's cornerstone in 1840 on its present site and consecrated the first church on Fifth Avenue the following year. Two silver alms basins that had survived the fire were brought along and placed near the entrance to Ascension's new nave.

This church had always been characterized by an outgoing spirit, and it soon became a dynamic and progressive force in the city. When German and Irish immigrants flooded New York during the 1850s, Ascension built model tenements for them on 43rd Street and Ninth Avenue. Free classes for the newcomers on a myriad of subjects were held, and a day nursery was opened. Records show that the nursery cared for 13,000 babies in one year. In 1907, at a public forum series sponsored by the congregation, Booker T. Washington delivered a lecture entitled "The Successful Training of the Negro." Charles Darwin's theory of evolution was also part of this series and drew Ascension into a raging debate. A consensus emerged that the church should recognize the contributions and value of science in improving the quality of life and that science should recognize the power of the church in matters of spirituality.

ARCHITECTURE

Richard Upjohn (1820–1878) designed the sandstone English Gothic Revival church at the same time he was planning Trinity Church (see entry) in the Wall Street area. Like a country church, Ascension is set back from the street amid a charming garden. Its parapet-topped bell tower holds five stained-glass windows with more than a hundred illustrations.

From 1885 to 1889 the dark and somber interior was remodeled by the firm of McKim, Mead and White. The design was created by Stanford White, who assembled a group of artisans to assist him. John La Farge painted the chancel's great mural, *The Ascension of Our Lord*, on a blank canvas that he hung above the altar. La Farge, who was well-known for reviving the art of stained glass, also created four exquisite windows: *The Good Shepherd*; *Mary Magdalene at the Sepulchre*; *The Presentation of Christ in the Temple*; and *Nicodemus Coming to Jesus by Night*.

D. Maitland Armstrong designed the altar and the striking marble reredos. A pair of horizontal angels by Louis Saint-Gaudens hold a chalice while a small inscription reads, "This do in remembrance of me." The dark oak pulpit, designed by Charles McKim and hand-carved by Joseph Cabus, is a memorial to the Reverend Eastburn, founder and first rector. Look for his name carved into the handsome facade. An oil painting on the north aisle, *The Angel with the Flaming Sword*, by Edwin H. Blashfield, was exhibited at both the Paris Salon of 1891 and the Chicago World's Fair of 1893.

For a more intimate spot, visit All Saints' Memorial Chapel, designed by Ralph Adams Cram and Samuel Ferguson. It holds an exquisite mosaic of Christ, the work of Bruno dePaoli (see Christ Church).

As you leave, look for a bronze plaque on the facade, which proclaims that President John Tyler (a widower with seven children), married the parishioner Julia Gardiner here in 1844. She bore seven more children for him. What a blessing Ascension bestowed on them!

ADDRESS: *12 West 11th Street, New York, NY 10011*

PHONE: 212-254-8620

HOURS: Daily: *12:00 P.M.–2:00 P.M. and 5:00 P.M.–7:00 P.M.*

Sunday Service: *11:00 A.M.*

HOLY TRINITY CHAPEL

AT NEW YORK UNIVERSITY
QUIET OASIS ON AN URBAN CAMPUS

Religion has been a foundation block of colleges and universities from the Renaissance to the modern day, with institutions of higher learning setting aside quiet oases for students and faculty to commune with the Creator. New York University, an urban campus in the heart of Greenwich Village, has just such a spot in the Roman Catholic Holy Trinity Chapel.

The private university, formed in 1831, always had a non-denominational course of study, but religion was important in its formative years. Many early chancellors were Dutch Reformed and Presbyterian ministers who fought to sustain the evangelical character of the university. One argument led to the resignation of Albert Gallatin, a founding father. Today NYU is one of America's prestigious nonsectarian universities, with more than 40,000 undergraduate and graduate students.

HISTORY

The chapel, sponsored by the Archdiocese of New York, opened in 1964 to enhance the spirituality of the college community. It was dedicated by Francis Cardinal Spellman and made possible by a donation from the Generoso Pope family. Pope (1891–1950) was a rags-to-riches immigrant from Italy who published a popular daily newspaper, *Il Progresso Italo-Americano*. He is remembered for organizing Italian relief efforts during World War II and establishing scholarship funds for Catholic students.

Members of the congregation participate in the Newman Club, which takes its name from John Henry Newman (1801–1890), an Anglican theologian and follower of the Oxford Movement (see Church of St. Mary the Virgin) who would later convert and be named a Roman Catholic cardinal. Newman was ordained nearby at St. Patrick's Old

Cathedral. Students from the club work in the chapel's soup kitchen and serve as tutors to local grade schools. The Thomas More Law Society, named after the sixteenth century English lawyer and statesman (see Church of St. Thomas More), provides a forum for future legislators to discuss ethical and social issues confronting today's legal community.

ARCHITECTURE

The New York City architectural firm of Eggers & Higgans (creators of Damrosch Park in Lincoln Center) designed Holy Trinity Chapel to complement the defunct Loeb Student Center next door, which was replaced in 2001. The compact, modern chapel is 82 feet long and 51 feet wide. Above a red-brick entrance sits *The Shield of David*, a stained-glass window that dominates the facade. It symbolizes the heritage of God's people from the House of David. Three rays, representing the Trinity, flow from a six-pointed yellow star whose surrounding black abstract shapes represent the interaction of Being and Life.

When you enter the concrete nave, you'll find it strikingly simple. Stained-glass windows hold symbols of fields of study offered at the university: law, theology, philosophy, and commerce, which shows cogs and wheels. Science uses an abstract nuclear symbol and literature, the Roman alphabet. The upper windows depict the Stations of the Cross (a modern representation of fourteen scenes portraying the agony and death of Jesus). A yellow mosaic cross represents Jesus; the color red symbolizes his Passion. High over the clerestory windows, pale blue glass adds beauty to the ceiling bays.

All who stop in Holy Trinity are captivated by the chancel's focus, the Great Mural. Towering over 30 feet, this concrete sculpture represents the Trinity, three beings in one God. At the top God the Father is represented with elongated shapes. The Son, Jesus, is shown as a cruciform figure reaching out to all. Drawn on his body are abstract figures showing that Jesus encompasses all people, who ascend to the Father through him. The Holy Spirit is presented as energy and light in colored rays; the red and green rays are the only color in the gray concrete masterpiece. Be sure to see an emotional rendering of *The Crucifixion* hanging on the chancel's wall. The work was donated by the artist Robert De Niro, Sr.(1922–1993).

As you leave the nave, stop by the wood frame sculptures of Mary with the Child Jesus on the right-hand side, and Joseph on the left. Fashioned in gilded styrofoam and standing more than 7 feet high, they were created in 1971 by Earl C. Neiman, who designed the interior and all the furnishings of the chapel; he also made the Great Mural, the large crucifixes, and all the stained-glass windows.

ADDRESS: *58 Washington Square South (at Thompson St.)*
   New York, NY 10012 Enter through Community Center on Thompson St.
PHONE: *212-674-7236 or 212-998-1065*
HOURS: *Mon.–Fri.: 9:00 A.M.–4:00 P.M.*
   Closed Sat. Sun.: 9:00 A.M.–2:00 P.M.
WEB SITE: *www.nyu.edu/pages/catholic.center*

CHURCH OF ST. LUKE-IN-THE-FIELDS

A GARDEN TO REPLENISH YOUR SPIRITUAL ENERGY

Wander into the garden that surrounds this Episcopal church and you'll be sure to replenish your spiritual energy. Two acres of lawns and flower beds hold a wide variety of American flora. Benches are placed along the paths for the visitor to rest and enjoy the greenery and quiet thoughts. The charm of St. Luke's is a reminder of a simpler life—when a garden was a place to be nearer to God.

HISTORY

St. Luke's Chapel was built on the bank of the North River (known today as the Hudson River) and facing an extension of downtown Hudson Street (named in honor of the English explorer Henry

Hudson, who worked for the Dutch and claimed the territory for the Netherlands in 1608). Since most of the colony was settled at southern tip of Manhattan, Hudson Street was cut through farm fields and had few residents. The area was used as an escape from the yellow fever that frequently broke out in the crowded downtown area. Catherine Ritter, an early village resident, was interested in establishing a parish church and held the first meeting in her home. Look for her memorial vault from 1828 inside the columbarium, where ashes of the deceased repose. With the building of St. Luke's in 1821 and of the Federal town houses nearby, the development of historic Greenwich Village had begun.

Clement Clarke Moore, the Poet of Chelsea (see Chapel of the Good Shepherd at General Theological Seminary), was a parish founder and served as first senior warden. St. Luke's included the surrounding grounds, intended for use as a cemetery. In 1891, when the congregation moved to Upper Manhattan and opened St. Luke's Church (see entry), they removed seven hundred bodies, including that of Moore, from the present grounds to the uptown cemetery surrounding the Church of the Intercession (see entry). The property was

Garden gate at St. Luke's

then bought back by Trinity Church and became a chapel for the immi-grants who were crowding into Greenwich Village. Not until 1976 would St. Luke-in-the-Fields become an independent church.

On the night of Friday, March 6, 1981, a fire destroyed the parish house and the front of the sanctuary, leaving only a brick shell. A sad-dened but determined congregation, using the school's gymnasium as a temporary home, completed rebuilding the church in 1986. During the

winter of that same year, the congregation addressed another devastating event: the AIDS epidemic that was pummeling its Greenwich
Village community. The church, faithful to its namesake, Luke, the
patron saint of medicine, launched an AIDS project, with volunteers
focusing on educating the community and providing hot meals to those
suffering from the disease. Little was known about the epidemic at that
time, but the congregation made a difference and became an impetus
for the entire city.

Be sure to stop by the basement thrift shop, which is filled with
used treasures. Proceeds are used for the church's outreach programs.

ARCHITECTURE

The Landmarks Preservation Commission describes St. Luke's as "a
charming little church which recalls the atmosphere of an earlier day in
its small scale and simple design." James N. Wells, after completing
several projects for Trinity Church, is credited as the builder. Federal
row houses, built from 1825 to 1834, surrounded the church; ten still
survive.

The red-brick exterior with white woodwork enhancements and
black wrought-iron railings are all elements of St. Luke's simple Federal
design. The interior, skillfully restored by the firm of Hardy Holzman
Pfeiffer, includes three antique sanctuary lamps that survived the fire.
A refurbished chancel holds a mahogany canopy topped on either side
by a pair of charming little angels poised to fly away on gilded wings.
The glass artisan Dale Chihuly filled the pulpit window with waves
of color. Don't miss the baptismal font at the entrance to the nave; its
unusual urn shape has been raised on a pedestal. The position of the font
is a reminder that baptism is the formal entry to Christian life.

In 1950 several old buildings on St. Luke's property were condemned, making way for the creation of the garden complex. The garden continued to be expanded from 1985 to 1993. Upon its completion
the community was invited into the South Lawn area. It is inspiring to
think of the generosity of St. Luke's congregation in offering their private garden for public use—a reminder of the Lord's generosity when
he gave Adam and Eve their gift of life.

ADDRESS: *487 Hudson Street (between Christopher & Grove Sts.)*
   New York, NY 10014
PHONE: *212-924-0562*
HOURS: *Tues.–Fri.: 9:00 A.M.–5:00 P.M. Sat.–Sun.: 11:00 A.M.–*
   4:00 P.M. Closed Mon.
Enter through the garden, which is accessible when the main gate is open
WEB SITE: *www.stlukeinthefields.org*

CHURCH OF ST. VERONICA-IN-THE-VILLAGE

PUBLIC STATEMENT OF COMPASSION

This Roman Catholic church was deeply affected by the advent of AIDS both within the Greenwich Village community and among its congregation. It responded with the example set by its patron, Veronica, the legendary woman who wiped the brow of Jesus on his tortured journey to Calvary. The Gift of Love, a shelter for homeless victims of AIDS, was opened in the rectory and an AIDS Memorial established as a permanent part of the church.

HISTORY

This parish was founded in January 1887, a time when Greenwich Village was blossoming as a community of elegant town houses, literary salons, and galleries for local artists. The area was also bursting with Irish, Spanish, and Italian immigrants working as longshoremen on the nearby piers of the North (Hudson) River. St. Joseph's Church on Sixth Avenue was not large enough to accommodate the huge crowds who came to worship. So, with money collected from neighboring parishes, the Reverend John Fitzharris from St. Joseph's Church established a new parish in a warehouse at the corner of Washington and Barrow Streets. In 1890 the cornerstone was laid on the present site, and a basement church was opened in October.

St. Veronica's upper church would take more time to build, for the congregation of Irish longshoremen and their families had to make great financial sacrifices to finish construction. On June 7, 1903, parishioners dedicated the church seen today and celebrated with a boat trip up the Hudson.

During World War I, eighty-five members of the congregation gave their lives in battle; they are honored with a plaque on west wall. Another plaque honors members who served in World War II and the Korean and Vietnam Wars.

In the late 1950s the Greenwich Village piers became obsolete, and the neighborhood changed from residential to commercial. Parishioners moved away, and St. Veronica's elementary school, which had educated local children for sixty-six years, closed. Among its alumni were Gene Tunney, world heavyweight boxing champion from 1926 to 1928, who graduated with the class of 1911. The building was sold to the Village Community School and still stands at 272 West 10th Street.

In 1985 John Cardinal O'Connor dedicated St. Veronica's Rectory, on Washington Street, as a residence for homeless AIDS

Church of St. Veronica

patients. The Gift of Love is tended by Mother Teresa's sisters, the Missionaries of Charity, and the Reverend Kenneth J. Smith, St. Veronica's pastor, whose humanitarian spirit is widely admired. An interfaith prayer service is held here every January and June. Today the neighborhood resounds with music tolling from the Blake Family Bells in the church tower. Its sound is a soothing reminder that St. Veronica's has survived gentrification and remains a compassionate haven for those seeking spiritual comfort.

ARCHITECTURE

The local architect John Deery designed this building in Gothic Revival style with Victorian touches. The red-brick exterior and wide towers are also reminiscent of Eastern European churches. Terra-cotta twin steeples cap the towers, which loom over low-rise buildings in the neighborhood.

Since the interior was designed before the advent of electricity, look for remaining gas jets on the back walls. The skylight (or oculus), holding a Dove of Peace, was placed in the center of the sanctuary to flood the nave with natural illumination. Half-moon windows over the side altars and a patterned skylight in the small baptistry also add filtered light. Be sure to see the image of John the Baptist anointing Jesus in the charming round window placed over the original marble baptismal font.

The chancel, faced with side altars, holds two tributes to the church's patron: a gilded-framed image of the face of Jesus that was left on Veronica's veil, and a full-length mural of Veronica holding her veil. Legend says that the veil became known as the *vera icon*, (true image), which might have been the derivation of the name Veronica. St. Veronica has also been identified with a group of women who were known disciples of Jesus.

A large stained-glass window on the right side of the nave again depicts Veronica offering her simple act of compassion to the suffering Jesus. Look above the window for an outstanding Stations of the Cross (fourteen scenes showing Jesus on the road to his death). The murals, painted on steel, were created in Germany and feature Veronica in the sixth station.

The sanctuary is almost a square, like the footprint of many classic Roman churches. Corinthian columns of gold scagliola marble (plaster that has been finished to resemble marble) line each side. Two tiers of galleries fill the back of the church. The top loft was once used by a children's choir from the elementary school; the lower gallery now holds the AIDS Memorial. In 1986, when the first annual AIDS Candlelight March and Vigil was held, hundreds of New Yorkers joined to share their grief. It became the wellspring for the AIDS Memorial at St. Veronica's. Individual brass plaques, fastened to the dark wood face of the balcony, bear the names of those to be remembered. The Reggie Fitzgerald Sanctuary Lamp, honoring a local neighborhood leader, contains an eternal flame and is suspended from the ceiling.

Persons wishing to have a name inscribed in the memorial can call the church for details. The message of the memorial is simple: "To live in the hearts of those we leave behind is to never die."

ADDRESS: *149 Christopher Street (between Washington & Greenwich Sts.) New York, NY 10014*
PHONE: *212-243-0265, 212-924-5628*
HOURS: *Mon.–Fri.: 8:00 A.M.–2:00 P.M. Sat.: 12:00 P.M.–6:00 P.M Sun.: 9:00 A.M.–2:00 P.M.*

BY THE WAY

As you make your rounds on the WEST SIDE, south of 103rd Street and down to GREENWICH VILLAGE, you may wish to visit other spiritual places. Some are public, others are open at special times. Be sure to call ahead.

ST. MICHAEL'S EPISCOPAL CHURCH: 1891. This Romanesque limestone design by R. W. Gibson seats 1,600. The square bell tower rises 160 feet on a corner site. In the apse a suite of seven Tiffany windows from 1895 features the story of Michael the Archangel and his victorious battle with the fallen angel Lucifer. Tiffany also created the lanterns and the chapel's magnificent mosaic. This congregation was founded in 1807 on old Bloomingdale Road (now Broadway) as a summer community for worshipers wanting to escape the oppressive heat of Lower Manhattan. St. Michael's was intimately connected with the development of the present area and remained involved in social reform issues. The church sponsored sewing and carpentry classes for immigrants and questioned the concept of class churches that separated poor from rich congregations. A cemetery originally surrounded the church but was moved to Astoria, Queens, in 1852.

225 West 99th Street (at Amsterdam Ave.) 212-222-2700

FIRST CHURCH OF CHRIST SCIENTIST: 1899–1903. This Beaux-Arts granite **landmark** was built by Carrère & Hastings of New York Public Library and Frick Museum fame. The architects are said to have been influenced by Nicholas Hawksmoor, a London builder of Baroque churches. An outstanding tower with elongated spire adds a powerful presence to Central Park West. The oldest Christian Science congregation met in 1887 and planned this church. The sanctuary with sculptured stone ceiling was decorated by the artist Charles Cottrell and seats 2,000. Look above the entrance door for the opalescent stained glass window, *Touch Me Not*, of the Risen Jesus and Mary Magdalene outside the sepulchre. Circassian walnut pews with carved siding and windows with designs from Michelangelo add quiet beauty. This sect was founded in 1875 by Mary Baker Eddy (1821–1910), a New Englander who wrote the Church's textbook, *Science and Health with Key to the Scriptures*. Services are led by two elected readers who give planned weekly readings from the Bible and the church textbook. There are no ordained ministers. Every Wednesday evening healing services are held. There is a unique memorial to World War II in this five-story building. Told to cover all lights, the congregation blackened out the stained-glass skylight over the top floor, but the paint was never removed.

1 West 96th Street 212-749-3088

CONGREGATION B'NAI JESHURUN: 1918. A conservative group of Jews named the congregation after Jacob, or Israel, whose sons comprised the Twelve Tribes of Israel. The name is translated as "Children of the Twisted One who Struggled with Righteousness." The red granite Romanesque Revival design by Henry Herts and Walter Schneider has a decorative limestone portal. This oldest Ashkenazic group was founded in 1825 by German and Polish Jews. They had left Shearith Israel Synagogue (see entry), the Sephardic Orthodox synagogue that was the only Jewish house of worship in New York City, because of differences in customs and rituals, and even objections to accents while speaking Hebrew. Their action would start the formation of other congregations who had political disputes and squabbles over interpretation of religious laws. In America, conservative groups were a compromise between the "radical" reform movement and the ancient Orthodox tradition that strictly follows rituals and dietary laws—but all groups were built around the Torah, which defines how life should be lived. Because the congregation numbers over 3,000, services are also held in the Church of St. Paul and St. Andrew (see entry). These two congregations met in 1991, when the synagogue's roof collapsed.

257 West 88th Street (between Broadway & West End Ave.)

212-787-7600

CHURCH OF ST. PAUL AND ST. ANDREW: 1895. Robert Henderson Robertson designed the fourth home for St. Paul's Methodist Episcopal Church, which was founded in 1834 on Mulberry Street as the Second Wesleyan Chapel. St. Andrew's parish on West 71st Street merged with St. Paul's in 1937; their 1890 building is now the **West Side Institutional Synagogue.** The congregation voted to demolish the present church in 1979, but the building was saved because of its designation as a **landmark**. The church petitioned the U.S. Supreme Court to ban preserving churches as an infringement of religious freedom under the First Amendment but lost. This yellow-brick chuch is an unusual combination of Italian and Spanish Renaissance, Romanesque, and Early Christian design. Look for the octagonal corner tower, Spanish tiled roof, terra-cotta angels on the facade, and marble cornerstone engraved with three dates. The interior space is shared with the Congregation **B'nai Jeshurun**, the **Korean Presbyterian Church**, and **Iglesia Cristo Vivo**, a gay and lesbian Hispanic church. It is also the center for the West Side Campaign

Against Hunger. Be sure to see the stained-glass window of the patron Paul before the Roman official, Agrippa.

540 West End Avenue (at West 86th St.) 212-362-3179

CONGREGATION RODEPH SHALOM (PURSUER OF PEACE): 1930. This Neo-Romanesque design is by Charles B. Meyers. The Reform congregation, founded in 1842, started its northerly move in 1886. The original synagogue from 1853 is still at 8 Clinton Street in Lower Manhattan and used by the **Congregation Chasam Sofer**. The smooth limestone facade is inscribed, "Do Justly— Love Mercy—And Walk Humbly with Thy God." In 1970 the congregation established the first Reform Jewish day school in North America.

7 West 83rd Street (off Central Park West) 212-362-8800

HOLY TRINITY ROMAN CATHOLIC CHURCH: 1900. This building by J. H. McGuire is an homage to the Byzantine design of Santa Sophia in Istanbul, Turkey. On the exterior intricate rust-colored brickwork is inlaid with white terra-cotta holding Greek crosses (with arms of equal length). Sculptured bronze doors from Florence enhance the entranceway. The empty niches were to hold bronze statues like those of the Apostles Peter and John that grace the facade. Near the rectory see the statue of Christ as King that never made it to the top of the building. Beige Guastavino tiles fill the square-shaped interior, whose dome, perforated by a stained-glass oculus, rises over 100 feet. Four arches rest on corner pillars. The sanctuary walls hold three groupings of sixteen stained-glass lancet windows designed by the Oidtmann Studio in Germany, which was destroyed in World War II. The Greek mosaic of God Pantocrator over the main altar is flanked by a lamb representing Jesus and the dove as the Holy Spirit. Symbols of the Holy Trinity fill the church; see the narthex window by Charles Connick as well as the chancel's statue of St. Patrick holding a three-leaf shamrock. Over the baptistry, a 3,000-pound bronze crucifix hangs with a Byzantine image of Jesus wearing a tunic and a crown. This church was founded in 1898 by German and Irish immigrants who first worshiped in the lower church, now the George Murphy Center, named after a beloved late pastor. Before you leave look up to the choir

loft to see an enormous silver-piped organ from 1998. It frames a color-ful roundel of St. Cecilia, the patron of music.

213 West 82nd Street (between Amsterdam Ave. & Broadway) 212-787-0634

WEST END COLLEGIATE CHURCH: 1893. Designed by Robert W. Gibson to resemble a colorful seventeenth-century guild hall in Holland, this brick **landmark** with tiled roof and step gables heralds New York's Dutch heritage (see Marble Collegiate Church). Many churches on the West Side were built during the 1890s as Broadway was widened and blocks of row houses were developed. In the rose-col-ored sanctuary be sure to see the Creed, basis of Christian faith, written in Gothic script in a huge gilded arch to the left of the altar. Heraldic shields of the United States, and the State and City of New York, along with symbols of the Dutch provinces that form the Union of Utrecht, are displayed in a colorful window over the choir loft. In 1940, following the Nazi conquest of the Netherlands, the church, under the leadership of Dr. Edgar Romig, became an important center for Dutch refugees and financial aid to the war-torn country. Today preschool programs, Bible study, choir groups, a center for the mentally and emotionally frail, and community meetings are all part of the church's ministry.

368 West End Avenue (at West 77th Street) 212-787-1566

ELEANOR ROOSEVELT MEMORIAL: 1996. By Penelope Jencks. Her great-granddaughter Phoebe Roosevelt sat as a model for this 8-foot bronze sculpture of the former First Lady Anna Eleanor Roosevelt (1884–1962), who was born in New York City. The memo-rial, initiated by the art dealer Herbert Zohn, sits in Riverside Park which runs four miles along the Hudson River. During the Depression Mrs. Roosevelt visited a nearby site called Hooverville to show her son Franklin the shacks of the unemployed. She never ceased to work for social justice and was widely known for her humanitarian efforts dur-ing and after her husband's presidency. President Harry S. Truman appointed her to the United States delegation of the newly formed United Nations, where she played a vital role in writing the Universal Declaration of Human Rights. The sculpture captures her wisdom, humility, and compassion. There is no pedestal.

Riverside Drive and West 72nd Street Public space.

STRAWBERRY FIELDS IN CENTRAL PARK: 1985. Garden memorial to the Beatle John Lennon was given by his wife, Yoko Ono. The couple resided in the Dakota, an apartment building overlooking this spot. The "Imagine" mosaic set into the walkway is a gift from the people of Naples, and is often covered with floral tributes.

At West 72nd Street inside Central Park Public space

BLESSED SACRAMENT CHURCH: 1917. Gustav Steinbach designed this French Gothic church in the fourteenth-century style of Sainte-Chapelle in Paris. This Roman Catholic parish was founded in 1887 with services held in the Havemeyer stable on West 72nd Street until the first church was built on the present site in 1900. A growing congregation made it necessary to build the present church, which seats over 1,500, but the magnificent facade with detailed tympani cannot be fully appreciated on such a narrow street. The interior, with an enormous polychrome crucifix above the chancel, is filled with beautiful artifacts. Three tapestries hanging behind the main altar tell the stories of Melchizedek blessing Abraham, the sacrifice of Isaac, and the Crucifixion of Jesus. Clement Heaton designed many of the figurative windows, including the rose window, a gift of the Heide family. A theater group rents the basement.

152 West 71st St. (between Broadway & Columbus Ave.) 212-877-3111

SHEARITH ISRAEL SYNAGOGUE (Remnant of Israel): 1897. The **landmark** filled with Tiffany windows is thought to be the first synagogue built in Roman Temple style; it was modeled after ruins uncovered in the late 1800s of the Second Temple in Jerusalem. This building was designed by Brunner & Tryon as its Orthodox congregation's fifth home. The oldest Spanish-Portuguese congregation in North America was founded in 1654 by Sephardic Jews from Brazil. Until 1825 this was the only Jewish congregation in New York City, with a membership since its inception equally split between those of Sephardic and Ashkenazic roots. Near the main sanctuary, which seats 700, is the Little Synagogue chapel. It measures 31 feet by 24 feet and is similar in size to the group's first haven, built in 1730 on Mill Street (now William Street), in Lower Manhattan. The *tebah* (reader's desk) bears its original railing; four Spanish brass candlesticks have been in use since services were held in private homes in New Amsterdam. A Torah soiled with blood and pierced by a bullet has been kept as a reminder of the synagogue's destruction by English forces when the American Revolution was brewing in colonial New York. Look for two old millstones (used for grinding grain) taken from the site of St. Nicholas Dutch Reformed Church within the Dutch fort, where all colonists had to worship. Synagogue members have included the U.S. Supreme Court Justice Benjamin Cardozo and the author Emma Lazarus, whose poem "The New Colossus" is inscribed on the base of the Statue of Liberty.

99 Central Park West (enter at office: 8 West 70th St.) 212-873-0300

The Ark at Stephen Wise Free Synagogue

STEPHEN WISE FREE SYNAGOGUE: 1941–1950. The fieldstone building by Bloch & Hesse is for a congregation from the neighboring Hebrew Union College–Jewish Institute of Religion (a center of the Reform movement) and was named for its charismatic leader, Rabbi Stephen

Wise (1874-1949). His followers established a free synagogue in 1907 with democratic leadership and no dues. They also set up a unique social service department in Bellevue Hospital to serve immigrant Jews on the Lower East Side. After worshiping in several places, including Carnegie Hall, (with World War II intervening) the congregation completed this new building dedicated to Rabbi Wise, who had just died. The blue-and-gold sanctuary holds a chapel with this inscription above the Ark: "Let there be Light."

30 West 68th Street (between Central Park West & Columbus Ave.) 212-877-4050

HOLY TRINITY LUTHERAN CHURCH: 1903. Neo-French

Gothic design by William Schickel.has a colorful rose window gracing the gray stone facade. Bright red entrance doors represent the blood of Christian martyrs. The intimate sanctuary, which seats over 300, has two Tiffany windows among its stained glass. Be sure to see the white marble chancel filled with colorful mosaics of the Apostles. Each portrait is placed in an individual marble niche decorated with miniature French spires. This parish was organized on West 21st Street in 1868 by a German congregation who wanted more conservative ideals. They left St. James' Church, founded in 1827, but reunited with the group in 1938.

3 West 65th Street (on Central Park West) 212-877-6815

CHURCH OF JESUS CHRIST OF LATTER-DAY SAINTS:

1975. This modern design fits comfortably into its Lincoln Center neighborhood. The thirty-six-story complex includes commercial tenants, rental apartments, and the Visitors Center, which holds a highly regarded genealogical library. The Museum of American Folk Art is located on street level. This sect, admired for its dedication to family life, was officially organized in 1830 in Fayette, New York. Mormon Christian congregations are led by a lay priesthood that is not a distinct class within the church. Joseph Smith (1805-1844) experienced a vision from God in 1820 and was told to restore the original church organized by Jesus Christ. Smith published *The Book of Mormon*, named for ancient American prophets and containing an eyewitness account of Jesus on the North American continent after his resurrection in

Jerusalem. In 1846 a church group from Illinois began traveling across the Great Plains to the Salt Lake Valley in Utah while a New York group chartered the ship *Brooklyn* and sailed from Old Slip in Lower Manhattan to California. A bronze plaque to mark this 20,000-mile religious exodus will soon be placed at Old Slip.

125 Columbus Avenue (at West 65th St.) 212-875-8197

SOCIETY FOR ETHICAL CULTURE: 1910. This limestone **landmark** is by Robert D. Kohn. Its abstract classical design was influenced by the Vienna Secession, an artistic reform movement around the turn of the twentieth century. Estelle Rumbold Kohn, the architect's wife, created the sculptures. The society was founded in 1876 in New York City by Felix Adler (1851–1933) and spread throughout the United States. Its purpose is to create a more humane society and "to work together to improve our world and the world of our children." Adler also founded the City Club in 1883 to fight political corruption, and taught political and social ethics at Columbia University. He was the son of Rabbi Samuel Adler, who was a leader of the Jewish Reform movement in Germany and at Temple Emanu-El (see entry). In 1927 the society opened Fieldston School for children in the Riverdale area of the Bronx. The group continues to examine and act upon moral dilemmas and holds lecture series open to the public. **The City Church New York** also meets in the oak-paneled auditorium, which seats over 700. The inscription in gilded letters on the stage backdrop reads: "The Place Where People Meet to Seek the Highest Is Holy Ground."

2 West 64th Street 212-874-5210.

ROBERT MOSES MEMORIAL: 1970. The triangular marble column by Albino Manca holds a bronze bas-relief of Robert Moses (1888–1981) "the city shaper" and "master builder," and is on the Fordham University campus. Moses served six governors, from Alfred Smith to Nelson Rockefeller, and five mayors, from Fiorello La Guardia to John Lindsay. He built thirteen bridges and tunnels and 28,000 public-housing apartments. His projects uprooted so many neighborhoods that controversy still swirls around his name. When 53 acres of West Side slums were cleared for the 18-acre Lincoln Center and other buildings, Moses displaced 7,000 families and 800 businesses. His legacy as a builder is unprecedented in the history of New York. Lincoln Center for the Performing Arts is just across the street.

Midblock on West 62nd Street (between Columbus & Amsterdam Aves.)

AMERICAN BIBLE SOCIETY: 1997. The curved glass facade, designed by Fox & Fowle, was added to a Skidmore, Owings & Merrill building from 1966. Television monitors form a 10-foot-by-12-foot wall and tell biblical stories. The society was founded in 1816 on Nassau Street in Lower Manhattan to publish and distribute Bibles to all Christian denominations (see Fifth Avenue Presbyterian Church). It was funded by a group of philanthropists including John Pintard, who also founded the New-York Historical Society. With its art gallery, archives, library, and Web site (www.americanbible.org), the society continues to distribute the Christian scriptures in many languages for adults and children. The library holds 52,000 Bibles in nearly 2,000 languages, and a collection of manuscripts including a fifteenth-century Torah scroll used by the Jewish community of Kai Feng Fu on the Silk Route of China. Be sure to visit the gallery, which usually has Judeo-Christian art exhibits, and the gift shop for a selection of "tools for spiritual growth."

43 West 61st Street (at Broadway) 212-262-2060

CALVARY BAPTIST CHURCH: 1930. This modern sixteen-story hotel-church replaced a sanctuary from 1883 on the same site. Salisbury Hotel was named for King Saul, the biblical monarch of Israel. After breaking away from Stanton Street Baptist Church of 1833, this group organized as Hope Chapel Congregation in 1847 and adopted the name Calvary Baptist in 1854. *The Calvary Hour*, a weekly radio program that originated in 1923, is still broadcast by the congregation.

123 West 57th Street (between Sixth & Seventh Aves.) 212-975-0170

ST. LUKE'S LUTHERAN CHURCH: 1922. E. L. Tilton and A. M. Githens, who specialized in libraries, designed this German Gothic building with no transepts, no flying buttresses nor a deep chancel. The charming Arts and Crafts interior includes stenciling, geometric designs, and warm wood wainscoting filling a sanctuary that seats 350. The stained glass was designed by F. X. Zettler from the

Royal Bavarian Company in Germany with clerestory windows lined with the names of the original German congregation. Be sure to see the iconography of the four evangelists that fills the 18-foot window above the entrance. Two smaller windows on either side feature the founder of the Reformation, Martin Luther (1483–1546) and Philipp Melanchthon, who wrote the Augsburg Confession in 1530 to explain Luther's theses to Charles V. The congregation was founded in 1850 after leaving a group on the Upper West Side and continues its long ministry of caring for the poor.

308 West 46th Street (between Eighth & Ninth Aves.) 212-246-3540

HOLY CROSS CHURCH: 1870. Henry Engelbert created a red-brick Romanesque design with a cruciform floor plan. The Roman Catholic parish was founded in 1852 by the Reverend Joseph A. Lutz. The present church rises to 148 feet and is the third building on the enlarged site. An 1885 renovation by the architect Lawrence J. O'Connor added 25 feet to the interior and a school on 43rd Street. At that time the chancel was filled with three murals of the Exaltation of the Cross and a semidome holding nine stained-glass windows by Mayer & Company of Munich. Louis Comfort Tiffany, assisted by Benjamin Eggleston, is credited with redecorating and painting the interior as well as designing the mosaics in the sanctuary. In 1921 the Reverend Francis Patrick Duffy (1871–1932), the famous World War I chaplain of The Fighting 69th Regiment of the New York National Guard, was appointed pastor and inspired the congregation with his tolerance and love of democracy. Be sure to stop at Duffy Square and see the statue created by Charles Keck of Father Duffy in combat uniform standing in front of a huge Celtic cross. The site also holds a booth selling half-price tickets to Broadway shows. A statue of George M. Cohan, a pal of Father Duffy and originator of the Broadway musical, guards the southern corner. Today, the parish plays host to theater programs featuring Broadway stars and budding talent.

329 West 42nd Street (between 8th & 9th Aves.) 212-246-4732
Duffy Square (between 46th & 47th Sts. on Broadway) Public Space

CHURCH OF THE HOLY APOSTLES: 1846. The architect Minard Lafever combined Romanesque Revival with classic Italian elements for this unusual design. A square brick tower topped by an octagonal steeple dominates the exterior. The sanctuary, which is lined with rounded arches and Italian Renaissance columns, has no pews. Transepts were added in 1858 by Richard Upjohn & Son. Be sure to see the window by Bruno Clagnan in tribute to the artisans and workers who helped rebuild the interior after a fire in 1993, as well as some original William Bolton windows. This Episcopal congregation serves weekday lunches to those in need and was among the first to use their nave for this ministry. The sanctuary is also shared with **Congregation Beth Simchat Torah**, a Jewish lesbian and gay congregation founded in 1973; this egalitarian community meets every Friday evening and offers an adult studies program and family support groups. The congregation also cares for a Sefer Torah from Kladno, Czechoslovakia, that was rescued after the Holocaust.

300 Ninth Avenue (at 28th St.) 212-807-6799 Synagogue: 212-929-9498

SERBIAN ORTHODOX CATHEDRAL OF ST. SAVA: 1855.

This English Gothic Revival **landmark** by Richard Upjohn was built as a chapel for Trinity Episcopal Church. In 1943, the Serbian Church acquired the property and added a richly painted iconostasis (altar screen) to the chancel and a golden mosaic of the patron above the main entrance. St. Sava, born in the late twelfth century, was a prince of Serbia. He fled, became a monk on Mount Athos in Greece, and returned to Serbia to establish the Orthodox Church. Every June the cathedral commemorates the Battle of Kosovo Field, which occurred in 1389. Most of the building's original details have survived, including the Upjohn rose window and the Rachel Richardson 9-foot interior murals, which are painted in niches that surround the long nave. The lancet windows are original except for five in the chancel that were destroyed when the nearby office of the American Communist Party was bombed in 1967. Each replacement holds a vibrant Byzantine image. When you leave look in the garden for the bust of Bishop Nikolai, who was the cathedral's first leader and preached the value of preserving both Old and New World traditions. Michael Pupin, a Serbian physicist who has a hall named for him at Columbia University, is memorialized in the church walkway. The need for restoration on this architectural masterpiece remains an enormous challenge for the congregation, as does the neighboring High Victorian clergy house, designed in 1860 by Jacob Wrey Mould.

15 West 25th Street (between Broadway & Sixth Ave.) 212-242-9240

ST. VINCENT DE PAUL CHURCH: 1857. A renovation in 1939 added this church's French Neoclassical facade and narthex by the architect Anthony De Pace. This Roman Catholic French congregation was established in 1840 by the French bishop Charles Forbin-Janson. The original church was built on a burnt-out lot at Canal Street left by the Church of the Ascension (see entry). Records show that John La Farge, Sr., the father of the famed stained-glass artist, was a founding member and treasurer, and that the first contribution came from Pierre Toussaint, a former Haitian slave and successful businessman (see St. Patrick's Old Cathedral). The commercialism of the area forced the Reverend Annet Lafont of the Fathers of Mercy, who served as the first pastor, to move north to the present site. The gracious interior is filled with artifacts. Look for enameled roundels of the Stations of the Cross, colorful murals, and French history featured in stained-glass windows. See a youthful St. Jeanne d'Arc (1412–1431), the heroine and military leader who was condemned for heresy and witchcraft and burned at the stake. The church remains a special haven for Francophiles. In 1952 Edith Piaf was married here with crowds of European journalists and Marlene Dietrich as witnesses. A French service is held every Sunday at 11:30 A.M.

West 23rd St. (between Sixth & Seventh Aves.) (office: 116 West 24th St.) 212-243-4727

SHEARITH ISRAEL CEMETERIES: These small graveyards are used by the oldest Orthodox congregation in North America. See Lower Manhattan for the first cemetery.

West 11th St. between Fifth & Sixth Aves. and West 21st St. between Sixth & Seventh Aves.

CHURCH OF THE GUARDIAN ANGEL: 1930. John Van Pelt designed this Romanesque red-brick and limestone church which has an interesting colonnade across the lower facade. Horizontal banding is filled with figurative carvings from Christian history. This Roman

Catholic parish was founded in 1888 on 23rd Street for Irish and Norwegian dockworkers. The original church was razed by the city for an elevated railroad and the group moved to the present site. Look for a stained-glass anchor and sailing ship by F.X. Zettler, and small plaques dedicated to seamen. Four life-size marble angels greet all who enter the nave.

193 Tenth Avenue (at 21st St.) 212-929-5966

ST. PETER'S CHURCH: 1838. This Gothic Revival building by James W. Smith sits on a site donated by Clement Moore. This Episcopal parish was started in 1831 at General Theological Seminary (see Chapel of the Good Shepherd) for the growing neighborhood. An exterior central tower with clock resembles one from Magdalen College at Oxford, but the finials on the rooftop weakened and were removed. Gothic entry porches on either side of the tower were also removed but may be duplicated in restoration plans. A wrought-iron railing was donated by the old Trinity Church of 1790, since Trinity was planning a new building (see entry). The interior, with a square floor plan and the original carved wood galleries by Samuel Smith, was redecorated many times. Be sure to see the Clement Moore white marble memorial tablet over the pre-Civil War baptismal font, and note the stone embedded in the wall. It is from Chelsea Old Church, which was destroyed by bombs in 1936 in London. Thomas Clarke, grandfather of Moore, attended Old Church before settling in 1750 on his American estate called Chelsea. In 1892 a new marble altar was installed along with a stained-glass window of Jesus calling to the patron, Peter, and his disciples, "Follow me and I will make you fishers of men." Note the gilded murals of individual saints on either side of the altar; they are thought to be from 1873, when James Wells, Jr., redecorated. Plain glass windows started to be replaced with colored glass beginning in the 1870s, but most memorial windows date from 1919. The figurative opalescent glass windows in the nave include several by Tiffany. The Greek Revival church, built in 1832, is now the rectory.

346 West 20th Street (between Eighth & Ninth Aves.) 212-929-2390

SHRINE CHURCH OF OUR LADY OF GUADALUPE: This brownstone residence was purchased in 1902 as the first National

Hispanic Roman Catholic church by the Reverend Venance Besset, a Frenchman and member of the Assumptionist Order. At that time the largest concentration of Hispanics lived between 12th and 16th Streets, surrounding Sixth to Eighth Avenues. The charm of a narrow floor plan that can accommodate 200 worshipers combines with spirited dedication to Mary, the Mother of Jesus, who appeared in the Mexican village of Guadalupe to the poor Indian Juan Diego in 1531. An annual feast on December 12 is celebrated with runners carrying a torch (Antorcha Guadalupe) through the streets of Manhattan to signify that the light from the sanctuary built on Tepeyac Hill, where Mary appeared, will be brought to all people. Celebrations often feature mariachi bands in traditional dress. Enormous groups of Puerto Ricans began to arrive in 1952, and the parish was again called upon to give spiritual comfort and help newcomers adjust to cultural differences. Dorothy Day, one of the founders of the Catholic Worker Movement, with houses still at 36 and 55 East First Street, frequently attended services here. Thomas Merton, Trappist monk and author, wrote lovingly about the church in his autobiography, *The Seven Storey Mountain*.

229 West 14th Street (between Seventh & Eighth Aves.) 212-243-5317

ST. BERNARD OF CLAIRVAUX: 1873. Gothic Revival design by Patrick Keely had its interior and roof restored in 1890 after a fire. The Roman Catholic parish first held services in 1868 at Knickerbocker Ice Company, an empty factory on West 13th Street. Most of the Irish families that made up the congregation were employed on the nearby docks. The symmetrical stone facade has twin towers, a tripartite entry, and a rose window. Read the detailed inscription on the corner-stone for a history of civil and religious leaders of the day, including the carpenter Patrick Reed and the brick mason Edwin Harlow. The Reverend Gabriel Healy, founding pastor, made sure all would be remembered. The patron, Bernard (1090–1153), is recognized as a great Christian reformer who founded the Cistercian Order and 160 European monasteries. Look for Bernard in the center mosaic over the main altar. The sanctuary is filled with murals, mosaics, and figurative stained glass, with clerestory windows from Munich installed in 1897. The artisan Jorge Miranda skillfully renovated the church in 1998.

328 West 14th Street (between Eighth & Ninth Aves.) 212-243-0265

METROPOLITAN-DUANE UNITED METHODIST CHURCH: 1853. Gothic granite and limestone building is home to two groups, which merged in 1939. The Metropolitan Temple, whose congregation built the church on the present site, was founded in 1833 as First Wesleyan Chapel. The Duane Church was organized in 1797 and named in honor of James Duane, mayor of New York City from 1784 to 1789. He was an important leader in the headquarters of the new American nation. Today Thomas Duane, representing the West Village area in the New York State Senate, carries on the family tradition.

201 West 13th Street (at Seventh Ave.) 212-243-5470

FIRST PRESBYTERIAN CHURCH: 1846. Gothic Revival brownstone design by Joseph Wells, with the south transept added in 1893 by McKim, Mead & White, sits in a large green garden. The congregation was started in 1707 by immigrants from Scotland and Ireland meeting in private residences. The first church (hence its name) was dedicated in 1717 in Lower Manhattan and used until it was destroyed by British troops during the American Revolution. The congregation then met in Trinity Church chapel until they received their charter from the new government and moved in 1811. The Great Fire of 1835 destroyed that building and the congregation made its final move to the present site. University Place and Madison Square Presbyterian Churches merged with this congregation in 1918 and greatly increased its size. The sanctuary seats over 1,200, and the chancel, which was added in 1919, holds oak chairs inscribed with the names of all the pastors. Musical instruments were forbidden in church until more liberal members were able to install an organ in 1886. Stained-glass windows were placed between 1893 and 1916. The Martin Luther window by Charles Lamb has Latin and German inscriptions, and the Tiffany window of Isaiah with the Books of Prophecy has panels of grapes and ivy. The artisan Maitland Armstrong designed both the English Protestant Reformation symbol, the Puritan, and the window of Admiral Gaspard de Coligny of the French Huguenots with shield and countryside prominently featured. Enter through the church house, designed in 1960 by Edgar Tafel, an apprentice to Frank Lloyd Wright.

12 West 12th Street (at Fifth Ave.) 212-675-6150

JEFFERSON COMMUNITY GARDEN: 1973. This garden is located behind the Jefferson Market branch of the New York Public Library, built in 1877 as a Victorian Gothic courthouse. An adjoining jail for women was demolished and replaced by the garden, which is cared for by neighborhood volunteers. The Greenwich Village Society for Historical Preservation installed the high black wrought-iron fence in 1998. Weather permitting, the garden is open from May until October on Wednesday, Saturday, and Sunday from 2:00 to 4:30 P.M. 18 West 9th Street (at Sixth Ave.)

ST. JOSEPH'S CHURCH IN GREENWICH VILLAGE: 1833. This Greek Revival temple with huge Doric columns was built by John Doran for a Roman Catholic congregation organized in 1829. The parish originally extended from Canal Street to 20th Street. The square-shaped interior was restored after a fire in 1885 and again several times later. Three crystal chandeliers enhance the austere blue sanctuary whose white wooden columns support the original balcony. A single mural of the Risen Christ is the only focus of the apse. The Reverend Thomas Farrell, pastor from 1857 to 1880, was leader of the Academia, a group of priests who focused on the role of the Roman Catholic Church in American culture. See the stained-glass window that was a gift to the congregation from Farrell, who also left a generous legacy to start **St. Benedict the Moor**, a parish founded in 1883 for the first black Roman Catholic group established north of the Mason-Dixon Line. It was led by the Reverend John E. Burke, who opened a home in the parish house for destitute black children who were not admitted into white orphanages.

371 Sixth Avenue (between Waverly & Washington Pls.) 212-741-1274

JUDSON MEMORIAL BAPTIST CHURCH: 1892. This church
was built by McKim, Mead & White in Early Christian and Italian Renaissance style. The Rockefeller family donated the corner lot to start a more diverse church that would care for both the Italian immigrants who were pouring into the Village and the wealthy neighbors who lived nearby. The Reverend Edward Judson planned the church and named it for his father, Adoniram Judson (1788–1850), who in 1811 became the first American missionary to travel to Burma. Look for the John La Farge suite of seventeen opalescent stained-glass windows placed in arched bays. The shape of the windows echoes Stanford White's Washington Square Memorial Arch sitting in the 9.5 acres of Washington Square Park, which borders this **landmark**. A charming bas-relief of floating angels by Augustus Saint-Gaudens guards the baptismal pool. Faithful to its history as a center for liberal politics, Judson has an energetic congregation that supports civil liberties and sponsors art festivals and recitals, poetry readings, and avant-garde lectures.

55 Washington Square South (at Thompson St.) 212-477-0351

SHRINE CHURCH OF OUR LADY OF POMPEII: 1926. This
Italianate building by Matthew Del Gaudio is the first one built for this Roman Catholic parish. It began in 1892 as the Raphael Society by the Missionaries of St. Charles in a private home on Waverly Place. Its mission was to assist Italian immigrants in obtaining jobs, skills, and education and to protect them from unscrupulous men who were exploiting newcomers. The society evolved into a church group and

Sanctuary angel at Our Lady of Pompei

had several homes before the last one was razed to make way for the extension of Sixth Avenue and the Holland Tunnel. The Raphael Society remains as the parish archives, an important reference library for scholars. The decorative interior seats over 1,200. Above the main altar hangs an oil painting of the Madonna of the Rosary, copied after one in Pompeii. Look in the stained glass for the legendary traveler Mother Frances Xavier Cabrini speaking to Pope Leo XIII about sailing to New York City. Nearby Father Antonio Demo Square is named for the beloved pastor who cared for the immigrant community from 1899 to 1933, and documented parish life. In 1906, Father Demo estimated that he had 30,000 members. Be sure to see the charming reminders of Italian heritage in stained glass over the entrance doors. One shows an immigrant family, several priests, and the Statue of Liberty; another shows Columbus and his mates with unfurled banner landing in the New World. The Sunday service at 11:00 A.M. is conducted in Italian.

25 Carmine Street (between Bleecker St. & Sixth Ave.) 212-989-6805

ST. ANTHONY OF PADUA CHURCH: 1886. This Italian Romanesque design by Arthur Crooks was culturally relevant to its Italian Roman Catholic congregation. In 1866 Franciscan priests organized a group who met in an abandoned Methodist church that was part of the present site. Stained-glass windows depict the life story of the patron, Anthony (1195–1231), who became the first preacher of the Franciscan Order. An elaborate marble altar holds a statue of Anthony with outstretched arms, kneeling before Mary, who is offering him her infant son, Jesus—a reminder to care for the spiritual and temporal needs of all children. Walk along Houston Street and see the statue of St. Alphonsus rescued from a nearby razed church. Also notice the grotto of Our Lady of Fatima, a bas-relief of Anthony holding the Child Jesus surrounded by images of the Church, the World Trade Center, and Empire State Building. For the feast day of St. Anthony, on June 13, there is a week-long celebration with daily services and a festive neighborhood procession that display the saint's relic.

154 Sullivan Street (at Houston St.) 212-777-2755

CREDITS

All photographs are by author except those noted below.

Maps: ©Darcy Pleckham
Back cover: ©Christopher Cook

LOWER MANHATTAN:
p. 4 ©Nat. Museum of the American Indian
p. 15 ©Frank Bauer: Trinity Archive
p. 26 ©Eldridge St. Project
p. 33 ©St. Mark-in-the-Bowery Archive

EAST SIDE:
p. 69/71 ©Leland Cook
p. 82/83/84 ©Leland Cook
p. 93 ©Saint Peter's Church Archive
p. 97 ©Christ Church Archive
p. 102 ©Will Brown:Congregation Emanu-El Archive
p. 112 ©All Souls Archive

UPPER MANHATTAN & HARLEM:
p. 157 ©John Frederick Herrold: Riverside Church Archive
p. 161 ©Joseph Pineiro

WEST SIDE:
p. 189 ©Office of Paulist History & Archives
p. 199 ©St. Francis of Assisi Archive
p. 205 ©St. Francis Xavier Archive
p. 208 ©Church of the Ascension Archive: Whitney Cox